Post-Exceptionalism

Incitements

Series editors: Peg Birmingham, DePaul University and
Dimitris Vardoulakis, Western Sydney University

Available

Return Statements: The Return of Religion in Contemporary Philosophy
Gregg Lambert

The Refusal of Politics
Laurent Dubreuil, translated by Cory Browning

Plastic Sovereignties: Agamben and the Politics of Aesthetics
Arne De Boever

From Violence to Speaking Out: Apocalypse and Expression in Foucault, Derrida and Deleuze
Leonard Lawlor

Agonistic Mourning: Political Dissidence and the Women in Black
Athena Athanasiou

Interpassivity: The Aesthetics of Delegated Enjoyment
Robert Pfaller

Derrida's Secret: Perjury, Testimony, Oath
Charles Barbour

Resistance and Psychoanalysis: Impossible Divisions
Simon Morgan Wortham

Reclaiming Wonder: After the Sublime
Genevieve Lloyd

Arendt, Natality and Biopolitics: Towards Democratic Plurality and Reproductive Justice
Rosalyn Diprose and Ewa Plonowska Ziarek

Worldlessness After Heidegger: Phenomenology, Psychoanalysis, Deconstruction
Roland Végső

Homo Natura: Nietzsche, Philosophical Anthropology and Biopolitics
Vanessa Lemm

Spinoza, The Transindividual
Étienne Balibar, translated by Mark G. E. Kelly

Uncontainable Legacies: Theses on Intellectual, Cultural, and Political Inheritance
Gerhard Richter

The Trial of Hatred: An Essay on the Refusal of Violence
Marc Crépon, translated by D. J. S Cross and Tyler M. Williams

Machiavellian Ontology: Political Conflict and Philosophy
Francesco Marchesi, translated by Dave Mesing

Post-Exceptionalism: Art After Political Theology
Arne De Boever

Visit the series web page at: edinburghuniversitypress.com/series/incite

Post-Exceptionalism

Art After Political Theology

Arne De Boever

EDINBURGH
University Press

Edinburgh University Press is one of the leading university presses in the UK. We publish academic books and journals in our selected subject areas across the humanities and social sciences, combining cutting-edge scholarship with high editorial and production values to produce academic works of lasting importance. For more information visit our website: edinburghuniversity press.com

Edinburgh University Press Ltd
13 Infirmary Street
Edinburgh EH1 1LT

First published in hardback by Edinburgh University Press 2025

Typeset in 11/14pt Bembo
by Cheshire Typesetting Ltd, Cuddington, Cheshire, and
printed and bound by CPI Group (UK) Ltd, Croydon, CR0 4YY

A CIP record for this book is available from the British Library

ISBN 978 1 3995 3969 2 (hardback)
ISBN 978 1 3995 3970 8 (paperback)
ISBN 978 1 3995 3971 5 (webready PDF)
ISBN 978 1 3995 3972 2 (epub)

MIX
Paper | Supporting
responsible forestry
FSC® C013604
FSC
www.fsc.org

Contents

Acknowledgments

I consider this book to be part of a trilogy on what I have been calling "unexceptional art". As such, it has clear connections to the trilogy's first and second volumes, *Against Aesthetic Exceptionalism* (University of Minnesota Press, 2019) and *François Jullien's Unexceptional Thought* (Rowman & Littlefield, 2020): my Introduction is a heavily revised version of *Against Aesthetic Exceptionalism*, and traces of that book can be found in Chapter 2 and my Conclusion as well. Some of what is in Chapter 4 appears in a very different form in *François Jullien's Unexceptional Thought*. Beyond that, and in ways that may be evident to me alone, there are more distant echoes from my books *Finance Fictions*, *Plastic Sovereignties*, and even (in Chapter 6) *States of Exception in the Contemporary Novel*. One might argue that taken together these three books—*Against Aesthetic Exceptionalism*, *François Jullien's Unexceptional Thought*, and *Post-Exceptionalism*—constitute a single work that is reflected in very different ways in each volume. That single work, however, does not exist; the trilogy offers only its original copies. An outtake from *Post-Exceptionalism*—a co-authored book about music—is in progress.

As some of this book's interlocutors know, I first drafted these pages while I was doing some house-painting. The timing of the writing with the painting was not a case of bad planning but a deliberate decision, one that was inspired by a story I was told when I was Visiting Professor at the Central Academy of Fine Arts in Beijing in Fall 2019. One day, my guide there—Haomin Xu—pointed me toward a student who was sweeping the campus roads. "That's a student of Song Dong's", he told me. "When he went to see Song to ask for advice about his art-making, Song suggested he start sweeping". Apparently the student has been sweeping ever since. The story resonated for me with my thinking about unexceptional art (in which Song's work has a prominent place); I wanted to balance out the activity of writing with a different, more manual task. This in fact brought great focus to the writing: I would think out during the painting how the writing would proceed, and once the time to write arrived, I would put to the page what I had thought out while painting. When other work—teaching, administration—distracted me from painting, the writing stopped. Ultimately, I could only write when I was painting—ceilings, walls, baseboards, trims, cabinets. Needless to say, I got a lot of painting done while I was working on this book.

The book owes much to my time in Beijing and Shanghai in 2017, and then again in Beijing in 2019. I am grateful to Zhang Ga for the invitations, to the students in my courses for their questions and comments, and to the audiences at my public lectures for their questions. I am also grateful to the graduate students in the "Duplitectures: Architecture, Art, and the Copy" seminar that I taught as Visiting Professor in the Department of Architecture and Urban Design at UCLA—thank you Michael Osman and Heather Roberge for the invitation, and thank you to my Teaching Assistant Giulia Amoresano for the stimulating conversations about architecture. A special thanks to Adam

Boggs for putting me on the track of provisional painting. My CalArts students are an inexhaustible source of inspiration: thank you in particular to those BFA students who took my class "Unexceptional Art", and to the MA and MFA students in my Spring 2020 "Critical Discourse in the Arts and the Media" class (with guests Nan Z. Da, Michael Nylan, and Robeson Taj Frazier) and Fall 2020 "Contemporary Aesthetic Theory" class. I learned much from our conversations. The artistic work of my former graduate student Lucinda Trask provided inspiration for the book as well. Winnie Wong, who visited my Fall 2020 class, kindly shared a syllabus with me at some point—several of the readings on it have worked their way into this book—and I've learned much (I hope) from her writing on copies in art and architecture.

Parts of this book were test-run as public presentations at the *boundary 2* Fall 2019 conference that I co-organized with Leah Feldman at the University of Pittsburgh, at the "Finance and Fiction" conference that I co-organized with Mikkel Krause-Frantzen at the California Institute of the Arts in Spring 2020, and in a lecture I gave at the Center for the Study of Theory and Criticism at Western University in Spring 2021 (thank you Allan Pero for the invitation). I also prepared a talk related to the book for the Twelfth East-West Philosophers' Conference, University of Hawai'i, Manoa, Summer 2020, but my presentation of those materials was postponed due to the pandemic. I am grateful to the California Institute of the Arts and the School of Critical Studies for their support of my research, and to my colleagues within and outside of the school who have expressed interest in this work—in particular Andrew Culp and Louise Sandhaus, who invited me to present some of this research in her class. The research for this book would have taken much longer without the expert assistance I received from my graduate students Carl Schmitz, Clara Wenrong-Lee, and especially Ling Tiong. Maisa Imamović expertly prepared the book's index.

I couldn't have written this book, and done the traveling that it required, without the support of Olivia C. Harrison, who covered for me at home. For Ada and Louise, I've tried to be the post-exceptional parent: "good enough". My own father, Wilfried De Boever, has often warned me for exceptionalism, and shown me through example what a commitment to the unexceptional looks like. My final thanks are to Count G, whose work put me on the tracks of unexceptional politics.

We need to cut off the King's head: in aesthetics, that still has to be done.

—after Michel Foucault

Introduction: Post-Exceptionalism and its Politics

A Thought Experiment

Consider a dubious thought experiment, one that I have tried numerous times in my graduate student classrooms: consider reading the first chapter of Carl Schmitt's *Political Theology: Four Chapters on the Concept of Sovereignty*, titled "Definition of Sovereignty," at the beginning of a course in "Contemporary Aesthetic Theory" to see what the chapter might have to say about our definition of art and the artist.[1] It's a dubious experiment, not in the least because of Schmitt's dark political affiliations: Hannah Arendt called him "a convinced Nazi."[2] Still, the experiment is not entirely outrageous. After all, political thinkers like Giorgio Agamben or Chantal Mouffe are frequently read at arts institutions, where they also visit as invited speakers and sometimes also teach, and both Agamben and Mouffe are sharp readers of Schmitt.[3] With one's graduate students, of course, one cannot just read Agamben and Mouffe; one must also read whom they have read so as to assess their take on those they praise or criticize. That would mean, in the case of Agamben and Mouffe, reading Schmitt (among others).

But the experiment might also reach further than that, into our very understanding of art and the artist. For by reading Schmitt in a course on aesthetic theory, one would also be pursuing Paul Kahn's provocative suggestion, in *Political Theology: Four New Chapters on the Concept of Sovereignty* (a rewriting of Schmitt's book for our time), that "the idea of creation links the political decision [promoted by Schmitt] simultaneously to God *and to the artist*" (emphasis mine).[4] "In each case," Kahn continues,

> the problem is to understand how the subject's will can bring something new into existence. This sounds more mysterious than it is. Artistic creation has a relationship to norms, but it is not simply the deductive application of the norm. We don't create art by following a set of rules. Similarly, we cannot explain art by analyzing its causes—although once again there is some relationship to causal factors.[5]

Reading Kahn's reflection on art back towards Schmitt, the conclusion would need to be that as such, artistic creation—tied here to divine creation—is linked to what Schmitt is writing about in *Political Theology*, which is the concept of sovereignty. Provocative as that claim might be in its connection of the aesthetic, the theological, and the political, how are we to understand it?

In this Introduction, I will execute the experiment I have proposed in a minimal form. After a brief discussion of Schmitt's chapter that lays out its central idea, I intend to consider how Schmitt's concept of sovereignty resonates in an aesthetic context, namely in a profile that the Norwegian writer Karl Ove Knausgaard wrote of the German artist Anselm Kiefer. You might object that "resonate" is too vague a term to establish relation, but apart from the fact that Knausgaard's piece really does operate by resonance (as I will show), you may find my approach less objectionable when you consider that Knausgaard—taking his cue from a lecture that Kiefer gave at the University of Freiburg—also explicitly discusses Schmitt in his profile. In short, Schmitt—and, specifically, Schmitt's concept of sovereignty—is both implicitly and explicitly present in Knausgaard's profile, and that presence will lead me to reflect not only on our understanding of art and the artist, but on the politics of that understanding as well. Schmitt's politics, as I've indicated, were dubious. But if we find that Schmitt's concept of sovereignty extends into our concept of art and the artist, what does that say about the politics of our aesthetics? This is the question that lies at the root of this book.

In a second move, I will consider how this question is played out around the aesthetic phenomenon of the fake whose scandal has strangely persisted in the art world, suggesting that postmodernism's critical project crucially missed something when it targeted the force of the original. The discussion of the fake and the copy will enable me to provide further evidence for my suspicion about the affinities between Schmitt's concept of sovereignty and the art world and enable me to sharpen my thinking about those. Finally, I will provide a brief overview of the project of this book and say a bit more about the post-exceptional politics that the book, in its thinking about unexceptional art, explores.

Definition of Sovereignty

Schmitt begins *Political Theology* with the claim that "Sovereign is he who decides on the exception."[6] The claim appears to come out of nowhere. Schmitt simply posits it, as a stand-alone sentence, at the very beginning of his text. While the sentence lays out, as a constative, an understanding of sovereignty as agentive, specifically as an agency that decides, and even more specifically that decides on the exception (in the German original, it says on "the state of exception," "Ausnahmezustand"[7]), it also reads as a performative, as a writerly enactment of that very act of decision, with the author deciding on the exception as one of the key components in his definition of sovereignty. The sentence is a sovereign performance.

This is the *only* definition, Schmitt continues—and it's worth noting that we are in the logic of the *one* here—that "can do justice to a borderline concept"[8]—and sovereignty is such a borderline concept. By this, Schmitt does not mean something vague; rather, he intends a concept that "[pertains] to the outermost sphere."[9] Taking our cue from the word "border," it can be helpful to think this territorially: sovereignty is a concept, Schmitt argues, that applies to the margin rather than the center, to the exception rather than the norm. It's associated with "a borderline case and not with routine."[10] If you want to see sovereignty in action, if you want to see who is sovereign, you ought to look at the border—not at routine. The extreme case rather than the normal situation. Sovereignty becomes visible in war rather than in peace—and even war, with all of the rules that, in Schmitt's analysis, apply to it, may not be the best situation to witness sovereignty. Sovereignty applies in what Schmitt very specifically calls a state of exception, which, he points out, is not just "any emergency decree or state of siege."[11]

So, what is the exception? The exception is something that cannot be derived from the norm. It is, rather, what comes first—it's the norm that comes after. It's only "[t]he decision on the exception that is a decision in the true sense of the word";[12] this is because a decision on the norm lies within the mapped totality of a situation, it is not a decision on something that is truly new. (One can see here one of the reasons why Schmitt's work stood out as interesting to Jacques Derrida.[13]) The question of sovereignty in truth only emerges, Schmitt suggests, in an argument about a "concrete application, and that means who decides in a situation of conflict what constitutes the public interest or interest of the state, public safety and order, *le salut public*, and so on."[14] The exception is a very specific instance of such a situation, "which is not codified in the existing legal order, [and] can best be characterized as a case of extreme peril, a danger to the existence of the state, or the like."[15] However, "it cannot be circumscribed factually and made to conform to a preformed law."[16] Schmitt argues that as such, it "makes relevant the subject of sovereignty," which decides on an emergency whose "precise details . . . cannot be anticipated" and whose actions in such a situation cannot be spelled out in advance. In that sense, sovereignty's power in such situations is absolute—"unlimited,"[17] as Schmitt also has it. Such actions are the actions of sovereignty: not subject to the "checks and balances" of "a liberal constitution."[18]

But whereas from the liberal constitutional point of view there would in such a case "be no jurisdictional competence at all," Schmitt's position differs from this, since he argues that while the sovereign "stands outside the normally valid legal system, he nevertheless belongs to it, for it is he who must decide whether the constitution needs to be suspended in its entirety."[19] Liberal constitutionalism seeks to eliminate this kind of power. But for Schmitt there is much more at stake than just a legal issue: "But whether the exception can be banished from the world is not a juristic question. Whether one has confidence and hope that it can be eliminated depends on philosophical, especially on philosophical-historical or metaphysical, convictions."[20] Later in the chapter, he will at several points suggest that what is at stake here is nothing less than "life."[21] For what raises its head in a state of exception, and by extension in the power that decides on it, is for Schmitt life itself, or at the very least something that with a "vital intensity" breaks through the crust of the boring everyday to bring something that arrives, as if from the future, unprecedented, not codified, not anticipated by the law—a true exception to which only a sovereign can, with absolute power, respond.[22]

It makes Schmitt sound like a science-fiction writer, and it's worth noting that he began his writing career publishing fiction, including one fascinating science-fiction story that deals, precisely, with the codification of the present, and specifically situations coming from the future.[23] That concern is markedly present in *Political Theology* as well, and it's in large part, I want to suggest, why Schmitt's chapter can appeal to its readers. Its attraction, for many, lies not so much in Schmitt's definition of a sovereignty that decides on the state of exception; it lies, rather, in his theorization of the exception as life breaking through the crust of the boring everyday. In other words, if Schmitt is a conservative, what appeals to readers in this chapter is his keen understanding, as a conservative, of that which is impossible to conserve or contain—that which always risks to come from afar, arrive unexpectedly, to shake everything up (that which "defies general codification"[24]). Schmitt has a keen appreciation of this, and in fact he designs his conservative concept of sovereignty in response, as an absolute power that can respond to such an exception. (Scholars have shown that this in fact needs to be understood as a conservative response to the work of Walter Benjamin, specifically Benjamin's essay "Critique of Violence" and the plea for a lawless, divine violence—which Benjamin calls "waltend," translated as "sovereign"—that it develops.[25]) The sovereign, as Schmitt puts it later in the chapter, is the one "responsible for that for which competence has not been anticipated."[26]

There are clear political dangers to this position, especially when you see Schmitt pursue the question of the extent to which the sovereign is bound to laws, a question that remains particularly pressing today for example in the United States where the situation is something like the inverse of what Schmitt was witnessing, with the executive branch having progressively done away with the checks and balances that were meant to contain it (as Dana D. Nelson in her work has shown[27]). Relying on the work of Jean Bodin, Schmitt suggests that in a state of exception, the sovereign is not bound by law, and moreover he posits that this is the core of any power called sovereign. In some cases, it becomes necessary for the sovereign to "violate"[28] his commitments to the people; those are exceptional situations in which sovereign power is absolute—not bound by such commitments. But if this of course leads to an understanding of sovereignty as the power that is able to suspend the law, Schmitt also points out that this names the same power that decided on the law in the first place: we have here sovereignty's transcendental force, as the condition of possibility for the law's institution *and* its suspension. The consequence Schmitt draws from this is that "the legal order rests on a decision and not on a norm."[29] It's the decision that institutes the norm.

The understanding of sovereignty that's laid out here is, overall, monarchical (it follows the logic of the one). Whenever monarchy comes up in the chapter, it has positive connotations, as in Schmitt's discussion of article 48 of the German constitution of 1919. He notes that the article stipulates that "the exception is declared by the president of the Reich but is under the control of parliament, the Reichstag, which can at any time demand its suspension."[30] But, Schmitt argues, this "control" that is expanded in liberal constitutionalism (which in his view has progressively shrunk the power of sovereignty) only applies to the "invocation of exceptional powers"; it does not apply to the "content" of those powers themselves.[31] Those are free from such hamperings. "Article 48," in Schmitt's reading, "grants unlimited power," the kind that is typically associated with a "monarch."[32] Whereas law certainly recedes in such a situation, it is not destroyed. "Order in the juristic sense still prevails, even if it is not of the ordinary kind"[33]. It's a moment in which the phrase "legal order" is split in two and the conceptual independence of law and sovereignty becomes clear. One consequence of this is that a state of exception is not anarchy and chaos, for the law is merely suspended—it has not been destroyed. We are at its limit, but not fully outside of it. We still stand in some kind of relation to it. Chaos is too extreme a term for such a situation—Schmitt, a conservative, cannot tolerate it. (Andreas Kalyvas has, in his work on Schmitt's book of democratic thought *Constitutional Theory*, characterized this as Schmitt's interest in the "extra-parliamentary."[34]) This indicates that the exception, exceptional as it is, still remains somehow tied to the norm, with the sovereign deciding "whether this normal situation actually exists," or, vice versa, deciding on the exception.[35]

Schmitt notes the eighteenth century's difficulties with thinking a law that can suspend itself. It's something that rationalism cannot get its head around. But, Schmitt writes, it should: it should be of interest to the rationalists that the law includes the possibility of suspending itself. How can the law have this force? What is the count of the law if it includes the possibility of the uncountable? To pursue such questions would mean to commit to "a philosophy of concrete life," and in the closing paragraphs of Schmitt's chapter, the emphasis on life becomes prominent.[36] "The exception," he concludes, "is more interesting than the rule":

> The rule proves nothing. The exception proves everything: It confirms not only the rule but also its existence, which derives only from the exception. In the exception the power of real life breaks through the crust of a mechanism that has become torpid by repetition.[37]

The last words of the chapter are quoted from the Danish philosopher Søren Kierkegaard and reinforce Schmitt's emphasis on—and, one might say, his perverse (given that he was a conservative) passion for—the exception as a manifestation of life.

That is, in sum, Schmitt's chapter, and it's a peculiar read. It seems strangely torn between, on the one hand, a passion for life and the unexpected; and, on the other, a commitment to a power called sovereign that would be able to respond to the emergency that life—life in the true sense of the word—poses. As I've indicated, the chapter has the marks of a conservative who has a keen appreciation for that which cannot be conserved. One may be weary of Schmitt's theorization of sovereignty as a power that is able to suspend the law, that is not beholden to the law in situations of emergency, because it tends—theoretically but also historically—fascistically. This is closely connected, of course, to the vitalist impulse in Schmitt's thought. And yet, the students in the thought experiment with which I began often assess the vitalism as separate from that; that is the part of the chapter that appeals to them, and that in fact they can associate quite easily with art.

The intimate, although troubling, connections between Schmitt's exceptionalist concept of sovereignty and our understanding of artists and art become even more clear when they are considered next to the more common conception of sovereignty as normative. Indeed, the sovereign is more commonly defined as whoever guarantees the law in the normal situation. The interesting thing about Schmitt, of course, is that he does not follow—or only partly follows: there is a normative dimension of sovereignty in Schmitt but it comes second to sovereignty's exceptionalism[38]—that common understanding; and what I am proposing in this Introduction is that by doing so, his conception of sovereignty in fact becomes legible as a theory of art.

Art: now *that* is what "breaks through the crust of a mechanism that has become torpid by repetition." And the one who decides on that—why, that's the artist. (Critics and curators will pitch in as well—but the initial decision, that's the artist's to make.) As Paul Kahn writes, art has a relation to the norm—but it does not derive from norms. Like the sovereign decision, it stands outside of those, has an independence in relation to those. Art has a close relation to the future, and the artist is tapped into that. An artist sees the future before it has arrived.[39] It's not that art is chaos or anarchy; it is rather, an extraordinary sense of order—order while the law is suspended. Art and the artist are, then, borderline concepts: they don't apply so much in a situation of routine but in extreme cases. That's at least a hallmark of what we think of as good art. Such statements on art and artists, such understandings of art and artists, are legion; one can find them everywhere in the art world and outside of it. Dear reader, you yourself may have said or written such things about art and artists! And while many of those making such statements, and promoting such understandings, may raise an eyebrow at a course that has Schmitt on its syllabus, and would likely disagree with Schmitt's politics, they nevertheless also promote Schmitt's thought, and by extension his politics, through the very ways in which they talk about art and artists.

Now, granted: art and artists are not political sovereigns. They do not have the same kind of power. But if we accept that there is a transfer between aesthetics and politics, that some of what goes on in art makes its way into politics and vice versa, shouldn't it also trouble us that we appear to celebrate in aesthetics what we criticize in politics? Doesn't that deserve a good bit of reflection? As an example of the prominence of a Schmittian take on art and artists, I propose to now consider one specific case of arts-writing in which Schmitt's relevance to aesthetics lies exposed, both through implicit and explicit references to Schmitt and the power called sovereign, and with reference to the historical context of fascism: the Norwegian author Karl Ove Knausgaard's profile of the German artist Anselm Kiefer.

"Like a King's Court"

Let us consider the thought experiment with which I started: let us try to find, as a way to test out my hypothesis about the widespread presence of Schmitt's thought in aesthetics, moments in Knausgaard's profile where Schmitt's thought resonates—or is explicitly present, even. Let us start with the moment where Schmitt explicitly appears: we are at the University of Freiburg (famous, of course, in the history of philosophy and the history of fascism) "just before Christmas," as Knausgaard notes, and

Kiefer is giving a talk "about his days as a law student there in the '60s."[40] You see, before Kiefer went to art school, he was a law student; he only went to art school after "dropping out of law school," as Knausgaard tells us a little later.[41] During his talk, Kiefer projects on a screen behind him "a picture of the young Kiefer in uniform, doing the Nazi salute."[42] One can imagine the shock that this image would have had on the large audience; it certainly caused an uproar in Kiefer's student days, when he presented as his final exam project a work called "Occupations" that "shows Kiefer giving the Nazi salute in various European countries that had been occupied by Germany during the war."[43] Knausgaard tells us that when these pictures were first published in 1975, "it became a full-blown scandal." "Who is this fascist who thinks he is an anti-fascist?" the artist Marcel Broodthaers asked.[44]

It's a good question—it will turn out to sum up my concerns with Knausgaard's profile. Standing in front of the picture of him giving the Nazi salute, Kiefer begins to talk about Schmitt, whom he read during his law student days. Knausgaard merely adds that Schmitt was "the crown jurist of the Third Reich"; but when he mentions immediately thereafter that Kiefer went to art school after "dropping out of law school," one senses how Schmitt's thinking about law and sovereignty's relation to law—the sovereign decision is made, as I have explained, outside of the law—"resonates" here.[45] It's the same when Knausgaard, when speculating about Kiefer's "Occupations" project and its engagement with fascism, notes that "Kiefer must have found something exceptionally interesting here."[46] "Exceptionally," yes—that would be the adverb to use on this occasion. The relations that we are asked to think are multiple: of art to law; of law to politics; of art to politics; of art to history. Does one have to drop out of law to make art? Does art mark, rather, an entering into law—but maybe another law? If one drops out of law to make art, does that mark art as political? What is politics' relation to law? The concept of sovereignty plays a major role in how these debates are played out in political theory, and Schmitt's work is an important reference in those. Knausgaard does not mention sovereignty by name—but it is everywhere in his profile.

To be sure, Kiefer emerges from Knausgaard's profile as an intensely sovereign figure. This is, of course, something that is obvious about how Kiefer and his work have been described—even if the exact term "sovereignty" may not have been applied to it: "Today," Knausgaard writes,

> Kiefer has long since been canonized, and his name has become a kind of trademark. If anyone is truly provoked by his work these days, it is by its price tag. And it's easy to find critical voices: There are plenty who say his art is that of a megalomaniac, that it consists of grand gestures and little else, that it is hollow and empty and perhaps not art at all but kitsch.[47]

I will return to the role of economics in this quote later in this Introduction. For now, let me place an emphasis on the megalomaniac and the grand, since I think they do apply (I disagree with descriptions of Kiefer's work as hollow and empty—those seem off the mark; moreover, they don't seem to name the same thing as megalomaniac and grand). While Knausgaard acknowledges the majesty of Kiefer's works, works in front of which the writer "[falls] silent,"[48] his profile also relates critically, I want to propose, to such majesty, confirming it in multiple ways while also laboring to undermine it. Indeed, there is a way in which Knausgaard's profile both confirms Kiefer's artistic sovereignty and undermines it. If it undermines the sovereignty of Kiefer as a person, it nevertheless still seems to confirm the sovereignty of art—it speaks of the artist and the artwork as some kind of vehicles through which something else, "art," or perhaps even "the cosmic," passes. One aspect of Knausgaard's profiling of Kiefer that is worth considering is Knausgaard's own status as one of the "gods" of contemporary literature: his six-volume autobiographical project titled *My Struggle* (after Adolf Hitler's flawed autobiography, which Knausgaard discusses in a 400-page-long essay that is included in the autobiography's final volume) has also been criticized as megalomaniac and grand. And what's with the reference to Hitler? *Who is this fascist who claims to be an anti-fascist?* Knausgaard may be writing about Kiefer—but he is also writing about himself.

When Knausgaard enters into the huge warehouse where Kiefer seems to work and live, he notes that it was "filled to the brim with art."[49] Knausgaard's description of it strikes one as a description of a cabinet of wonders, those famous rooms in the castles of medieval princes that, through their collection of myriad objects of all kinds, appeared to contain in their microcosm the macrocosm of the universe. The warehouse becomes a bit of a castle, then—and one other castle will appear later in Knausgaard's text, one that has an actual cabinet of wonders—especially when Knausgaard, looking at the art in the warehouse, notes that "It was as if our whole culture surged through this hall, raw and wild, like its subconscious. Could all this really come from one person? Who was this man?"[50] Knausgaard is writing these words anno 2020, but they would not have been out of place in the Middle Ages, in the writing of someone who had just stepped into the cabinet of wonders of a medieval prince. Following these associations, Knausgaard describes Kiefer as a "cult leader"; but he also does not forget that we are, after all, in a warehouse: Kiefer is also "an engineer."[51] When lunch is served in the living quarters of the warehouse, Knausgaard notes that "it looked strange, as if someone had planned an elegant meal [prepared by a cook] in an auto-repair shop."[52] The exceptional confronts the unexceptional, if you will. Both are on display.

The reference to a cult, while evoking the "theology" that is part of Schmitt's book title and that runs through Knausgaard's profile, is picked up immediately after this, when Knausgaard is presented with a book of Kiefer's watercolors that is titled "*Ich bin der ich bin*."[53] Earlier on in the text, the watercolors were presented as strangely disarming: wonderfully personal pieces as opposed to Kiefer's grand works. But the title of the collection seems to undermine that: "It's what God said to Moses when he asked for God's name," Kiefer explains.[54] Trying to find the term to describe God's enigmatic formula, he calls a friend, referred to in Knausgaard's text as "a university professor." The professor delivers: "Tautology," Kiefer explains—"that's the word to describe a formula like 'I am who I am'."[55] When a moment later Kiefer wants to know about an old German song referencing a girl called Heidi (the name of one of Knausgaard's daughters), he calls the professor again, who dutifully sings the song over the phone. Thankfully, the profile does not mention the professor's name: who would want to be at the beck and call of this kind of man? When a few pages later, Knausgaard seeks to describe Kiefer's entourage, the people flocking around him after his talks and joining him for celebratory dinners et cetera, he mentions that it was "like a king's court."[56] The university professor, then, is at the king's beck and call. When Kiefer calls, you pick up the phone, and you deliver—no questions asked.

These are features of the artist that resonate with the concept of sovereignty, and Knausgaard oscillates between "aesthetic" and "political" articulations of these features. For example, there is a moment early on in the profile where Kiefer talks about how, during the time when he studied law in Freiburg, he thought he was "a genius."[57] That's what he wrote down in his notebooks of the time: "In one of those books I wrote once, 'I'm the greatest painter, and there's no doubt'"—this followed by laughter (Kiefer's laughter punctuates the text, often destabilizing the grand things he has just said). "Today I wouldn't say that, it is complete nonsense," he continues. "What is 'the best'? But in those days, I believed it. I wrote it down like a law case, you know? That there's no doubt, that I am the best."[58] The statement "I'm the greatest painter" does not sound much like a law case, however. It sounds, rather, like a sovereign declaration (the profile is full of them). (When Kiefer makes another such sovereign declaration elsewhere in the text—"Napoleon was a feminist"—Knausgaard adds in parenthesis that "The fact checkers for this article looked this up, and in fact the situation seemed to be much more complicated" than Kiefer made it appear. Now *this* is more like a law case![59]) A similar declaration appears a little bit later in the text, this time attributed to Kiefer as "a little boy": "I thought that the best thing is to be an aristocrat. They don't work, and they are born with it all. And I thought to be an artist is like to be an aristocrat. Not like . . . no, no, no. It is to be *out of* classification. And I like to be out of any classification."[60] Here, the terminology is more political. The idea of the artist as aristocrat—which, etymologically, evokes the idea of "the best" that is present in Kiefer's earlier discussion of himself as a genius—is not characterized as non-sense but it is rejected nevertheless, this time in favor of an idea of the artist as "out of any classification." Knausgaard continues by saying that Kiefer realized this. But it's worth asking what has been realized: out of any classification. "The best" is obviously still a classification. Kiefer, however, is outside of that—is higher than, or if not that, than at least next to, outside of "the best." This is, arguably, something that is even greater than genius. It is not about being the best, which is, in a sense, a classification that remains within the law. ("The best" can, in Kiefer's opinion, be written down like a law case.) But the "outside" with which Kiefer associates the artist here—now that is something altogether different. Given Knausgaard's language and references elsewhere in the text, one would have good reason to call it "sovereign."

Kiefer takes Knausgaard to visit an actual aristocrat in the profile, at an actual castle, which has an actual "cabinet of curiosities, a collection of creatures from far and near, from a time when the world had not yet been fully mapped and science had not subjugated everything."[61] Kiefer is dressed for the visit like a priest, wearing an "ankle-length black robe and a black hat that resembled a skullcap."[62] Visiting the cabinet of wonders, Kiefer picks up "a bludgeoning weapon with spikes at the top": "He grinned and lifted it above his head as if to strike. Dressed in his black, priestlike robe and with his black headwear resembling a skullcap, he looked completely crazy."[63] When they notice his interest in the weapon, the aristocrats tell Kiefer he can keep it. He ultimately walks out of the castle holding "the club in one hand and an old-fashioned pair of scales with two bowls in the other."[64] For anyone familiar with images of sovereignty, it's hard not to read this as such an image. Specifically, one is reminded of the frontispiece of Thomas Hobbes' 1651 classic work of sovereignty, titled *Leviathan*, in which the Leviathan/ sovereign is shown holding a sword in their one hand, and a religious staff in the other, as the symbols of military/worldly and religious power. But in another version of the frontispiece that Horst Bredekamp includes in his book *Thomas Hobbes' Visuelle Strategien*, the sovereign is shown holding a sword and a pair of scales. If Knausgaard had taken a picture of Kiefer leaving the castle, it would have had an uncanny resemblance to this other version, underlining further Kiefer's association with sovereignty in the text.

Now, about Knausgaard's relation to his profile of Kiefer-the-artist-as-sovereign, I remain uncertain. On the one hand, the profile construes Kiefer as such; the resonance of Schmitt and of the concept of sovereignty in the profile is undisputable. This is explicitly tied to the question of fascism, and Broodthaers' response to Kiefer's "Occupations" project—who is this fascist who thinks he is an anti-fascist?—certainly applies when it comes to asking about the politics of the figure of the artist-as-sovereign. On the other hand, Knausgaard's profile also undermines Kiefer's sovereignty—there are plenty of petty aspects of his personality that are highlighted, raising the question with which the profile begins, namely how can *that* great art come from *this* petty person? Ultimately, then, one gets the sense that while Knausgaard may be undermining the sovereignty of the artist in his text, the text very much confirms the sovereignty of art—of something greater, sublime, that works through Kiefer, but in relation to which Kiefer is really only a small fry. We may be able to posit, then, a chain of exceptionalisms that can be traced back to the exceptionality of art that Knausgaard keeps intact: that of the artwork and the artist; that of the curator and the art critic; that of art's spectators. All of those figures, in different degrees, participate in art's exceptionalism. Indeed, it may be part of the reason why many people are into art: because they too want to be exceptional. All of those figures participate in the maintenance of an exceptionalism that extends from art's sovereignty to the much lesser sovereignty of art's spectators—but even they maintain a minimal edge, still, in relation to those who do not appreciate art. This is, I would argue, the foundational architecture of the art world. It is a world built around the exceptionalist sovereignty of art. And this very fact, given its close associations with Schmitt, of course begs the question of the art world's politics. What is this fascist world that claims to be anti-fascist? One thing is certain: "the death of the star-system"[65] never truly arrived in art.

The Toporovski Affair

There is a phenomenon in art where the art world's structuring logic of exceptionality is nicely exposed, and that is the fake. While the fake is a subject that, according to one critic, has begun "to look like one of those scenic spots of nature where too many vacationers have had a picnic,"[66] its scandal strangely persists in the art world and returning to it once again will enable me to substantiate further the claims about the art world's exceptionalism—and, by extension, the exceptionality of the artwork, the artist, the critics and curators, and the spectators of art—that I proposed above. Consider, as an another (after Knausgaard on Kiefer) example, the exhibition titled "From Bosch to Tuymans: A Vital Story," which opened on October 20, 2017 at the Museum voor Schone Kunsten (Museum of Fine Arts) in Ghent, Flanders (Belgium), where it was supposed to run through February 28th, 2018. Curated by the internationally recognized art critic and art historian Catherine de Zegher, who had become the museum's director in 2013, the exhibition included works of early twentieth-century Russian avant-gardist art attributed to Wassily Kandinsky and Kazimir Malevich amongst others. Through those works, de Zegher ambitiously sought "to rewrite the history of the Russian avant-garde." Not part of the museum's permanent collection, the works had never before been publicly exhibited. It was revealed that the museum had them on loan from the Dieleghem Foundation, a charity established by the Russian/naturalized Belgian Igor Toporovski who (with his wife Olga Toporovski) owns the castle in Belgium after which the charity is named.[67]

However, as soon as—and even before—the works from the Toporovski collection had gone on show, doubts were raised about their authenticity. After all, if the works included in the exhibition were authentic, the museum would have had the exhibition of the century, one for which major institutions in major cities would have *killed*. Something about the works just seemed "too good to be true." Moreover, the Toporovskis' record in the art world wasn't exactly clean: some ten years earlier, the discovery of a fake Malevich and Kandinsky had been traced back to a sale by . . . Igor Toporovski.[68] Shortly after the exhibition opened, a public letter appeared in *The Art Newspaper*, signed mostly by art dealers and collectors (as well as a few art historians, curators, and one independent scholar), which claimed that the works from the Toporovski collection featured in the show were "highly questionable."[69] If de Zegher, when she became the museum's director in 2013, had said she wanted to create an "open museum," the letter pointed out that surely *this* was not the openness she would have wanted.

That letter landed on the desk of a politician, the Flemish Minister of Culture and the Media, the liberal Sven Gatz.

Apparently, it had been Gatz who had initially put de Zegher in touch with the Toporovskis after he had seen some of the Toporovskis' art collection at their home. Because the Toporovski affair was taking on larger proportions by the day—because it was turning, precisely, into an *affair*—Gatz decided to become involved again, this time as a politician who knows nothing about art and whose hands were therefore clean in the entire situation: he had merely put de Zegher and the Toporovskis in touch. Gatz now pressed the city of Ghent to put together a commission to investigate the works in the exhibition.

Another public letter followed in the Flemish newspaper *De Standaard*, signed not by dealers and collectors this time but by representatives of important institutions in the Flemish art world.[70] It too openly questioned the authenticity of the exhibited works but it specifically charged the museum and its director with having neglected all deontological codes and rules during the preparation of the exhibition. Rather than being concerned with the authenticity of the works, the letter focused on the *modus operandi* of the museum and how it reflected back on the Flemish museum world in general.

An adjusted commission was created to do just that, and during questioning de Zegher confirmed that the museum had most certainly followed standard procedure during the preparation of the exhibition. Very quickly, however, it was revealed that the experts she claimed had been consulted during the vetting of the questionable works' provenance, had in fact not actively been involved in that process at all.[71] On the basis of this new information, and due to increased media pressure, de Zegher was then temporarily suspended as museum director, even if during that time she remained an official of the city of Ghent, which is technically her position (the city "lends" her to the museum as director). On March 14, 2018 newspapers revealed that Ernst & Young had been engaged to do an audit of the museum to see whether proper procedures had indeed been followed during the preparation of the exhibition.[72] After months of silence, another open letter was published on October 10, 2018 in which many major artists, art critics, and curators expressed their support for de Zegher and criticized the curator's "trial by media."[73] At this point, the museum audit had not yet been concluded; there was still no news about the authenticity of the works.

On October 17, 2018 de Zegher and Toporovski held a press conference to announce that a material and technical analysis performed in European laboratories on ten of the works that had been exhibited, proved that the works are authentic. It is unclear what exactly was meant by "authentic": while such analysis may prove that the works date from the 1920s, it does not necessarily prove that they were made by the actual artists to whom the museum had ascribed the works.[74] In a letter titled "Fake Art or Fake News?"[75] that was made available at the press conference with the promise of later publication in the art magazine *Hart*, de Zegher recounted some of the facts of the case—the letter did not comment on the Toporovskis' reputation in the art world—and pointed out its economic (financial) and political dimensions. She highlighted, for example, that it was initially art dealers who questioned the work and notes the implications of the affair and her "trial by media" for "our democracy."[76] The letter also announced that a book would be published in Spring 2019 detailing all of the facts of the affair, including all the art historical, archival, literary and material and technical evidence proving the authenticity of the works in question.

At the end of 2019, the Toporovskis were arrested and put in provisional detention at the prison of Ghent awaiting trial for forgery, among other crimes. The newspapers reported that they were released in January 2020 under specific conditions, in anticipation of a trial. At this time, the book that de Zegher had announced for Spring 2019 had not yet appeared.

Why have a picnic here again? In this kind of book, I don't want to cast judgment on the works from the Toporovski collection or even on the museum. I leave that to the art *connoisseurs* and the politicians (given that a public institution is involved), although I should add that de Zegher's qualities as an art critic and curator are, in my view, beyond doubt—even if she may have been fooled on this occasion. The starting point for this book is instead philosophical, and takes its cue from de Zegher's comments about the economic and political dimensions of the affair. This involves asking a transcendental question: How is this Toporovski trouble made possible? My suggestion is that the Toporovski affair is enabled by what I call *aesthetic exceptionalism*, something that we can see powerfully at work in Knausgaard's profile of Kiefer as well.[77]

The phrase sounds ugly and difficult, like a piece of theory-jargon that ought to be assigned to the trash heap of contemporary thought. However, many of us are no doubt familiar with the beliefs I would associate with this notion—indeed, we may even (uncritically) share them. I am thinking for example of Alain Badiou, who in his book *The Century* understands the effect of art as "forcing a thinking to declare, in its area of concern, the state of exception"[78]—and he values this effect positively. When Steven Corcoran characterizes the connection between aesthetics and politics in Jacques Rancière's thought, he suggests (but I will have to nuance this suggestion later) that in Rancière "art and politics can be understood, such that their specificity is seen to reside in their contingent *suspension* of the rules governing normal experience."[79] Art and politics find each other in the fact that both depend on "an innovative leap from the logic *that ordinarily governs human situations*."[80] Art and politics find each other, it seems, in their shared exceptionality. But where have we heard this before? In an early response to Badiou's book *Being and Event*, Jean-François Lyotard suggests that Badiou's theory of the subject strangely "mirrors" Schmitt's theory of the sovereign as he who decides on the state of exception.[81]

Something of this applies in the Toporovski affair as well, which of course reveals the need for a decision on the work of art: Is it a fake? Or not? The power to decide is in part that of the curator, the art critic, the art dealer, the politician, the scientist (who will be doing the material-technical analysis of the works)—but the objectivity of those decisions is, in each of these instances, at least partly in question (even if the material-technical analysis proves beyond a doubt that a work is from the time that its owner claims it to be, that still does not prove that the artist to whom it is attributed actually painted it). I consider the fake here because it enables us to push this question about "who" decides further, towards the question of "what" it is upon which these various would-be sovereigns are taking a decision. That is, of course, the work of art, and a specific aspect of the work of art: its originality. The latter is evidently also made up of more than one element—in addition to the evidence that a material-technical analysis can provide, there is the question of authorship, which may be harder to answer—but its force is nevertheless clear. What makes the Toporovski affair possible? What enables the scandal of the fake? It is the art world's attachment to the original, something that seems almost too obvious to mention—except that it is curious that it would persist to this day. To this day, the structuring logic of the art world—of the artwork, the economics of the art world, its aesthetics (how do works receive aesthetic appreciation?—originality plays a major role in that, with spectators stopping to appreciate a work of art they may have liked before as soon as it is revealed that it is a fake), its politics—appears to be organized around the exceptionality of the original.

Now, I am not saying there is anything inherently bad about the art world's attachment to the original. I too would not want my work to be presented as someone else's; I wouldn't want to present someone else's work as my own. I understand that someone else's appreciation of my own work will depend on the fact that it is indeed my own—that, if it were exposed that my work is not my own, someone else's appreciation for it may disappear. We can, of course, discuss the extent to which anyone's work is really "their own," especially when it comes to thinking and writing which are both influenced by the thoughts and texts of so many other people that it may become difficult to truly claim a work as one's own—witness the acknowledgments to most published books. (The only thing people truly claim as their own is their errors.) Still, at the end of the day, I will be marked as the author of "my own work," indebted to others as it may be. Authorship and originality conquer—even if many a writer and artist has of course tried to mess with the power those notions hold.

My critical question pertains to assessing, if indeed exceptionalism—the sovereignty of the artist, the originality of the work of art—centrally structures the logic of the art world, what that makes us realize about that world's politics. I am suggesting, following a thought experiment that read the figure of the artist through the lens of Carl Schmitt's theory of sovereignty, that the logic of sovereignty still reigns supreme in the art world. Given Schmitt's troubling politics, that has meant—especially in my discussion of Knausgaard's profile of Kiefer, in which this problematic is prominent—asking whether the art world tends fascistically. This is a provocation, of course; I am not saying that the art world is fascistic. Certainly it is worth noting its often emphatic declaration of anti-fascism, or its equally emphatic association with democracy. My question is whether those emphatic declarations are in line with the art world's simultaneous, continued celebration of the sovereign figure of the artist and the originality of the work of art. Can such aesthetic exceptionalism be squared with the art world's claim to a democratic politics? Does it evoke, rather, the specter of fascism? Often, the response of those accused of messing with this structuring logic, purposively or not, does not free us from the logic: de Zegher, for example, in response to accusations of having publicly shown fakes, responds by insisting on the original, on proving that the works were original. It seems to me that the more interesting conversation to have is why we still value so much that very notion, not only to question why we do—as I've indicated, I see clear and good reasons for that—but to then also draw appropriate conclusions about the art world's politics, conclusions that may be relevant outside of the art world as well. "Democracy," as Kenneth Goldsmith has observed, "[is] generally a recipe for disaster when it comes to art."[82] How are we to take the measure of this provocation?

Vandal, Forger, Sage

One thing that will be clear from the above is that if the art world remains attached to the exceptionality of the artwork, the artist, and art—if its fundamental approach to those figures remains within what I have characterized (following Stathis Gourgouris[83]) as the logic of the *one*—these attachments are obviously phantasmatic and in (often no doubt knowing) denial of a reality that is much more plural, both when it comes to deciding who the author of a work of art is and whether a work of art is original. Like any creator, artists are influenced by other artists, to just name one influence; the originality of an artwork has been subjected to such intense deconstruction that it seems almost absurd—though again, it clearly has some value as well—to even insist on a work's originality. This means that, in the political terms I used in the previous sections, "the democratic" always haunts "the fascistic," the plural always haunts the logic of the one. This seems to be a fact that is difficult to escape and that, if it were fully recognized, would destabilize the art world—our understanding of the artwork, the artist, and art and the economics, aesthetics, and politics that are built on it.

Strangely, or perhaps not, this realization seems to already be present in the famous image of sovereignty that I brought to your attention earlier on, from Hobbes' *Leviathan*. The issue of plurality is present within the image, of course, in the sense that Hobbes designed his theory of sovereignty to promote a logic of the one, in response to the division of a two that he feared—specifically, the situation of civil war to which his book responded. But it is interesting to see what happens when different editions and translations of Hobbes' book are published: its frontispiece gets adjusted, undergoing sometimes minor, sometimes major changes, constituting what Bredekamp refers to as a group of sovereign "brothers" whose plurality—a gendered plurality, to be sure—begins to undermine Hobbes' theory of the sovereign as one. The pluralization of the image of sovereignty can be read as an uncanny aesthetico-political anticipation of the history of sovereignty itself, which morphs from the monarchical to the popular, and while maintaining some ideal of unity becomes pluralized. This pluralization writes, I would argue, sovereignty's *fact* rather than its *phantasy*, and it is a fact that can be read back to the art world and the way in which the concept of sovereignty is operative there—as a phantasy of unity that is undermined by the fact of plurality.

The challenge, then, politically, would be to insist on this plurality in our aesthetic discourse about the artwork, the artist, and art. How to talk about these in the plural? How to allow for some unity—originality and "the author" surely ought to retain some of their importance?—in an overall situation of plurality? This is, in the terms that I seek to develop in this book, a question of unexceptionalizing the art world and, by extension, its politics. It is a question of largely leaving aesthetic exceptionalism behind in order to try something else. It's not as if this hasn't been tried before—this book will rely on many previous such attempts, and also indicate that the very project to attempt this as something "new" can perhaps only make sense within a Western tradition that has held the exception so dear. But exceptionalism's dogged persistence suggests that we are not quite done with it—and perhaps there are good reasons why we shouldn't be (these too I will consider). Still, the Schmittian resonances in aesthetic theory ought to give us much to think about, and in what follows I focus on three figures to organize such a project: the vandal, the forger, and the sage. In Knausgaard's profile of

Kiefer, Kiefer is quoted as saying that "all artists are iconoclasts" in response to Knausgaard questioning why Kiefer is putting a brown sticky substance on one of his paintings.[84] Why would he destroy such a beautiful work? That's what artists do, Kiefer appears to be saying, thus bringing the artist in close connection to the vandal. Starting from this suggestion, which one finds echoed elsewhere in art history and aesthetics as well, I want to begin by exploring the relation between the understanding of the artist as vandal and that of the artist as sovereign. Does the former confirm or challenge the latter? How does this question enable us to understand something about vandalism, sovereignty, and the artist? I will pursue such questions by thinking about art's connection to on the one hand, the smooth (recognized by some as "the signature of our times") and, on the other, injury. These connections will extend from the artwork to what is shown within the artwork as well as our thinking about the artist. Ultimately I will be interested in the politics of such a project.

One particularly interesting question, in view of my discussion of the fake, that will come up in the context of my discussion of vandalism and art's connection to injury is the observation, made by one critic whose work I will engage with, that copies and fakes are somehow less susceptible to vandalism than originals. Apart from confirming the exceptional status of the original, that critical observation also seeks to distinguish between different kinds of vandalism (something I will have already discussed when I considered the vandal in their relation to art and sovereignty). These considerations will beg a further examination of the fake and the copy; specifically, I am interested in how these can be read not so much as tributes (as they often are) but as acts of vandalism themselves—against originality.

The reason why vandalism may not be as effective with a copy or fake would not so much be, then, because those works are not originals, but because the copy and the fake are vandalizations already—and to vandalize something that's already broken is just not as effective as vandalizing something that is whole. Continuing my reflections about an aesthetic of the smooth versus an aesthetic of injury, I intend to consider specifically the role of the nude in Western art history as a figure of the smooth, original idea/ideal that, as such, says something central about the Western art historical tradition in which the copy and the fake have always remained unreconciled. Taking my cue from other critics, my thinking will be directed towards Chinese art history and the difference in thinking about the copy that it reveals, and I will focus on Chinese landscape painting and the tension in which critics have observed it to exist with Western painting and specifically the tradition of the nude (which is absent in Chinese art, even if Chinese art does show naked bodies; landscapes are of course central to Western art history as well but as we will see these are different landscapes from Chinese landscape painting). Weary of the risk of orientalism in this context, which would simply turn China into "the opposite" of the West, I will nevertheless acknowledge divergences in approach and emphasis and, indeed, show how some of the West's most influential thinking about the copy and the fake found its origin in an encounter with Chinese landscape painting.

Such a consideration will be continued in an extended reflection about the figure of the sage from ancient Chinese thought. While obviously a figure of cultural elitism, as several have noted, and as such a figure of exceptionality, ancient Chinese thought and specifically daoism have been praised for drawing out the unexceptional. As such, they place a markedly different emphasis from what is dominant in Western thought, even if there is exceptionalism in Chinese thought and even if unexceptional thinking is prominent in the West as well. My goal will be to explore the politics of unexceptionalism which has, in studies of daoism, been associated with "anarchy." More recently, however, it has also become associated with neoliberalism. What to make of these associations in the wake of a global pandemic that required, for the greater safety of all, exceptional intervention of the sovereign nation-state? Mapping out these connections and engaging such questions will enable me to get a better grasp on unexceptionalism's politics, which will be central to my explorations of the sage.

I will then continue this investigation with a close reading of two case-studies, Bianca Bosker's study of architectural copying in China and Winnie Wong's art historical study of the mass copying of Western paintings in China. While both of these studies confirm many elements of my own work, they also enable me to enlarge the deconstructive, non-orientalist approach that I pursue by highlighting the exceptionalism in both China's approach to architectural copying and the copying of Western paintings that Wong discusses. Both Bosker and Wong show, in different but complementary ways, that exceptionalism can be found in very unexceptionalist places, indicating the persistence of exceptionalism even in places where it is sometimes—superficially—deemed not to exist. While these are extremely valuable insights of fact, they are also highly valuable from the methodological point of view, because they make an orientalism in this context—any simple opposition of the West to China on the count of exceptionalism—impossible. Rather, what my own study discovers is not so much essences but tendencies, in both the West and China, to undermine exceptionalist conceptions of the art world and the politics that is tied to them. These tendencies will be further explored in the very last section of the book, where I intend to run through a series of cases to put some of the thinking that I have developed in the book to the test.

Post-Exceptional Politics

Taking my cue from understandings of daoism as "anarchist," I intend to develop the notion of "democratic anarchy" as an effective antidote against exceptionalist thinking, one that can begin to resonate in both the West and the East. Defined by Stathis Gourgouris (who is in dialogue with Emily Apter on this count) as an unexceptional politics, specifically as a politics that does not grant anyone any particular privilege to rule, democratic anarchy will connect in my reading to Giorgio Agamben's theorization of "destituent power" as what would break the spell that sovereignty has cast over our theories and practices of politics.

In the last volume of Agamben's *Homo Sacer* series, which lays bare the fundamental biopolitical operation of sovereignty (its internal exclusion or exception of what Agamben after Walter Benjamin calls "bare life" within the limits of the *polis*, thus turning the *polis* into a camp[85]), Agamben describes a kind of power—or perhaps better, potential—that he dubs "destituent."[86] With this notion, Agamben wants to take on precisely the sovereign exceptionalism that I have associated with Schmitt. In the earlier volumes of his project, Agamben had traced such an exceptionalism back to the fact that the Greeks, in his analysis, had two words for life: *zoe*, or the simple fact of living shared by animals, humans, and gods; and *bios*, which refers to the qualified life of an individual or group—ethical or political life. The tragedy of Western power, as Agamben sees it, is played out in the dynamic between those two notions of life, with for example political protection being granted to living subjects as an addition to their *zoe*, thus including *zoe* within the sphere of *bios* only by virtue of its exclusion. "[I]n this mad world," as one of Agamben's major influences, Hannah Arendt, writes in a text titled "We Refugees," "it is much easier to be accepted as a 'great man' than as a human being."[87]

Agamben understands this internal exclusion to be an exception, and refers to the general state in which such a political logic is the case as "the state of exception." Whereas the latter, in Schmitt, tends to be associated with emergency situations, according to Agamben it has become the rule in contemporary Western societies. If the concentration camp is an extreme example of such a state, where its underlying logic is unsparingly laid bare, modern political societies have in fact continued to operate according to this rule, which is the rule of the exception. According to Agamben, the only way out of such a situation is to neutralize the vicious dynamic between *zoe* and *bios*, between the simple fact of living and its form, life and the form of life. To accomplish this, he develops in *The Use of Bodies* the enigmatic notion of form-of-life (with the hyphens), which had already come up at various other places in Agamben's work.

If the separation between *zoe* and *bios* can be traced back to a hylemorphic Aristotelian ontology (an ontology that is founded in the distinction between matter and form), as Agamben convincingly argues, form-of-life is meant to displace the basic opposition of that ontology by "contract[ing] into one another in a peremptory gesture" the notions of *zoe* and *bios*, thus "taking leave of classical politics."[88] In Agamben's view, this "points toward an unheard-of politicization of life as such":

> The wager here is that there can be a *bios*, a mode of life, that is defined solely by means of its special and inseparable union with *zoe* and has no other content than the latter (and reciprocally, that there is a *zoe* that is nothing other than its form, its *bios*). Precisely and solely to the *bios* and *zoe* thus transfigured do there belong the attributes of political life: happiness and autarchy.[89]

It is this new form of contract-theory (as I have characterized it elsewhere) that Agamben finds in form-of-life (with the hyphens marking the contraction, visualizing it on the page).[90]

Exceptionalism, for Agamben, can thus be traced back to the dynamic between *zoe* and *bios*. Translated into aesthetic exceptionalism, I want to propose an analogy with the dynamic between the original and the copy, with the art world—in parallel to modern Western states—emerging as what Agamben calls a camp, where works (*zoe*) are only included by virtue of their being labeled original and authentic (*bios*), an inclusion that truly operates as an internal exclusion or exception given that when works—even if they are good works—are exposed to be forgeries, they will be banned from the art world.[91] Here, it becomes clear that the distinction between a good and bad work of art ultimately operates in a different way from that between the original and the copy. Whereas the former comes about by subjective determination, whether individual or collective, the latter can be objectively determined. As such the logic of exceptionalism is much more effective in the latter than in the former, even if traces of the exceptional are of course retained in any aesthetic judgment.

The post-exceptional would need to be conceived, in Agamben's terms, as a kind of "destituent potential" that would unwork the Aristotelian ontology underlying Western politics—an ontology that is very much present in the valuation of the original over the copy that structures the Western art world, its aesthetics, economics, and politics. For Agamben, it is "destituent potential" that unworks political exceptionalism of the kind that can be found in Schmitt. This involves, he suggests, "think[ing] entirely different strategies": it is not about "revolutions, revolts, and new constitutions," the dynamic between constituting and constituted power.[92] When it comes to bringing "destituent potential" in conversation with an already existing political name, the closest Agamben comes to that is in his turn towards "anarchy," towards an "anarchist tradition" that has "sought to define [destituent power] without truly succeeding in it."[93] In a way, Agamben can be considered to be taking up that anarchist project, even if in the closing pages of *The Use of Bodies* that particular challenge ultimately remains undeveloped. Indeed, the book reads not so much as a concluding volume to a series but as a text in which the project of the series is "abandoned," as Agamben puts it in a Prefatory Note.[94]

In order to pursue this suggestion of an "anarchist" politics further, let me loop back to the political references that I used earlier. Schmitt, and by association a thinker like Badiou, are inconceivable within post-exceptionalist thought. However, and this is where I would counter the reading that Steven Corcoran provides of his thought, Rancière could perhaps still fit, given that he claims to reconceptualize the exception precisely *not* like Badiou. Possibly recognizing the potential problems of Badiou's thinking on this count, Rancière has in an interview insisted that if there is an exception in his theory, it is different from Badiou's theory of the event: for him the exception is always ordinary, he insists, coming "not out of a decision or out of a radical rupture" but out of a "multiplicity of small displacements."[95] Rancière's theory of transformation marks, in that sense, an unworking of a Western theologico-political thought of the exception.

But this is ultimately not convincing. Consider how the notion of "anarchy" appears in this context.[96] When in his "Ten Theses on Politics" Rancière seeks to characterize "democracy," he mentions Cleisthenes' famous democratic experiment, wherein "democracy is characterized by the drawing of lots, or the complete absence of any entitlement to govern. It is the state of exception in which no oppositions can function, in which there is no principle for the dividing up of roles . . . Democracy is the specific situation in which it is the absence of entitlement that entitles one to exercise the *archè*."[97] Rancière takes this exceptionalist understanding of democracy from Plato's *Laws*, in which Plato "undertakes a systematic inventory of the qualifications (axiomata) required for governing and the correlative qualifications for being ruled."[98] Plato retains seven, four of which (Rancière notes) are based on "natural difference, that is, the difference of birth."[99] "The fifth qualification . . . is the power of those with a superior nature, of the strong over the weak."[100] The sixth, which Plato considers most worthy, is that of "the power of those who know over those who do not"[101]—hence, his preference for philosopher-kings. But, Rancière notes, Plato adds a seventh qualification which produces what he considers a "break in the logic of the *arkhè*."[102] Plato calls this seventh qualification "the choice of God" or "the drawing of lots."[103]

This is how Rancière arrives at his understanding of democracy as "the state of exception." If such a democratic state is "anarchic," this is not because of its total absence of *archè*, but because it produces a break in the *logic* of *archè*, in that *it turns the absence of the entitlement to rule into the entitlement to rule*—into a "commencement without commencement, a form of rule (*commandement*) that does not command."[104] In other words: there is rule, but not as before. This is a state of exception, as Rancière sees it, but one "that more generally makes politics in its specificity possible."[105] This is why democracy for Rancière is not so much a political regime but the name of politics as such. Democracy, like politics, is what produces a break within the logic of ruling as such. This has something to do with the particular anarchy that it brings. Anarchy, then, does not so much refer to the absence of all rule but to the democratic break in the logic of a rule that is exercised by one "determinate superiority" over "an equally determinate inferiority."[106] It refers to the rule of equality.[107] In other words: Rancière claims democracy as anarchic and in that sense as politics due to its rule of equality, a rule that is based on the absence of any entitlement to rule. While such a position obviously marks a kind of shock, and an exception in this sense—it does, after all, accomplish a break in the logic of the *arkhè*—it is worth noting that such a shock or exception does not do away with all rule. Indeed, it is folded back within the rule—a wholly transformed rule.

It is no wonder that Agamben has revealed himself to be rather critical of Rancière given that, first of all, Rancière is still an exceptionalist thinker and, second, he is ultimately attached to some form of constituted power.[108] While everything political in Rancière challenges constituted power, which Rancière associates with the police, politics also always moves in the direction of a newly constituted—but more equal—order. With the notion of destituent potential, Agamben is precisely trying to steer clear from this.

In his thought about anarchist democracy, the already mentioned Stathis Gourgouris may have drawn the right conclusion on the basis of Rancière's central idea. If in an anarchist democracy as Rancière describes it everyone is equally entitled to govern, Gourgouris argues, then anarchist democracy is precisely unexceptional—for everyone, *without exception*. Following Emily Apter,[109] he embraces the notion of an unexceptional politics:

> I favor this notion because for me democracy is precisely the regime that does not make exceptions, if we are to take seriously Aristotle's dictum of a politics where the ruler learns by being ruled, making thus the ruled simultaneously the rulers, in a determinant affirmation of an *archè* that has no precedent and no uniqueness but is shared by all. No exceptions. The obvious politics of partiality and discrimination or exclusion in so-called modern democracies testifies to their fraudulent use of the name. Contemporary democratic states are no more than liberal oligarchies.[110]

As Gourgouris sees it, unexceptional politics goes against the theologization of politics (which he associates with Schmitt):

> I am interested instead in a politics where nothing is miraculous, where indeed nothing is sacred, where there is no *Homo Sacer* [this is a reference, obviously, to Agamben's project]. This would be an unexceptional politics, an untheologized politics. It would have to be necessarily an anarchic politics, as democratic politics is at the core, insofar as *archè* is unexceptionally shared by all and therefore lapses as a singular principle. Anarchy as a mode of rule—democratic rule par excellence—raises a major challenge to the inherited tradition of sovereignty in modernity.[111]

When it comes to politics, many artists would be ready to embrace this. They would be ready to embrace the post-exceptionalism of such an anarchist democracy. However, when it comes to art, the situation appears to be very different. Unlike "unexceptional politics," "unexceptional art" receives a much less warm embrace, if it is welcomed at all. People, in particular artists, tend to find "unexceptional art" offensive. To think of art as unexceptional—now that goes against the very core of what we believe art is!

But that difference in reception leads to the strange situation—central to this book—that in art we praise what in politics we find dubious. To be fair, art and politics *are* different—so perhaps it is just fine to find dubious in politics what we praise in art. Perhaps we can pursue in art what we think can't be pursued in politics, and perhaps it is better to pursue those things in art rather than in politics. Perhaps art is where we can exorcise the demons by whom we'd prefer not be haunted in politics. But to the extent that both art and politics operate in the imaginary, and in that sense mutually support each other (with artistic imaginaries passing into politics, and political imaginaries into art), art is not separate from politics—and vice versa. In part, that means one can expect some consistency between the two realms. When it comes to exceptionalism, it seems there is little: exceptionalism is treated as suspicious in politics, but loved in art. This book reconsiders whether that ought to be so.

To end, let me address—entirely in line with this project—the inevitable accusation that risks to come my way, namely, that my plea for unexceptional art is nothing new but has a longstanding history in the arts—that it is a copy, and therefore inferior. I want to acknowledge that history from the outset, and I will return to it throughout this book, even if the elements from it that I will highlight may not be the usual ones. Indeed, and in some tension with the accusation that this book says nothing new, for art history readers my book will likely seem to combine an unusual, even idiosyncratic range of references; and the same may be true for scholars of exceptionalism in political theory, and those interested ancient Chinese philosophy and art.

To some, the book may seem to have something like a three-body problem, to echo the title of a celebrated Chinese science-fiction novel: engaged in art history, political philosophy, and Sinology, it never—and could never—cover the ground of each of those disciplines in a way that is satisfactory to all of those scholars. While the book does cover a lot of ground, and also builds on ground that I have already begun to cover elsewhere, the fact remains that it ultimately takes several risks in order to make its intervention. Discussions of originality and authorship as well as the copy and the fake are legion in the arts, but I am resituating them here within debates about exceptionalism and political theology. Exceptionalism is a major topic in political philosophy, but I am tying it to conversations in the arts with which, to my knowledge, it has not previously been associated in this particular way—that is, with a focus on political theology. "China" obviously is a field on its own; I am not *forcing* it onto the work I am doing but *finding* it in the sources that I consult and *following* the fact of its reference from text to text, exploring this reference in fields with which it is not usually associated. None of those separate fields is fully grounded by the standards of each discipline in this book. This means that I discuss Carl Schmitt in this Introduction, a thinker on whom I have spent a lot of attention elsewhere, not in order to cover all the published scholarship on Schmitt or even situate him in a tradition of political thought, but for the purpose of illuminating how Schmitt's thought appears in a perhaps surprising place—Karl

Ove Knausgaard's profile of Anselm Kiefer. It means that in my engagement with what I call post-exceptionalism in the arts, I do not seek to provide an overview of other work in art history that may have already laid bare an aspect of such post-exceptionalism, for example through its focus on labor in the arts or the politics of conceptual art (with which I am familiar; I have engaged with it in my work on finance). Much of that other work *will* be referenced along the way, *but* my goal is not to provide an overview of it; instead, as I already said, I am setting up a constellation of references in my opening chapter whose reverberations I then pursue to the end. Finally, I should note that while most of my attention in the book is on the visual arts, my training is in the literary arts, and as such the book springs from an engagement with a contemporary novelist—an art-critical essay they wrote about art vandalism. This arguably introduces a fourth body into the picture that may throw off each of my three other audiences.

Let me return to the charge of the copy, dubious as it may seem in light of the work I accomplish in this book: even if it were true that with my plea for post-exceptionalism in the arts, and my exploration of the politics that it may mark, I would merely be repeating pleas that have been made many times before, the question remains worth asking why it is that this plea would have had to be repeated again and again, as if it had never been said before? In other words, why is it, in spite of the fact that this plea has obviously been made several times, that its target—exceptionalism—has somehow prevailed? From Walter Benjamin to Hito Steyerl to Byung-Chul Han, Winnie Wong and others: it's the engagement with and in several of those instances defense of the copy, over and over again, in response to tendencies of thought, art, and politics that Benjamin perceptively labeled "fascistic" (as I will discuss). Even if what I have to say here strikes you as no more than a copy, that alone is worth considering—including in relation to your charge that this book is a copy.

Dear reader, why are you protesting so much? What is the politics of your protest? In what kind of thinking about art and the artist is it grounded? Furthermore, why do the idiosyncracies of this book trouble you, the risks it takes with disciplines? The thinking that's developed here is obviously not formless—I hope we can agree on that; instead, it seeks to establish another kind of form. As I explain in Chapter 5, I consider this to be critical to the future of any discipline.

Ultimately this book wasn't written for any of the above audiences. It was written for artists. If I am taking a risk putting this book out there, I am doing so largely because I have seen the effect of this thinking on the many young artists with whom I have worked over the years. They have responded to it with great enthusiasm, explaining to me that they found in it not only a book but something like an attitude that changed their relation to their own work, that of others, and the institutions in which they were being educated. If that is bad education, then good education may be worse.

Notes

1 Carl Schmitt, *Political Theology: Four Chapters on the Concept of Sovereignty*, trans. George Schwab (Cambridge, MA: The MIT Press, 1985), pp. 5–15.

2 Richard Wolin, "Carl Schmitt: The Conservative Revolutionary Habitus and the Aesthetics of Horror," *Political Theory* 20:3 (1992), p. 426.

3 See, for example: Giorgio Agamben, *Homo Sacer: Sovereign Power and Bare Life*, trans. Daniel Heller-Roazen (Stanford, CA: Stanford University

Press, 1998); Chantal Mouffe, ed., *The Challenge of Carl Schmitt* (New York: Verso, 1999).

4 Paul Kahn, *Political Theology: Four New Chapters on the Concept of Sovereignty* (New York: Columbia University Press, 2012), p. 128.

5 Kahn, *Political Theology*, p. 128.

6 Schmitt, *Political Theology*, p. 5.

7 Carl Schmitt, *Politische Theologie: Vier Kapitel Zur Lehre Von der Souveränität* (Leipzig: Duncker & Humblot, 1922), p. 9.

8 Schmitt, *Political Theology*, p. 5.

9 Ibid.

10 Ibid.

11 Ibid.

12 Ibid., p. 6.

13 Jacques Derrida, *Politics of Friendship*, trans. George Collins (New York: Verso, 1997).

14 Schmitt, *Political Theology*, p. 6.

15 Ibid.

16 Ibid.

17 Ibid., p. 7.

18 Ibid.

19 Ibid.

20 Ibid.

21 Ibid., p. 13.

22 Ibid.

23 See: Joseph Owen, "Details, Details, Details: Carl Schmitt's Critique of Borderline Anticipation," *boundary 2 online* 5:2 (2020). "Frictionless Sovereignty," special issue, ed. Ryan Bishop, accessible: http://www.boundary2.org/2020/08/joseph-owen-details-details-details-carl-schmitts-borderline-critique-of-anticipation/

24 Schmitt, *Political Theology*, p. 13.

25 See: Samuel Weber, "Taking Exception to Decision: Walter Benjamin and Carl Schmitt," in: Harry Kunneman and Hent de Vries, eds., *Enlightenments: Encounters Between Critical Theory and French Thought* (Kampen: Kok Pharos, 1993), pp. 141–161; Giorgio Agamben, *State of Exception*, trans. Kevin Attell (Chicago, IL: University of Chicago Press, 2005).

26 Schmitt, *Political Theology*, p. 10.

27 Dana D. Nelson, *Bad for Democracy: How the Presidency Undermines the Power of the People* (Minneapolis: University of Minnesota Press, 2008).

28 Schmitt, *Political Theology*, p. 9.
29 Ibid., p. 10.
30 Ibid., p. 11.
31 Ibid.
32 Ibid.
33 Ibid., p. 12.
34 Andreas Kalyvas, "Carl Schmitt and the Three Moments of Democracy," *Cardozo Law Review* 21:1525 (1999–2000), pp. 1525–1565.
35 Schmitt, *Political Theology*, p. 13.
36 Ibid., p. 15.
37 Ibid.
38 On this, see: Arne De Boever, *Being Vulnerable: Contemporary Political Thought* (Montreal: McGill-Queen's University Press, 2023).
39 Armen Avanessian's book *Future Metaphysics* has made a major contribution to this kind of thinking about art. Schmitt comes up in his book, but curiously this dimension of his thought—which is quite close to Avanessian's—is not considered. I intend to come back to the Avanessian-Schmitt connection at length elsewhere. See: Armen Avanessian, *Future Metaphysics*, trans. James C. Wagner (Cambridge: Polity, 2020).
40 Karl Ove Knausgaard, "In Search of Anselm Kiefer," *New York Times Magazine* February 16 (2020), pp. 26–33, pp. 59–62, here p. 33.
41 Knausgaard, "In Search of," p. 33.
42 Ibid.
43 Ibid.
44 Ibid.
45 Ibid.
46 Ibid.
47 Ibid., p. 28.
48 Ibid.
49 Ibid.
50 Ibid., p. 29.
51 Ibid.
52 Ibid.
53 Ibid.
54 Ibid., pp. 29–30.
55 Ibid., p. 30.
56 Ibid., p. 32.
57 Ibid., p. 30.
58 Ibid.

59 Ibid., p. 60.
60 Ibid., p. 32.
61 Ibid., p. 60.
62 Ibid.
63 Ibid., p. 60–61.
64 Ibid., p. 61.
65 Julio García Espinosa, "For an Imperfect Cinema," *Jump Cut: A Review of Contemporary Cinema* 20 (1979), pp. 24–26, accessible: https://www.ejumpcut.org/archive/onlinessays/JC20folder/ImperfectCinema.html
66 Rudolph Arnheim, "On Duplication," in: Dennis Dutton, ed., *The Forger's Art: Forgery and the Philosophy of Art* (Berkeley: University of California Press, 1983), pp. 232–245, here p. 232.
67 Apparently, the Toporovskis are planning to turn the castle into a museum to exhibit their extensive art collection. See: Colin Gleadell, "Experts Say Russian Modernism Show at Ghent Museum is 'Highly Questionable,'" *Artnet News* January 15 (2018), accessible: https://news.artnet.com/exhibitions/experts-say-russian-modernism-show-ghent-museum-highly-questionable-1198757
68 See: Sarah Cascone, "Belgian Museum Removes Show of Disputed Russian Avant-Garde Works after Damning Exposé," *Artnet News* January 30 (2018), accessible: https://news.artnet.com/exhibitions/russian-avant-garde-exhibition-closes-expose-1210742. For a more extensive account in English, see: Simon Hewitt, "The *Art Newspaper* Exposé Helps Close Dubious Avant-Garde Art Display in Belgian Museum," *The Art Newspaper* January 29 (2018), accessible: https://www.theartnewspaper.com/news/the-story-behind-the-dubious-russian-avant-garde-art-show-in-ghent-museum
69 See: "Arts Professionals Accuse Ghent Museum of Exhibiting Unauthenticated Works," *Artforum* January 16 (2018), accessible: https://www.artforum.com/news/arts-professionals-accuse-ghent-museum-of-exhibiting-unauthenticated-works-73539
70 See: "De Imagoschade Na Toporovski is Groot," *De Standaard* March 5 (2018), accessible: http://www.standaard.be/cnt/dmf20180304_03390328
71 See: Geert Sels, "De Zegher Loog Gentse Politici Voor," *De Standaard* March 7 (2018), accessible: http://www.standaard.be/cnt/dmf20180306_03394363
72 See: gvds, "Ernst & Young Doet Audit in MSK Ghent," *De Standaard* March 14 (2018), accessible: http://www.standaard.be/cnt/dmf20180314_03409354

73 Sarah Cascone, "Luc Tuymans, Giuseppe Penone, and Other Art-World Figures Defend Museum Director After Russian Forgery Scandal," *Artnet News* October 11 (2018), accessible: https://news.artnet.com/art-world/artists-art-professionals-defend-ghent-museum-director-russian-forgery-scandal-1369207

74 See: Geert Sels, "Toporovski en de Zegher Claimen: 'Werken Zijn Authentiek,'" *De Standaard* October 17 (2018), accessible: http://www.standaard.be/cnt/dmf20181017_03852188

75 I think de Zegher is making a category mistake when she associates fake art with fake news. Fake art is still within the realm of the aesthetic. Fake news is no news at all.

76 Catherine de Zegher, "Fake Art or Fake News?," accessible: https://www.scribd.com/document/391046833/Tekst-De-Zegher#from_embed

77 I am not the first to use this term in print but, as far as I know, the content I give to it is original. Jon Robson already used the term as the title for a chapter he contributed to the book *Art and Belief* (Ema Sullivan-Bissett, Helen Bradley, and Paul Noordhof, eds. [Oxford: Oxford University Press, 2017]). Robson's work is in aesthetic epistemology, however, and pursues a related but different angle into the issue of aesthetic exceptionalism through its focus on "belief pessimism" in relation to aesthetic judgment.

78 Alain Badiou, *The Century*, trans. Alberto Toscano (Cambridge: Polity, 2007), p. 160.

79 Steven Corcoran, "Editor's Introduction," in: Jacques Rancière, *Dissensus: On Politics and Aesthetics*, ed. and trans. Steven Corcoran (London: Continuum, 2010), p. 1.

80 Ibid.

81 Philippe Lacoue-Labarthe, Jacques Rancière, Jean-François Lyotard, and Alain Badiou, "Liminaire sur l'ouvrage d'Alain Badiou 'L'être et l'évènement,'" *Le Cahier* (*Collège Internationale de Philosophie*) 8 (1989), pp. 201–225, pp. 227–245, pp. 247–268.

82 Kenneth Goldsmith, *Uncreative Writing: Managing Language in the Digital Age* (New York: Columbia University Press, 2011), p. 10.

83 Stathis Gourgouris, *The Perils of the One* (New York: Columbia University Press, 2019). I will engage with this text in detail in Chapter 1.

84 Knausgaard, "In Search of," p. 30.

85 On this, see: Agamben, *Homo Sacer*.

86 Giorgio Agamben, *The Use of Bodies*, trans. Adam Kotsko (Stanford, CA: Stanford University Press, 2016), p. 263.

87 Hannah Arendt, "We Refugees," in: Marc Robinson, ed., *Altogether Elsewhere: Writers on Exile* (Boston, MA: Faber and Faber, 1996), pp. 110–119, here p. 115.

88 Agamben, *Use*, p. 219.

89 Ibid.

90 For Agamben, such a contraction is a Platonic gesture, but to understand this one must delve into his idiosyncratic reading of Plato, which I will leave for another time.

91 Agamben comes closest to this analogy in his book: *The Man Without Content*, trans. Georgia Albert (Stanford, CA: Stanford University Press, 1999). Following this analogy, one must risk to rewrite Schmitt's famous dictum about all significant modern concepts of the state as follows: all significant modern aesthetic concepts (concepts of the museum and the gallery, if you will) are secularized theological concepts. Doing so would then in turn lead one to consider the residue of sovereignty, and monarchical sovereignty in particular, in modern aesthetics.

92 Agamben, *Use*, p. 266.

93 Ibid., p. 275.

94 Ibid., p. xiii.

95 Abraham Geil, "Writing, Repetition, Displacement: An Interview with Jacques Rancière," *Novel* 47:2 (2014), pp. 301–310.

96 This paragraph as well as the following are taken from: Arne De Boever, "Art and Exceptionalism: A Critique," rev. Santiago Zabala, *Why Only Art Can Save Us: Aesthetics and the Absence of Emergency* (New York: Columbia University Press, 2017), boundary 2 45:4 (2018), pp. 161–181.

97 Jacques Rancière, *Dissensus: On Politics and Aesthetics*, trans. Steven Corcoran (London: Continuum, 2010), p. 31.

98 Rancière, *Dissensus*, pp. 30–31.

99 Ibid., p. 31.

100 Ibid.

101 Ibid.

102 Ibid.

103 Ibid.

104 Ibid.

105 Ibid.

106 Ibid., p. 30.

107 This understanding of anarchy is clear throughout Rancière's work, from his book *The Ignorant Schoolmaster: Five Lessons in Intellectual Emancipation* (trans. Kirstin Ross [Stanford, CA: Stanford University

Press, 1990]) onwards. In the first chapter of that book, for example, Rancière develops a criticism of the "*archè*" of "explication." This is clear from the fact that he distinguishes the following two dimensions of explication: "On the one hand, [the explicator] decrees the absolute beginning" (Rancière, *Ignorant Schoolmaster*, p. 6)—"*archè*" in the sense of "beginning." "On the other," he continues, the explicator "appoints himself to the task of lifting [the veil of ignorance that s/he has cast over everything that is to be learned" (ibid., pp. 6–7). This is "*archè*" in the sense of "rule"—the master rules through appointing her-/himself this task. This is what Rancière later calls the "hierarchical" set-up of explication. Of course, by making the case for an ignorant schoolmaster, Rancière seeks to intervene in this. But how exactly? He proposes a kind of an-archy, but not the loose sense of anarchy that gets rid of the master altogether—it's an an-archy that is "not . . . without a master" (ibid., p. 12), as he points out. This is the anarchy of an emancipatory teaching situation, of an equality and democracy of intelligences, freed from the hierarchy of *archè*—or, rather, operative after a radical transformation in the logic of *archè*.

108 Giorgio Agamben, *The Time that Remains: A Commentary on the* Letter *to the Romans*, trans. Patricia Dailey (Stanford, CA: Stanford University Press, 2005), pp. 57–58.

109 Emily Apter, *Unexceptional Politics: On Obstruction, Impasse, and the Impolitic* (New York: Verso, 2018).

110 Stathis Gourgouris, "The Question Is: Society Must Be Defended Against Whom? Or What?" *New Philosopher*, May 25 (2013), accessible: http://www.newphilosopher.com/articles/the-question-is-society-defended-against-whom-or-what-in-the-name-of-what/

111 Gourgouris, "The Question Is."

Part I

The Vandal

1

Damage Art

America likes and demands a clean art.[1]

—W. H. de B. Nelson, "Aesthetic Hysteria" (1917)

"All artists are iconoclasts"

There is a moment in Karl Ove Knausgaard's *New York Times Magazine* profile of the German artist Anselm Kiefer when Kiefer states: "All artists are iconoclasts."[2] The artist laughs after he says it, so it's not clear whether the statement can be taken at face value. It may be a mere platitude that Kiefer offers in response to Knausgaard's *petit bourgeois* objection to the artist starting to apply a sticky brown substance along the edge of what Knausgaard thinks is a beautiful painting: "The painting, about 12 feet long and six feet wide, depicted a forest at the far end of a snow-covered field. No people, no animals, no sky. Just the field and the trees."[3] Why would Kiefer put that brown stuff on something so beautiful? Why would Kiefer vandalize such a painting—Knausgaard notes, in an interesting aside, that "I would have given my right arm to make such a picture"[4]—why would he destroy it? The moment arrives immediately after their discussion of Kiefer's use of lead in his paintings. Kiefer likes lead in part because "it's the matter of alchemists" (those who sought to turn stone into gold) but also because "it's toxic!": "I like this. I like this poison thing. Because it has an edge . . . I like this dangerous stuff."[5]

Those final lines remind one of the heroic, masculinist, and what in my Introduction I analyzed as "sovereign" concept of the artist that circulates in Knausgaard's profile. "Sovereign," the troubling constitutional scholar Carl Schmitt tells us, "is the one who decides on the exception," and the exception, as the situation that defies general codification, always has something of the intensity of life to it—of the danger of life, which is also the danger of death. Indeed, the opposition that structures Schmitt's *Concept of the Political*—published after his *Political Theology*, from which I drew in my Introduction—is that between friend and enemy, with the enemy being defined as the one who poses the threat of the real possibility of killing.[6] Such a real possibility is most palpably present in a situation of war. One does not determine who the sovereign is in a routine situation, but in an emergency that takes place at the border of the law. Overall, as scholars like Stathis Gourgouris have observed, Schmitt's concept of sovereignty follows the monarchic logic of the one,[7] and in situating this "one" at the limit of the law, partly inside of it and partly outside, the concept tends fascistically—a tendency that was borne out by history. This makes it all the more troubling that Schmitt's concept of sovereignty is (at least by the account that I offer in this book) widespread in the art world.

While Schmitt's concept of sovereignty is prominently present for example in Knausgaard's profile of Kiefer, it does not appear to fit with Kiefer's supposed use of the line "*all* artists are iconoclasts" (emphasis mine) to describe his own artistic practice. If one learns anything from Knausgaard's piece, it's that Kiefer's practice, and his understanding of himself, is precisely *not* of the order of the "all." "Genius," "aristocrat," "outside of classification":[8] Kiefer is precisely *not* someone to whom such a democratizing statement would apply. *All* artists may be iconoclasts—but Kiefer is definitely *not* all artists. Hence, perhaps, his laughter.

Taking my cue from Kiefer's statement, however, I propose to continue my investigation of the connections between Schmitt's concept of the sovereign and the figure of the artist by adding the figure of the iconoclast, and specifically the vandal, to this configuration. The iconoclast is someone who attacks the image, an attack in which historically "the sacred" has often played a role. The vandal, as one who deliberately destroys private or public property, is a more secular version of the same figure, an iconoclast who does not necessarily target the sacred—unless, of course, "property" is considered the sacred value of capitalist societies. (Consider here the relations of the vandal to more "political" figures like the rioter and the looter.) Kiefer's claim—whether serious or not—invites one to pursue two paths of investigation: on the one hand, the possibility that artists are exceptional, sovereign figures who stand outside of the law in the vandalistic destruction they practice through their creations. On the other, and given that Kiefer claims "all" artists are such vandals, there is the possibility that artists by bringing such destruction are merely doing what all artists do—and that they are, in that sense, entirely unexceptional, at least as far as artists go. As such, the artist-as-vandal may be an exceptional or an entirely unexceptional figure. It may be, as Knausgaard's profile of Kiefer suggests, that the real artist, the artist called Kiefer, is in fact outside of such classifications—that the real artist names a supreme vandalism outside of such critical distinctions. This may be where Kiefer's sovereignty truly lies (or, where his true sovereignty lies).

Exploring these connections from the side of the vandal in their relation to art, two options need to be considered: on the one hand, there is a vandalism that has marked art history, and has easily become appropriated as the next big thing in art. One could rewrite recent art history, as the U.S. poet, critic, and novelist Ben Lerner does, as a series of acts of vandalism (vandalism gets appropriated here as exceptional art). On the other, this narrative of appropriation may also hint at the existence of another kind of vandalism, one that is not so easily appropriated by art (vandalism that remains outside of art's exceptionalism). Perhaps, then, one would have to cross the terms: unexceptional vandalism is vandalism that is all too easily turned into exceptional art. Exceptional vandalism is vandalism that refuses such appropriation. Both of these positions, however, are haunted by an even more superior exceptionality that a figure like Kiefer risks to bring to this configuration: the figure of an artist whose sovereignty, and whose vandalism, stands outside of these positions altogether.

I want to begin, however, by asking whether in the twenty-first century vandalism is indeed still a mark of the artist. Are artists still iconoclasts? Or has our time perhaps done away with such an understanding of those who make art? What might be the consequences of such a consideration for our continued figuration of the artist as sovereign?

Art and Injury

In his book *Saving Beauty*, the German (Korean-born) philosopher Byung-Chul Han asserts that "Without injury, neither poetry nor art is possible."[9] "Thinking," he continues, "is also sparked by the negativity of injury. Without pain and injury, the same, the familiar, the habitual continue."[10] This is a striking transcendental claim—one reviewer calls it "hyperbolic"[11]—not only about thought, art, and poetry, but also about ethics, since it implies that *in*vulnerability precludes otherness. It's a claim that obviously takes it up for the vandal—and I will return to that later. For now, however, I want to note how in the opening paragraph of Han's *Saving Beauty*, the philosopher lays out what he perceives to be the counter-figure of injury: the smooth. Han writes:

> The smooth is the signature of the present time. It connects the sculptures of Jeff Koons, iPhones and Brazilian waxing. Why do we today find what is smooth beautiful? Beyond its aesthetic effect, it reflects a general social imperative. It embodies today's *society of positivity* [which Han has written about elsewhere]. What is smooth does not injure. Nor does it offer any resistance. It is looking for *Like*. The smooth object deletes its *Against*. Any form of negativity is removed.[12]

Han goes on to mention the LG G Flex smartphone, which is "covered with a self-healing skin which makes any scratch, that is, any trace of an injury, disappear within the shortest of times," noting that it is "invulnerable, so to speak."[13] Discussing the work of Jeff Koons, he contrasts it to that of Andy Warhol, who "also professed his commitment to beautiful, smooth surfaces, but his art still had the negativity of death and disaster inscribed into it."[14] (Han mentions Warhol's *Death and Disaster* series specifically.) Roland Barthes' discussion in *Mythologies* of "the new Citroën D.S." also passes the *revue* as an example of the smooth. Like Koons' sculptures, one wants to touch it (Han writes of a haptic compulsion that is exercised by the smooth); Koons' works even make you want to "suck them."[15] They are "seamless sculptures" similar to "bubbles made of air and emptiness."[16] Han notes how they "confer a feeling of perfection, of lightness in a magical sense."[17] As such, they are all "surface, without depth and shallows."[18] In a mirror-like Koons sculpture, you see only yourself. Koons' work thus becomes a figure for Han of an art in which the alterity or negativity of the other and the alien is eliminated.

Philosophically, Koons' art is art that conveys "an agreeable feeling" but it "cannot be connected with any meaning or profound sense."[19] Koons' art merely "exhausts itself in a 'wow,'" Han writes: it lacks the negativity that for him is essential to art and thought. In such work, "[a]estheticization turns out to be anaesthetization; it sedates our perception."[20] Aesthetically, this makes the experience of beauty "impossible."[21] Towards the end of his chapter, Han returns to the example of Brazilian waxing and also associates the smooth with the eclipse of "[d]irty eroticism" by "clean pornography": "Depilated skin, in particular, gives the body a pornographic smoothness which is felt to be pure and clean."[22] Interestingly, but also problematically, Han then connects this discussion of what, with Vasco Medeiros, one might call "aesthetic hygienism"[23] to dataism, to the dominance of data and information in our contemporary societies: "Information is a pornographic form of knowledge"[24] that is associated with the smooth. Han, by contrast, takes it up for injury.

While I do not agree with all of Han's rather large claims—I will discuss later in this book Hito Steyerl's approach to data and information, which moves away precisely from understanding them as "smooth"—his overall position that the smooth has become the signature of our time appears to make some sense and seems to be evidenced in contemporary society, in particular if one considers the aesthetic of technological devices (both the hardware and the software) that Han discusses (ranging from smartphones to electric cars). This is so in spite of the fact that we know very well, and experience on a daily basis, the friction that such supposedly smooth devices produce: the fact they are, precisely, not smooth—their smoothness is an ideal projection, a kind of absolute that does not correspond to reality. One has to wonder, however, whether Han's claim about the dominance of the smooth applies in the realm where, because of his extensive discussion of Koons' work, he seems to want to make it apply: art. As the title of Han's book indicates, the philosopher is very much concerned in his book with saving beauty—a beauty that he considers to be conditioned by injury. But is such beauty really on the way out? Has art history really become dominated by the Koons-es of the contemporary art world? The claim holds water when one considers an artist like Anish Kapoor, for example; but it would be difficult to use Kapoor or Koons as stand-ins for the entirety of contemporary art. One need only think of the notion of the "unmonumental" for example—referring to art that is not "market-friendly"; not "dewy with high-production values"; not "slick"; without a "beautiful finish"; "jerry-rigged, ramshackle, accumulative, eroding, and chancy," as the Phaidon guide to art speak has it[25]—as one small marker of art that breaks with the smooth and that, as in the 2007–2008 exhibition "Unmonumental: The Object in the 21st Century" at the New

Museum in New York, "describes an age of crumbling symbols and broken icons."[26]

"Wow"

Indeed, from another point of view, much of the history of contemporary art—say, twentieth-century art and after—could precisely be written as a history of art's relation to injury. The problem here is not so much art's association with the smooth. It's the more critical problem of *how* to conceive art's relation to injury. This adds a dimension to Han's striking claims. In December 2019, perhaps in response to the "Art Under Attack: Histories of British Iconoclasm" exhibition that was on at the Tate Modern at the time,[27] the poet, novelist, and critic Ben Lerner recalled art's long-standing relation to iconoclasm in an article titled "Damage Control: The Modern Art World's Tyranny of Price."[28] "Much of the story of twentieth-century art,"[29] Lerner begins, "can be told as a series of acts of vandalism"[30]—as acts involving the deliberate destruction of or damage to public or private property (as the definition of vandalism goes). Lerner lists the work of Pablo Picasso, Paul Cézanne, Robert Delaunay, Marcel Duchamp, Andy Warhol, Jean Dubuffet, Andres Serrano, Jackson Pollock, Robert Rauschenberg, Gustav Metzger, Jean Tinguely, Yoko Ono, Vito Acconci, and Chris Burden as examples. Duchamp's assisted readymade *L.H.O.O.Q.*, in which Duchamp drew a mustache on a reproduction (the size of a postcard) of the *Mona Lisa*; Rauschenberg's erasure of a de Kooning drawing; Serrano's *Piss Christ* (a photograph of a plastic crucifix submerged in a container of the artist's urine): those are all examples of by now established works of art that resulted from acts of "[d]emolition, defacement, and debasement."[31] And those were acts they suffered, in this case, not at the hands of vandals (as Lerner points out) but artists. Vandalism is the art that is on display in these works.

But Lerner quickly turns his interest to something else. "It's against this backdrop," he writes, "that vandals often claim to be artists,"[32] and he mentions Vladimir Umanets, Uriel Landeros, Pierre Pinoncelli, Cia Yuan and Jian Ju Xi, Tony Shafrazi and Laszlo Toth as examples. Umanets wrote on a Rothko, Landeros spray-painted a Picasso, Pinoncelli urinated in Duchamp's *Fountain*, Cai and Xi did the same, Shafrazi sprayed Picasso's *Guernica*, Toth attacked Michelangelo's *Pietà* with a hammer. The vandal's claim to be an artist—and the knee-jerk resistance to this claim that Lerner also records—introduces an interesting problem, as Lerner notes:

> If we resort to claiming that what sets vandals apart is that they compromise valuable objects, that the originals aren't their property, or that they violate the contract between the museum and the public, we run up against the fact that the rejection of beauty and resistance to the market have been rhetorical staples of avant-garde art for half a century or more.[33]

In other words, the vandal is simply a figure who "takes literally"[34] the avant-garde project. It won't do to set vandals and artists apart on those grounds—the avant-garde won't allow it.

It's worth noting that all of the works Lerner discusses are paintings or sculptures: commodities that are easy to deface. None of Lerner's examples are artworks that escape the realm of the commodity: works of media art, for example, that incorporate the digital or exist as digital works (this the case at least in this text—I will turn to another text by Lerner later in this book in which a work of media art—Christian Marclay's "The Clock"—*is* considered). This raises the question of whether there are certain kinds of art that are less susceptible to vandalism, of whether an art that moves away from the commodity-form somehow also moves away from vandalism. This question will continue to concern me in what follows. At one point—and it's a crucial moment in his article—Lerner does consider performance art's relation to injury, but the consideration remains very much within the realm of the commodity. This is when he discusses the story of Dorothy Podber, "a self-described witch and performance artist",[35] visiting Andy Warhol's factory:

> Podber asked whether she could "shoot" a stack of his Marilyn paintings. Warhol, apparently believing she meant to photograph the paintings, consented. Podber then removed a pistol and fired at the stack, damaging several canvases.[36]

So Podber, too, shot Andy Warhol—not Warhol the person (that was Valerie Solanas), but several Warhols, several works by Warhol.

Lerner's ultimate point about this act of vandalism, however, is that it isn't one: he argues that because it increased the value of the shot painting (when "Shot Red Marilyn" was auctioned at Christie's in 1989, it went for twice the expected price, with "Shot Orange Marilyn" far surpassing that amount at an auction nine years later), Podber's shooting wasn't vandalism. This shifts the conversation about iconoclasm to the question of art's relation to value. It introduces economics into the consideration of vandalism. Vandalism is not really vandalism, Lerner argues, if it increases value. Value controls the damage that vandalism brings. This too introduces an interesting problem:

> [I]f we ultimately believe a vandal is a vandal and not an artist because he devalues someone else's property, then art-world radicalism doesn't look very radical at all. If we believe it's vandalism because it destroys a thing of beauty as opposed to creating more of it, then many vanguard artists who employ destruction need to be reclassified.[37]

Many vanguard artists might, in other words, not be quite as avant-garde as we—or they themselves—believe.

Ultimately, this comes down to a question of distinguishing, specifically distinguishing between different kinds of vandalism (it is, in other words, a question of critique). What counts as vandalism? It appears there are vandalisms that can be recuperated as art, and others that can't. Lerner's criterion for distinction is "value": when considering the relations between vandalism and art, he proposes that there is an inverse relation between vandalism and value. Vandalism is, essentially, what brings down value. Its target is value—if it is not, it is not vandalism. Unexceptional vandalism, one might say, is recuperated as exceptional art; exceptional vandalism, on the other hand, remains unexceptional art—if it is even art at all. To avoid confusion, let's say that such vandalism opens a vista onto the post-exceptional: onto the exceptional quality of resisting the exceptionalization of art. Lerner's final question, then, is the logical conclusion of his pursuit: "What would it mean to think beyond the economics of the art world, to move beyond both vandalism and the market it exposes?"[38]

Lerner answers this question through an example: the Polish artist Elka Krajewska's "*The Salvage Art Institute*," a project that Lerner also writes about in his auto-fictional novel *10:04*. In the novel, "Elka" becomes "Alena" and her project is retitled "The Institute for Totaled Art," but the idea behind the fictionalized and real projects, however, is the same: Lerner presents us with an institute that collects artworks that have been deemed to be of zero value—for example, a valuable painting that "is damaged in transit or a fire or flood, vandalized, etc."[39] It's deemed to be of zero value when "an appraiser agrees with the owner of the work [it's worth noting that the artist is not involved] that the work cannot be satisfactorily restored, or that the cost of restoration would exceed the value of the claim."[40] Like with a car that is declared totaled, such works are "declared to have 'zero value.'"[41] Such works, however, are not destroyed by the insurer but stored, not as valuable artworks but as "indeterminate objects: works by artists, many of them famous, that, after suffering one kind of damage or another, were formally demoted from art to mere objecthood, and banned from circulation, removed from the market, relegated to this strange limbo."[42] Lerner's narrator—also called Ben—is fascinated by this. He finds in these "valueless works" an art outside of the market. Alena's/Elka's project was to set up an institute to show these valueless works to the public, and at her request "the insurer agreed to donate a gallery's worth of 'zero-value' art" to the institute, "even [covering] the cost of shipping," as the narrator points out. The language is worth pausing over: What does it mean to "donate" "a gallery's worth" of "'zero-value' art," in other words to donate something that has been declared worthless? The donation really consists in covering the cost of shipping—there is an actual price on that. As for the art, it's priceless: "it's worth nothing."[43]

That is in fact Alena's determination when, at the institute, she picks up a piece from a broken Jeff Koons sculpture and "hurled it onto the hardwood, where it shattered."[44] It's not the shattering that produces the reduction in value—the work was already without value before. The shattering is merely one injury upon another. Lerner's narrator finds it "wonderful to see an icon of art world commercialism and valorized stupidity shattered."[45] In Byung-Chul Han's terms, he finds it wonderful to see Koons' art of the smooth returned to injury. If Koons' works in Han's analysis exercise a haptic compulsion on the viewer that Han values negatively, Lerner has a character quote Lerner's own poetry—"Why not let the children touch the paintings?"[46]—as part of what seems to be the opposite argument: touch is associated with injury here. It's worth noting, however, the discourse that the narrator uses to recuperate the project of returning the smooth to injury, and thereby taking art outside of value: "Not for the first time, I wondered if she was a genius,"[47] the novel reveals. A few pages later, after a discussion of totaled art being "art before or after capital," art from which "the twenty-one grams of the market's soul had fled," the narrator can only manage: "Wow."[48]

That single word, if it is one, takes us back, however, to Han's criticism of Koons, whose sculptures—in Han's analysis—exhaust themselves into precisely such a "Wow." Together with the introduction of the term genius, the narrator's "wow" can be said to return this art outside of value, this art of injury, right back to the realm of the smooth and the realm of value. It turns out the market's soul is not so easily chased away—at least not in the way in which the narrator talks about his friend Alena's project. Even the Institute for Totaled Art is at the risk of being reappropriated into precisely what it seeks to escape. The narrator wants the Institute for Totaled Art to accomplish what he characterizes (problematically, as I've argued elsewhere[49]) as a "reversal of the kind of recontextualization associated with Marcel Duchamp":[50] not into the museum, but in exodus from it. Not just outside of the market, but also outside of art, clearly. Krajewska of course refers to the works on show at her institute as "No Longer Art." But can this be true, if she is building a practice around them? Can it be true if Lerner is writing about them? Am I by writing about them now contributing to their reappropriation by the logic of value and the smooth? It seems exceptionalism may have the last word in this conversation towards post-exceptionalism.

Ultimately, Lerner is interested in how his own novel, *10:04*, could find its place in the Institute for Totaled Art, and I've discussed *10:04*'s elaborate negotiation of that issue at length elsewhere.[51] Lerner is obviously focused on value in this context—a focus that situates his argument, broadly speaking, within the realm of the economic. But one might also consider the artist Noah Davis' project "Imitation of Wealth," which has affinities with Krajewska's *Salvage Art Institute* but nevertheless does something different. "Imitation of Wealth" was a project Davis proposed for "The Underground Museum," which he founded in Arlington Heights, Los Angeles with the goal of bringing high art to a "traditionally African-American and Latino working class neighborhood," as the project's webpage explains.[52] Because no museums "were willing to lend major works to be exhibited at this location," Davis set out "to recreate iconic artworks by famous artists such as Marcel Duchamp, On Kawara, and Jeff Koons." The goal was to break down "the class and ethnic barriers to high culture." Lerner does not talk about ethnicity at all, and his argument tends to operate at the level of ontological, not historical, vulnerability. If Lerner's focus is ultimately economic, in Davis' project this also gets tied to a concern with ethnicity (race), and this enables a more intersectional approach to the issues under consideration here. There is, of course, a way in which the economic works its way back in: What about the gentrification that is often spurred by projects such as Davis'—opening an art gallery in a neighborhood like Arlington Heights (listed in recent studies of gentrification with Highland Park, Boyle Heights, and other neighborhoods as quickly upscaling)? There is a dialectic at work here that needs to be considered.

Perhaps a little cynically—like Lerner, I admire Krajewska's project, even if I am more reluctant to accept what Lerner deems to be its "messianic"[53] promise—I might suggest that the problem on display can be succinctly captured by the England-based street artist (sometimes also described as a vandal) Banksy and his work "Love is in the Bin." (People have in fact used Banksy's name to label the problem; it's come to be called "the Banksy effect."[54]) One needs to consider "Love is in the Bin" as part of a group of works, the first one of which is "Girl with Balloon," itself part of a series of works by Banksy that have been showing up as stencil murals in London since 2002. The "Girl with Balloon" I have in mind appeared as a print in an ornate frame at a Sotheby's auction on October 5, 2018. After the print was auctioned, an alarm went off and the print started sliding outside of its frame, which appeared to have been outfitted with a shredder. The shredding stopped, however, before the print had slid outside of the frame entirely, leaving the partially shredded print hanging at the bottom of the frame. This produced a new work, titled "Love is in the Bin."

After this event, Banksy posted a video[55]—arguably, a third work—showing how he had installed a shredder inside the print's frame and noting that in rehearsals the shredding had worked every time, the suggestion being that the shredding was supposed to have been complete. But the video includes more than that: it also explicitly laughs at the art world, specifically the world of galleries and auctions, where the rich—who often know nothing about art—hang out. That was, evidently, what the shredding of his work was meant to target: it was meant to destroy the thing of value that some rich person had just acquired. In this way, it continues a key component of Banksy's practice who, early on in his career, did not sell any work and has shown himself to be very critical of the art market in his later work.

As such, however, the transformation of "Girl with Balloon" into "Love is in the Bin" was not successful. It's worth noting that the sale of the artwork went through at the price that was agreed to before the partial shredding. Writing in *Art Monthly* about the Banksy stunt, the art lawyer Henry Lydiate suggests that the "transformed work . . . may already have a market value of three times its hammer price."[56] And isn't it convenient from this perspective, that the piece was only *partially* shredded, leaving the print somehow intact as a partially shredded work of art? It's art and injury put together as art—as partial injury, but *wholly* art. For Lerner, of course, the question of value would be a determining factor in this case: Did the vandalism of the shredding push up the value of the work, or not? Some also questioned Banksy's own involvement in all of this: Sotheby's, they argued, must have been in on the stunt, since the Banksy piece was only auctioned all the way at the end, and was presented as hanging on the wall in the back of the auction room rather than in the front, where the other auctioned pieces were shown. Auctioning the piece earlier would have disturbed the entire auction, which some clients may have considered to effect the rest of the proceedings; having the piece hanging on the wall in the back made it easily removable after the shredding had happened. Reports also surfaced of a person holding a remote control and a bag in the auction room; Sotheby's normally does not allow bags in its auction room. In other words: Banksy is not a vandal. The Sotheby's stunt marks the end of his street cred, if he still had any. Importantly, that does not make him an artist either. Far from being a work of injury, "Love is in the Bin" should be categorized under the sign of the smooth. According to Han, that means it *isn't* art.

Disability Art (Part One)

Ultimately, this issue—represented best by Banksy's "Love is in the Bin"—comes down to a question of definition, specifically to the definition of injury. What counts as injury? It appears there are injuries that can be recuperated as art, and others that can't. Banksy, like Lerner, appears to be in pursuit of the latter, but neither Banksy nor Lerner quite achieves it. Considering their work in fact greatly complicates the plea for an art of injury that Han develops. Han claims there can be no art without injury; but not all injuries are art, and not all injuries are proper injuries, even (consider also, for example, Jacqueline Humphries' *pre-vandalized* paintings, which take the sting out of the wound). Han's work needs much more elaboration.

I want to complete this picture for now by introducing a third perspective that rehearses what has come before, but also refracts it into another direction that will prove to be central for the further development of this book: Tobin Siebers' work on disability aesthetics. Siebers' chapter "Disability and Art Vandalism," which was published in his book *Disability Aesthetics*,[57] includes several of the same examples as Lerner—Siebers begins with a discussion of Laszlo Toth's vandalization of Michelangelo's *Pietà*, for one—and also makes the point that the avant-garde should be understood as an approved instance of what, in another context, would be understood as vandalism.[58] But Siebers makes these points within a different framework: that of disability studies. Vandalized images, he argues, shift our focus on art away from the able body to the disabled body. Moving away from the question of art and value, injury is returned in Siebers' work to the place where one might have expected it all along: the body.[59] This shifts the question of exceptionalism towards a conversation about how it applies in discussions about ability/disability, and how such discussions are relevant to representations of the body in art history.

Rather than asking whether vandalized images are "disabled images" (as for example Lerner seems to do), Siebers asks whether vandalized images might become "images of disability"?[60] Furthermore, Siebers wonders how the issue of disability in relation to vandalized images reflects back on the "makers of these images"?[61] Are vandals somehow considered "disabled" as well? How so? What is the effect of this on the discourse about "their acts of destruction and creation"?[62] This opens up a host of other interesting questions. Once a work has become vandalized, it no longer represents the same thing as it did before. Yet we usually resist this: our inclination is to get the work restored. (Siebers suggests that we could also just move the vandalized work of art for example from the gallery of sixteenth-century paintings to the modern art section of the museum . . . .) We precisely do not take the vandalized image to have a new referent. But, Siebers leads us to ask, what if the new referent of a vandalized image were the disabled body? One could then read the vandalized image as a critique of the exceptionalist dominance of the able body in art history, a dominance that is no doubt marked especially by the dominance of the nude as a figure of the ideal form in Western art history. It would then be shown, rather, and this is in line with Lerner's claim that the history of twentieth-century art is a history of acts of vandalism, that the *disabled* body has in fact been dominant, or at least has been prominently present, in Western art history all along.

What if the referent of the *Venus de Milo* were a double amputee (Siebers discusses a performance by Mary Duffy—"born without arms"[63]—that drew this out)? Do we find this statue beautiful because we project the ideal form of an able body into it? Do we find it beautiful as the body of a double amputee? If art shows us disabled bodies, then one approach may be, as Siebers points out, that we learn from art how to view disabled bodies as beautiful, as art.[64] It would simply be a question of coming to appreciate those distortions and defects that we praise in art as beautiful, in real bodies. But Siebers prefers another approach: why, he asks, would disability need to be made prettier?[65] Why can it not make things stranger[66]—in other words, liberate us (and, by extension, art) from beauty itself—from beauty as ideal *form*? Such changes might also effect the maker of the artwork, the artist, who would be liberated in turn from the straightjacket of the able body and the ideal form. Usually, however, vandals—real vandals—are not considered artists. Their work is considered an act of lunacy, not genius. Moreover, vandals—real vandals—are sometimes denied a range of intelligence and mental activity that our understanding of art-making assumes (but should it?). If art is at the same time understood to produce a shock—still an exceptionalist understanding of art, to be sure—what would it mean to shock these very assumptions, both about the work and about its maker? To shock them *beyond shock*, if the target here ultimately is exceptionalism itself? Those are some of the issues that Siebers brings to our attention and from where we can begin to challenge the centrality of the able body, and the ideal form—more generally, of exceptionalism—in Western art. It is injury that, in Siebers, puts us on the track of this.

Let's point out here as well, as I did in my discussion of Lerner, that by and large, Siebers' examples are works of art that take the commodity-form, suggesting that works of art who don't might somehow be immune to vandalism, or be outside of the sphere of injury or—in Siebers' framework—disability.

From another perspective, the fact that the focus here is so much on art*works* may also explain some of the dialectic that we have been confronting: perhaps the avant-garde's target was precisely not so much art but the realization of art as work, as Agamben in an essay that I already referenced earlier on has suggested. (Agamben relies for this point on a study by Robert Klein, "The Eclipse of the Work of Art," which suggests precisely this argument.[67]) It is thus the commodity, the work, that is the avant-garde's target; not so much art itself. Agamben brings in as an example the Situationists, who—in Debord's proclamation—"want at the same time to abolish [the work of art] and realize [art]."[68] Art realizes itself not so much "in a work but in life (the Situationists intended to produce not works but situations)."[69] Siebers' focus on disability, however, and the particular take on vandalism that it enables him to develop, goes further than this, because it targets the notion of art itself, not just the *work* of art. But that also means it would be good to look further than art that takes the commodity-form, as I will do in the next chapter where my focus will be on a work of media art.

Art's Own Political Theology

After considering these various ways in which the figure of the artist and the vandal intersect, I want to place my final focus more directly on how the figure of the sovereign—and in particular the problem of aesthetic and political exceptionalism, which I've brought up several times in the above—intersects with the figure of the artist-as-vandal. This of course means questioning sovereignty's relation to the aesthetics that have been central to this chapter: that of the smooth, and that of injury.[70] Han perceives the smooth to reign supreme in our time: it's our time's *signature*, as he puts it; it's our time's *author* and *creator*. Han gives us enough evidence to conclude that this is probably right in terms of our time's aspirations even if, as I have pointed out, it also does not fit its realities and can hardly stand in for our time as a whole. When it comes to the concept of sovereignty, while it is phantasized as smooth, I have shown elsewhere how, specifically within the framework of Carl Schmitt's thought, it most certainly is not—in other words, the sovereignty of the smooth that Han imagines is not compatible with Schmitt's thinking of sovereignty, which even in its simplest definition—"sovereign is who decides on the exception"—has nothing smooth to it: it is a statement, rather, of the cut, of the injurious border rather than the smooth center.[71] Schmitt's thinking is striated, not smooth, to evoke the terms of Gilles Deleuze and Felix Guattari (who take a keen interest in Schmitt when they are developing these notions[72]). All of this then points us in a troubling direction, namely towards the consideration that Han's plea for an art of injury, Han's defense of the vandal against an art of the smooth—one that is typical, I would say, of much twentieth-century art theory and would typically be associated with an ethics and politics of "otherness" that disrupts the dominance of "the same, the familiar, the habitual"[73]—in fact reveals complicities with Schmitt's thinking of sovereignty. It is, indeed, the call for a break with the smooth, with the same, the familiar, the habitual, that we find in Han that resonates most strongly with Schmitt's philosophical and legalo-political appreciation for an intensity of life breaking through the crust of the boring everyday. By insisting on injury, then, by promoting the figure of the vandal, Han also takes it up for Schmitt's concept of sovereignty. Perhaps this is why Lerner, when he turns towards Krajewska, states that he wants to move not just "beyond value" but also "beyond vandalism": *perhaps the vandal ultimately remains too problematic a figure in this context to be allowed to stand.*

I acknowledge that this may seem like a strange conclusion to reach. Consider, for example, how Han writes in a sharp criticism of the work of the contemporary theorist of sovereignty Giorgio Agamben in his book *Topology of Violence* that:

> The society of sovereignty has long belonged to the past. Today, no one is politicized "through an abandonment to an unconditional power of death." There is no longer any exterior, no transcendence, no sovereignty of power to which one would be subjugated and exposed as an obedience subject. Contemporary society is not a society of sovereignty. We now live in a society of achievement. The achievement-subject differs from the obedience-subject in that it is the *sovereign of itself*; as the entrepreneur of itself, it is *free*.[74]

While this passage testifies to Han's perceptive analysis of the society of achievement that he has also presented elsewhere, for example in his book *The Burnout Society*, it also immediately strikes the reader as self-contradictory, however, since it *both* claims sovereignty to be a thing of the past *and* turns the subject who is the sovereign of itself into the society of achievement's characteristic subject. Clearly, then, sovereignty is *not* a thing of the past.

Moreover, while Han's description of the society of achievement and its subjects, who are the sovereigns of themselves, no doubt matches *some* people's experience—and perhaps all people's experience to a certain extent—it would be hard to argue that today, as Han puts it, "*no one*" is politicized through brute exposure to sovereign power. One need only consider the state of black lives in the U.S. to see how narrow-minded Han's claim really is. Or just imagine Han proposing that sovereignty is a thing of the past to those who are exposed to drone violence.

This not-quite-pastness of sovereignty also reveals itself in Han's work in a more dubious way, due to his peculiar reliance on Schmitt's work. There is a way in which Han, in his analysis of the society of achievement as having overcome the society of sovereignty, in fact returns to some aspects of the society of sovereignty to combat the society of achievement. In *The Burnout Society*, for example, Han follows Schmitt's *Theory of the Partisan* to criticize Facebook.[75] In *The Transparency Society*, Schmitt becomes an ally in Han's criticism of transparency—and this time it's Schmitt's more problematic *The Crisis of Parliamentary Democracy* that is quoted.[76] In the already quoted *Topology of Violence*, which includes Han's longest engagement with Schmitt so far, the discussion is definitely more critical, with Han writing skeptically about Schmitt's criticism of parliamentary democracy for example and characterizing Schmitt (again, critically) as "a true land creature" who "has no concept of the floating or indistinguishable."[77] But while Han criticizes the violence that in Schmitt's theory is spent outwards, against an external enemy, the discussion also takes a turn when Han praises the inwardly stabilizing effect of this outward violence: Schmitt's attachment to character is at odds with the lack of character in today's achievement society, and Han sharply criticizes the latter. Thus, and in tension with the quote about "floating" from *Topology*, in *Saving Beauty* Han can praise Schmitt's criticism of water as "lacking character."[78] Instead, Schmitt is associated with "solidity and permanence" which "are not conducive to consumption." Immediately after this association, *Saving Beauty* repeats the Schmitt quote from *The Burnout Society*, and once again in a positive light. Han, then, turns out to be a Schmittian in his defense of injury, and this raises major questions about whether the vandal is a figure that leads away from the widespread presence of a Schmittian concept of art. Perhaps it merely continues it—perhaps it marks, indeed, following Lerner's conception, the very core of twentieth-century art.

In "For an Imperfect Cinema," a text towards which I will turn in Chapter 2, Julio García Espinosa makes the point that one can find a long-standing preference for "suffering" in Western art history, one that he considers to be related "to Christian tradition—which identifies seriousness with suffering": "Only in the person who suffers do we perceive elegance, gravity, even beauty; only in him do we recognize the possibility of authenticity, seriousness, sincerity."[79] Imperfect art, for Espinosa, must end that tradition—and that partly means turning away from Europe as the center of art history, and from a European standard for aesthetics. Espinosa allows us to articulate the political suspicions I have raised about injury as the transcendental condition for art in a geo-political framework, one that I will consider in more detail in the next chapter as an important aspect of any theory of unexceptional art.

But end it how? The answer to these problems with injury obviously cannot be a simple turn towards the smooth, which has its own problems, as Han analyzes. Rather, it would need to be to move beyond vandalism altogether, into a framework for thinking about art that troubles the Schmittian politics that the figure of the vandal has risked to perpetuate. If anything, my study of the artist-as-vandal across different texts and examples has made clear that vandals cannot so easily be set aside from the aesthetic exceptionalism they attack.

Stathis Gourgouris has made this point about the issue with which I began, iconoclasm—but his argument, in my view, does not reach deeply enough into art's own exceptionalism, its own political theology. In the closing pages of his book *Perils of the One*, in a section titled "Idols of Unrepresentability," Gourgouris explores two counter-intuitive theses. The first is announced earlier in his book and pertains to what Gourgouris refers to as "iconoclasm's own political theology," one that is active (he adds) "not just in the domain of religion but in the secularist framework itself, where the politics of unrepresentability continue to hold sway, unchallenged."[80] Gourgouris' position on this issue is clearly stated at the beginning of "Idols of Unrepresentability," and can be presented here as a first thesis: "[T]he prohibition of images is a radical notion only when it operates in a desacralized universe."[81] When it does not, "iconoclasm merely reorients idol worship from the utterable and representable to the unutterable and unrepresentable".[82] The positives may have been turned into negatives, but the logic remains the same. It's idols across the board. Gourgouris, by contrast, is interested in a "desacralized universe of meaning" that "reconfigures the meaning of both iconoclasm and the sacred."[83]

Perhaps unsurprisingly, given his interest in the political theology of iconoclasm, Gourgouris shows himself to be particularly drawn to icons—images, and by extension artworks—that *both* foreground the sacred status of the image *and* break it down. He quickly mentions Dadaism and Marcel Duchamp as examples—"Duchamp's ready-mades," he writes, "are iconic renamings"[84]—and then dedicates a few paragraphs to how Maurizio Catellan's art, suspended with steel cables from the ceiling of the New York Guggenheim museum for Catellan's exhibition *All*, "exposes and thus incapacitates . . . the latent idolatrous desire of the presumed secular spectator."[85] The work Gourgouris focuses on has explicit religious content: *La Nona Ora* (*The Ninth Hour*, from 1999) shows Pope John Paul II crushed by a meteorite. In Gourgouris' reading, however, that religious content becomes a red herring. He insists that the violent response this piece received when it was shown in the Pope's native Poland cannot be explained away as a response to blasphemy. Rather, the work's vandalization reveals the sacred logic of the demand that such a thing *not* be shown: "iconoclasm's own political theology." The iconoclast maintains the exceptionalism of the theological.

However, and on this count I am pushing Gourgouris a bit, Catellan's work also invites a reflection on the artwork's *own* relation to the sacred: Gourgouris refers to *La Nona Ora* after all as Catellan's "most iconic"[86] work, a superlative that begs the question of how to distinguish the "most iconic" from the "idol." *La Nona Ora* is not so much about its religious content but about the sacrality of the idol, its prohibition, *and* the icon/work of art. In Gourgouris' reading, then, which I am expanding here in the context of my own argument about aesthetic exceptionalism, the meteorite in *La Nona Ora* turns out to be a boomerang: it crushes the Pope and those who argue that such a thing ought not to be shown; but while crushing the sacred across the board—in crushing both the idol and its prohibition—it also ends up crushing the sacrality of art itself. The artwork's iconoclasm ends up hitting the artwork in the face.

It's worth noting how Gourgouris' argument about *La Nona Ora* differs from the one he develops (in close relation to his discussion of *La Nona Ora*—they are at one point treated in the same paragraph[87]) about the *Jyllands-Posten* controversy, which involved the cartooning of the Prophet Mohammed. The response to the cartoons, he argues, cannot be explained away with blasphemy—in that case, we would be dealing with a response that is entirely within the logic of the sacred. Rather, the issue with the cartoons is the violation of the representation of the Prophet by "the racist impulses against specific peoples still caught in the living history of colonial domination."[88] That is what explains the reaction they received. The issue is not simply idolatry versus iconoclasm. One can only arrive at that insight, however, by practicing what Gourgouris—via Jan Assman—refers to as an "iconic literacy"[89] or also an "iconic intelligence":[90] a mode of reading or thinking/knowing that would apply outside of the visual realm as well. If this is a lesson of secular criticism, one that seeks to go beyond both idols and idols of unrepresentability, it is one that Gourgouris attributes to Edward Said, whose influence is clear in *Perils of the One*.[91]

Part of the project of deconstructing the opposition of idolatry versus iconoclasm, and of rethinking the meaning of the sacred and iconoclasm, is to lay bare what Gourgouris refers to as "a certain vulnerability" of the image—something that, he adds, "cannot be abolished or transcended even by means of mechanical reproduction."[92] This is in fact what brings us to the second, much less developed, thesis in the book's closing section: even the idol, as a representation of the divine, exceeds the divine and therefore presents a threat to it. Another way of saying this is that the idol is always already desacralizing. Hence the need to forbid the idol, as Gourgouris notes, within the logic of monotheism—because monotheism follows the logic of the one, and the idol always inevitably adds to that: it turns the one into two. It is this simple fact of addition, of the artwork's power of presentation (as Gourgouris also calls it), that renders the artwork vulnerable, turns it into something that invites destruction—a destruction that, as per thesis one, might be even more theological than the idol itself. This would explain, then, Gourgouris' focus on unrepresentability: representation (or even just presentation) is always inevitably desacralizing; as such, it is rendered vulnerable and invites the anti-(re)presentational response; and it is the latter, rather than the former, that thus most deserves the scrutiny of Gourgouris' lesson in secular criticism. The sacred is at its most intense not in the image but in the image's prohibition. Representation/presentation and art always already have a tie to desacralization.

Of course, *La Nona Ora* shows us that art is not so easily situated on the side of desacralization. Part of the point of Catellan's work—perhaps the work's ultimate point—is in fact to unwork *art*'s tie to the sacred.[93] To paraphrase Gourgouris: to unwork *art's own political theology*. Art's challenge to the divine, to the logic of the one, is not so much established but something to be achieved. The project is perhaps especially urgent when it comes to big art-world names like "Catellan," who take on quasi-theological status, no matter their own iconoclasm. Consider, for example, Knausgaard's profile of Kiefer, which has this kind of sacralization of the artist on full—and, I as have shown, critical—display. Or consider another artist who has featured prominently in this chapter so far and will return throughout this book: Marcel Duchamp.

When it was photographed by Alfred Stieglitz in his studio, Duchamp's *Fountain* was renamed by Stieglitz and Duchamp "Madonna of the Bathroom" due to how the shape of the urinal resembles that of icons featuring the Virgin with Child.[94] "Buddha of the Bathroom" was one of the other titles that have been given to the piece: in the eyes of some, the shape of the urinal resembles a sitting Buddha.[95] It's worth noting that, usually, Duchamp's readymades are considered to mark an ascending move (that is, for example, how Ben Lerner's narrator critically presents them in Lerner's auto-fictional novel *10:04*): they seek to transform a found object—say, a urinal bought at J. L. Mott Iron Works—into an original work of art by adding a signature to it ("R. Mutt") and placing it in the gallery or museum. While it seems doubtful that this reading can cover the full extent of Duchamp's project—Stephen Barker has argued that a readymade was always already a replica: impossible to turn it into an original[96]—the iconic interpretation of Duchamp's project still seems right. Consider, for example, Duchamp's most famous readymade: as William Camfield has detailed, the original work, famously photographed by Stieglitz, has gone lost. Broken? Hidden? Stolen?[97] What we have, instead, is later versions, "fabricated replicas"[98] of the celebrated readymade. Of those replicas, however, including those of other works by him that have been lost, Duchamp apparently "made it absolutely clear that the copies were not meant to replace the originals."[98] In other words, the 1917 work was the original—the later versions did not exist at the same level. Duchamp said "that despite everything, 'a copy remains a copy.'"[99]

The artist and art vandal Pierre Pinoncelli, who urinated in Duchamp's *Fountain* and on another occasion also took to it with a hammer, reminds us of this when he defended himself in court against the charge that he attacked "state property": in response he pointed out "that what he had attacked was a fake, was not Duchamp's urinal . . . It was not the original it pretended to be."[101] If it may seem "ironic," as Leland de la Durantaye has suggested, that Pinoncelli refers to *Fountain* from 1917 as an original work—ironic because that work "prided itself on its lack of originality"[102]—Camfield's research indicates that there is also truth to this, that Pinoncelli was right to insist on originality because Duchamp's attachment to it in the case of *Fountain* was real.[103] As the art forger Ivan Friedland summarizes it in Daniel Kehlmann's novel *F*:

> Admittedly, an ironic free spirit once displayed a urinal in a museum to mock the institution and all its holy affectations and artistic pieties, but he also wanted money and honors and, above all, he wanted to be admired in the traditional way, and so a replica of the original still stands on its plinth, surrounded by holy affectations and artistic pieties. Although the theory that the museum has outlived itself is correct, the museum has in fact won, the urinal is exclaimed over, and as for the theory behind it, only students in their second semester still wonder about it.[104]

Leaving that last claim aside, Gourgouris—and others, like Ben Lerner—are clearly not wrong to draw out the idolatry in Duchamp's art. Indeed, and speaking more generally, if Duchamp sometimes does not seem to consider readymades as art, Camfield recalls that he also "stressed that readymades were not 'trivial' but, to the contrary, represented 'a much higher degree of intellectuality,'"[105] adding about himself that

"I'm nothing else but an artist, I'm sure, and delighted to be."[106] It's Duchamp's acknowledgment that he still finds "magic" in the readymade—something that Camfield captures with the wonderful but contradictory post-Benjaminian phrase "readymade aura"[107]—that puts one on the trace of exceptionalism in Duchamp's work.

Pushing Gourgouris' insightful analysis of iconoclasm further leads into my own consideration of art's own political theology, of the aesthetic exceptionalism—resonant with Schmitt's political exceptionalism of the sovereign, as I have shown—that structures the art world. If the iconoclast and the vandal are important figures in such a consideration, this chapter has also shown that their relation to political and aesthetic exceptionalism is by no means straightforward, but must be critically negotiated.

I might respond, then, to Gourgouris with two theses of my own to conclude the work that I have done in this first chapter on the artist's relation to the vandal, and the vandal's relation to the sovereign. First, the artwork is not so easily placed on the side of desacralization even if iconoclasm shows that it has a possible (but not necessary) relation to it. Second, if—big IF—what Gourgouris calls the artwork's "representation" or "presentation" poses a possible threat to the sacred (a thesis that Gourgouris pursues in the context of the re/presentation of the divine in particular), let us double that thesis and consider the threat posed by an artwork's re/presentation not of the divine but *of another artwork* (a stand-in for the divine, in my framework). Let us consider, in other words, a *copy* of an artwork, or even a forgery or fake, and consider its relations to aesthetic exceptionalism.

Notes

1 W. H. de B. Nelson, "Aesthetic Hysteria," *The International Studio: An Illustrated Magazine of Fine and Applied Art* 61: 241, 242, 243, 244 (March–June 1917), pp. ccxxi–ccxxv, here p. ccxxv.
2 Karl Ove Knausgaard, "In Search of Anselm Kiefer," *New York Times Magazine* February 16 (2020), pp. 26–33, pp. 59–62, here p. 30.
3 Knausgaard, "In Search of," p. 30.
4 Ibid. I find this aside interesting because the idiom suggests Knausgaard would be willing to suffer bodily injury in order to be able to make such a work of art.
5 Ibid.
6 See: Carl Schmitt, *The Concept of the Political*, trans. George Schwab (Chicago: University of Chicago Press, 1996).
7 See: Stathis Gourgouris, *The Perils of the One* (New York: Columbia University Press, 2019).
8 For a discussion of how these terms appear in Knausgaard's profile, see my Introduction.
9 Byung-Chul Han, *Saving Beauty*, trans. Daniel Steuer (Cambridge: Polity, 2018), p. 35.
10 Han, *Saving Beauty*, p. 35.
11 Lillian Wilde, rev. Byung-Chul Han, *Saving Beauty*, *Philosophy Now* 130 (February/March 2019), p. 47.
12 Han, *Saving Beauty*, p. 1.
13 Ibid.
14 Ibid., p. 2.
15 Ibid., p. 3.
16 Ibid., p. 4.
17 Ibid.
18 Ibid.
19 Ibid., p. 3.
20 Ibid., pp. 6–7.
21 Ibid., p. 7.
22 Ibid., p. 9.
23 See: Vasco Medeiros, "A Obra de Arte Na Era Da Sua Selfiezação: Empoderamento, Enxames Sociais E Higienismo Estético," *Art is On* 7 (2018), pp. 178–192.
24 Han, *Saving Beauty*, p. 10.

25 See: https://www.phaidon.com/agenda/art/articles/2012/april/11/the-phaidon-guide-to-art-speak-unmonumental/
26 See: https://archive.newmuseum.org/exhibitions/918
27 See: https://www.tate.org.uk/whats-on/tate-britain/exhibition/art-under-attack-histories-british-iconoclasm
28 Ben Lerner, "Damage Control: The Modern Art World's Tyranny of Price," *Harper's Magazine* 12 (2013), pp. 42–49.
29 It's worth noting that the history of attacks on art far exceeds the twentieth century. Lerner's thinking about art vandalism does not consider for example sixteenth- or seventeenth-century iconoclasm and the reasons behind it. In fact, Lerner seems to consider art vandalism within the limits of the aesthetic; he does not consider the religious or political motivations for it (I am thinking for example of the Sufragette Mary Richardson's slashing of Velázquez's *Rokeby Venus* in 1914). When Lerner moves outside of the aesthetic, it is to consider the economic dimension of art vandalism.
30 Lerner, "Damage Control," p. 43.
31 Ibid., p. 44.
32 Ibid.
33 Ibid., p. 45.
34 Ibid.
35 Ibid., p. 47.
36 Ibid.
37 Ibid., p. 48.
38 Ibid.
39 Ben Lerner, *10:04* (New York: Faber and Faber, 2014), p. 129.
40 Lerner, *10:04*, p. 129.
41 Ibid.
42 Ibid., p. 130.
43 Ibid., p. 132.
44 Ibid.
45 Ibid., p. 131.
46 Ibid., p. 132.
47 Ibid.
48 Ibid., p. 134.
49 Giorgio Agamben's assessment of this is more correct. Writing about Duchamp in an essay titled "Archaeology of the Work of Art," he suggests that while Duchamp makes art outside of art, "What happened later is that a gang, unfortunately still active, of skilled speculators and fools have

transformed the 'ready-made' into a work of art" (Giorgio Agamben, *Creation and Anarchy: The Work of Art and the Religion of Capitalism*, trans. Adam Kotsko [Stanford, CA: Stanford University Press, 2019], p. 12).

50 Lerner, *10:04*, p. 133.

51 See: Arne De Boever, *Finance Fictions: Realism and Psychosis in a Time of Economic Crisis* (New York: Fordham University Press, 2018).

52 See: https://theunderground-museum.org/Imitation-of-Wealth. All quotes are taken from the website description of this project.

53 Lerner, *10:04*, p. 134.

54 Lexa Brenner, "The Banksy Effect: Revolutionizing Humanitarian Protest Art," *Harvard International Review* XL:2 (2019), pp. 35–37.

55 See: https://www.youtube.com/watch?v=vxkwRNIZgdY&feature=emb_title

56 Henry Lydiate, "Love & Money," *Art Monthly* 421 (2018), p. 45.

57 Tobin Siebers, *Disability Aesthetics* (Ann Arbor: University of Michigan Press, 2010), pp. 83–99.

58 Siebers, *Disability Aesthetics*, pp. 94–95.

59 It is worth pointing out that although the word injury might be considered synonymous with "trauma," a Greek term that translates as "wound," I want to emphasize given that term's psychoanalytic overtones that I am not interested here in psychic wounds but in injuries upon the body—of a work of art, or other being.

60 Siebers, *Disability Aesthetics*, p. 84.

61 Ibid.

62 Ibid.

63 Ibid., p. 86.

64 Ibid., p. 85.

65 Ibid., p. 87.

66 Ibid.

67 Agamben, *Creation and Anarchy*, p. 3.

68 Debord qtd. ibid., p. 3.

69 Ibid.

70 A special issue of the journal *boundary 2 online* is fully dedicated to this question: Ryan Bishop, ed., "Frictionless Sovereignty." *boundary 2 online* 5:2 (2020), accessible: https://www.boundary2.org/frictionless-sovereignty-dossier/

71 See: Arne De Boever, "Futures of Sovereignty (Necropolitics in America)," *boundary 2 online* 5:2 (2020), accessible: http://www.boundary2.org/2020/08/7529/

72 I engage with this in detail in a chapter titled "The Wall" of my book: *Being Vulnerable: Contemporary Political Thought* (Montreal/Kingston: McGill-Queen's University Press, 2023).

73 Han, *Saving Beauty*, p. 35.

74 Byung-Chul Han, *Topology of Violence*, trans. Amanda DeMarco (Cambridge, MA: The MIT Press, 2018), p. 126.

75 See: Byung-Chul Han, *The Burnout Society*, trans. Erik Butler (Stanford, CA: Stanford University Press, 2015), p. 40.

76 See: Byung-Chul Han, *The Transparency Society*, trans. Erik Butler (Stanford, CA: Stanford University Press, 2015), pp. 6–7.

77 Han, *Topology*, p. 43.

78 Han, *Saving Beauty*, p. 49.

79 Julio García Espinosa, "For an Imperfect Cinema," *Jump Cut: A Review of Contemporary Cinema* 20 (1979), pp. 24–26, accessible: https://www.ejumpcut.org/archive/onlinessays/JC20folder/ImperfectCinema.html

80 Gourgouris, *Perils*, p. 136.

81 Ibid., p. 191.

83 Ibid.

83 Ibid., p. 192.

84 Ibid.

85 Ibid., p. 193.

86 Ibid.

87 See: ibid.

88 Ibid., p. 194.

89 Assman qtd. ibid., p. 195.

90 Ibid., p. 195.

91 The book's first chapter especially carries Said's imprint, and Gourgouris mentions in his acknowledgments that Said discussed the first draft of the chapter with him in 2003; see: ibid., p. xxiii.

92 Ibid., p. 195.

93 This is an argument that I have developed further in a review of a book that, coincidentally (or not?), has Catellan's *La Nona Ora* featured on its cover: "Art and Exceptionalism: A Critique," rev. Santiago Zabala, *Why Only Art Can Save Us: Aesthetics and the Absence of Emergency* (New York: Columbia University Press, 2017), *boundary 2* 45:4 (2018), pp. 161–181.

94 William Camfield, "Marcel Duchamp's *Fountain*: Aesthetic Object, Icon, or Anti-Art?," in: Thierry de Duve, ed., *The Definitively Unfinished Marcel Duchamp* (Cambridge, MA: The MIT Press, 1991), pp. 133–178, here p. 141.

95 Camfield, "Marcel Duchamp's *Fountain*," p. 140.

96 Stephen Barker, "Unwork and the Duchampian Contemporary," *boundary 2* 44:1 (2017), p. 53–78.

97 Camfield, "Marcel Duchamp's *Fountain*," p. 133.

98 Ibid., p. 162.

99 Ibid.

100 Ibid., pp. 162–163.

101 Leland de la Durantaye, "Readymade Remade: Pierre Pinoncelli and the Legacy of Duchamp's 'Fountains,'" *Cabinet* 27 (2007), accessible: http://www.cabinetmagazine.org/issues/27/durantaye.php

102 Durantaye, "Readymade Remade."

103 I would like to thank my graduate student Patrick Vogel for a productive conversation about Pinoncelli's art vandalism.

104 Daniel Kehlmann, *F*, trans. Carol Brown Janeway (New York: Vintage, 2015), p. 189.

105 Ibid., p. 165.

106 Ibid.

107 Ibid., p. 135.

2

The Copy's Blow

Copy Art!

In the previous chapter, I have shown that while the vandal at first sight may seem to pose a threat to the sovereignty of art, art history in fact reveals that vandalism has easily been reappropriated as art, with many of what are now recognized to be the major artists of the twentieth century appearing as vandals in their time. If that close relation of vandalism to art may have weakened in the twenty-first century, which (following Byung-Chul Han) one may characterize as an era in which the smooth reigns supreme, Han's plea for injury as art's condition of possibility—for an art that would break with "the same, the familiar, the habitual"[1]—could then be said to hearken back to an understanding of art as vandalism, a return that some may consider to be embedded in the West's Christian tradition. Triangulating the figures of the artist and the vandal with the figure of the sovereign that I introduced through a close reading of a chapter from Carl Schmitt's *Political Theology* in my Introduction, the question then becomes how to situate this third figure in relation to the previous two.

I have suggested that it is actually the figure of the artist as vandal, of the one who breaks with the same, the familiar, the habitual, that comes closest to Schmitt's conceptualization of the sovereign as one who decides on the state of exception and thus introduces a rupture—the cut of a decision—into the fabric of the everyday. Evidence of this can be found wherever there is talk about artists and art—I have considered the examples of Karl Ove Knausgaard's profile of Anselm Kiefer, and the Toporovski affair involving curator Catherine de Zegher at the Museum of Fine Arts in Ghent (Belgium). A Schmittian concept of the sovereign—that is, a conception of sovereignty that is non-normative, or normative only in a secondary way—rules over the ways in which artists and art are conceived—even today, after postmodernism. Far from necessarily marking the unexceptionalization of the artist and art, the vandal and Han's notion of injury—and, in another register, the historical issue of iconoclasm, as Stathis Gourgouris among others has shown—can also *contribute* to their exceptionalization. In the fourth chapter of his book *Disability Aesthetics*, titled "Disability and Art Vandalism," Tobin Siebers for example discusses injury not so much as what challenges the exceptionalism of the original work of art but establishes it: "[F]orgeries are often detected," Siebers writes, "because it is so difficult to reproduce the effects of deterioration."[2] While possibly associated with unexceptionalism, then, injury does not *necessarily* unexceptionalize, and injury, the vandal, and iconoclasm reveal themselves to be fundamentally critical notions whose relations to exceptionalism need to be carefully distinguished.

I ended the previous chapter with a proposal for an inquiry that emerges out of what I consider to be the foundational premise of this book, namely my claim that Schmitt's concept of sovereignty rules even today's discourses about artists and art. This can be seen, for example, in Knausgaard's critical construction of Kiefer as a genius-like person—a king, as I've discussed—outside of all classification; or in the fact that the fake's role in art discourse remains unreconciled—art discourse remains organized, in other words, around the fundamental value of the original. Both of these examples indicate how art discourse operates in the monarchical logic of the one, which tends fascistically. It is *not* the plural discourse of democracy with which the arts are frequently associated. And yet, art is only with difficulty contained within such a discourse of the one. Neither the artist nor the work of art, as I have already shown, are easily comprehended by it. This is why art has often appeared suspicious to theology: because its very act of representation, and even simply of presentation, poses a risk to the logic of the one. To bring this risk, then, to art itself, I ended the previous chapter by proposing a simple experiment: that we explore how the artwork responds to its own representation, or even simply presentation, in another work of art. This introduced into my thinking the notion of the copy, of the forgery and the fake to which this chapter is dedicated.

Traces of such a notion can, however, already be found in some of the materials I worked with in the previous chapter. Consider, for example, how Siebers claims in "Disability and Art Vandalism" that the effect of vandalism is blunted by the use of forgery and the copy.[3] In other words, the injury that vandalism inflicts is somehow less injurious if it is inflicted upon a forgery or a copy. Is this true? It's worth noting that Siebers is not consistent in drawing out this element in his chapter. One of the examples of art vandalism that he discusses, namely Hans-Joachim Bohlmann's acid attack on Peter Paul Rubens' "Portrait of the Archduke Albrecht," should have mentioned that the Rubens that Bohlmann attacked was most likely not by Rubens himself but by Rubens' studio, an important element to consider if the effect of injury is indeed blunted by this kind of information. Like many readers (I assume), I did not know the Rubens painting was not by Rubens himself when I was first reading about the acid attack; but I mourned its destruction nevertheless. In other words, I am not sure that the mere fact that the destroyed work of art is a forgery or a copy does indeed weaken the effect of vandalism. Presumably Siebers thinks that this is so because the forgery or the copy are not originals, in other words Siebers' claim adds evidence to the continued importance of the original as the art world's foundational concept, and by extension to my own claim about aesthetic exceptionalism.

But there may be another reason why vandalism effects the forgery or copy less strongly: because *the forgery or the copy themselves can already be considered forms of vandalism*, doing damage to the stature of the original. To vandalize a forgery or copy means to attack an image that is itself already an attack on an image—it's iconoclasm against iconoclasm. Often understood as tributes that further sediment the stature of the original, the forgery or the copy are at the same time also a vandalization of the very work to which they appear to pay tribute, and this is due to the fact that they undermine that work's exceptional status. In the forgery or the copy, then, we find that peculiar kind of tribute that, while delivering praise, is also landing a blow. And it is that blow to which I would like to pay closer attention so as to further my inquiry into the prominence of Schmitt's concept of sovereignty in the arts. After triangulating the sovereign and the artist with the vandal, then, I am now triangulating those two figures with the forger and the copyist—a subcategory, one might argue, of the art vandal—in order to see what such a project might yield for the unexceptionalization of art.

Walter Benjamin's celebrated essay "The Work of Art in the Era of Mechanical Reproduction" cannot be avoided in this context, and I begin the chapter by considering that essay again—but through the lens of Benjamin's established dialogue with Schmitt, one that is usually limited to the early 1920s but whose traces can be found in much later key essays by Benjamin as well, such as the "Work of Art" essay or also Benjamin's last text, the "Theses on the Philosophy of History." In Benjamin's notion of "divine violence" as laid out at the end of his 1921 essay "Critique of Violence,"[4] and characterized there as "sovereign" ("waltend"[5]) because of how it applies outside of the law, one can arguably hear an echo of Benjamin's "Theses," where he calls for "a real state of exception"[6] to counter the state of exception that he associates with fascism. This is Benjamin calling for an even greater sovereignty, one that he associated with the divine (in "Critique of Violence") and with the messianic (in the "Theses") to counter the Schmittian sovereignty of the state of exception. It is in response to Benjamin's conceptualizations of a violence outside of the law (labeled "waltend" by Benjamin, and rendered as "sovereign" by Benjamin's English translator) that the conservative Schmitt, as we know, proposed his concept of sovereignty as a power that would be able to decide on the state of exception. Schmitt sought to bring Benjamin's radical notion back into the law—as the legally guaranteed possibility to act outside of it, as I've shown in my Introduction. In Benjamin, as was previously (but differently) the case in Kiefer, we find the problem of *an even greater vandal*, whose vandalism would stand outside of an art history that easily reappropriates vandalism as art. Benjamin was trying to position himself outside of such a history. I present Benjamin's Marxist-Communist approach to the copy in response to fascism as an approach that counters what I call aesthetic exceptionalism, one whose project remains far from realized in the arts.

In a second part of the chapter, I consider Hito Steyerl's updating of Benjamin's essay for the digital era, looking specifically at how Steyerl's notion of "the poor image"—also presented as part of a Marxist-Communist position—is modeled after Benjamin's notion of the copy, and adds a new twist to what is probably the most famous term from Benjamin's essay: that of the aura of the original work of art. Steyerl argues that the poor image allows for a new kind of aura in the digital age. Using Steyerl's essay as a guide, I then pursue my thinking about the art copyist and forger in relation to a work of media art, Christian Marclay's "The Clock." Paying close attention to Ben Lerner's discussion of this work in his auto-fictional novel *10:04*, I explore the ways in which this work can be read as a copy, and even a forgery or fake, that undermines the notion of originality. From one point of view "The Clock" is, I argue, an example of what Steyerl calls the poor image. From another, Marclay's strict conditions for how the work is to be shown also maintain originality, or—in Benjamin's terms—the artwork's aura. While the work projects an image of the smooth, specifically of real time fusing with the time shown in Marclay's work, in fact such a projection always collapses into the gap between art and life, with art and life continuing to appear as distinct realities. Ultimately, this opening up towards the poor image is reappropriated by Marclay, however, into what one might call "the rich image" of "The Clock."

In the chapter's third section, I will look at "The Clock"'s failure anew from a point of view that considers life as unexceptional process (rather than as a sovereign, exceptional event) and seeks to rethink art in relation to that consideration (in other words, outside of the sovereign framework, and towards the unexceptional). Returning to Byung-Chul Han on this count, this time his book *Shanzhai: Deconstruction in Chinese*, I consider how Han in a typically orientalist fashion locates such another point of view in China, or what he also calls "the Far East" (he also includes examples from Japan in his writing). While it cannot be denied, I think, that the role of the copy in Chinese art history is not the same as it is in Western art history, and while some of the conclusions of Han's orientalist compare-and-contrast will turn out to be helpful to rethink both our notions of life and of art, my discussion of Han's work is really only the beginning of the development of a non-orientalist perspective that finds such new notions of life and art within the Western art history—and, more broadly, thought—as well. If most of what I will have to say in this chapter will pertain to the copy, in closing I will foreground the figures of the forger and the fake—related to, but also substantially different from, the copy and the copyist—that will take up a central role in the second part of this book.

In Praise of the Copy

Let me start by turning to a commonplace in theoretical debates about the copy, namely Walter Benjamin's celebrated essay on "The Work of Art in the Era of Mechanical Reproduction" in the hopes of shedding some new light on it.[7] In what way is Benjamin's essay a study of the blow that the copy delivers to what I call aesthetic exceptionalism? It should be noted first of all that Benjamin is no stranger to the thinking about exceptionalism that I am pursuing. Contemporary debates about exceptionalism are often traced back to Benjamin's back-and-forth with Schmitt on this very topic, with Benjamin's "Theses on the Philosophy of History" often playing a key role in this genealogy.[8] This is because Benjamin writes there, somewhat enigmatically (as he often does), about what he calls "the real state of exception," which he considers the key tool in the fight against fascism.

I recall the "Theses" and their political project because Benjamin's "Work of Art" essay pitches itself against fascism as well. The essay, which is dated 1936, opens with a quote by Paul Valéry:

> We must expect great innovations to transform the entire technique of the arts, thereby affecting artistic invention itself and perhaps even bringing about an amazing change in our very notion of art.[9]

It's a quote that has become only more urgent over the years. Benjamin opens his essay with those lines because he wants to argue that "the developmental tendencies of art under present conditions of production . . . brush aside a number of outmoded concepts, such as creativity and genius, eternal value and mystery—concepts whose uncontrolled (and at present almost uncontrollable) application would lead to a processing of data in the Fascist sense."[10] As his language reveals, Benjamin is writing from a Marxist point of view. The "present conditions of production" are those of the "mechanical reproduction" named in his title. It's mechanical reproduction—in other words, the capacity to mechanically copy—that in his view is getting rid of what he characterizes as the outmoded concepts of creativity and genius, eternal value and mystery, all associated (in their uncontrolled application—something he perceives to currently be the case) with fascism.

Schmitt may not explicitly appear in this essay, but what Benjamin is targeting under different terms is the notion of sovereignty. Another way of saying this is that he understands the era of mechanical reproduction to be in direct tension with sovereignty.

Of course, Benjamin knows very well that the possibility to reproduce a work of art is nothing new. He notes, in fact, that "[i]n principle a work of art has always been reproducible."[11] But he adds that "[m]echanical reproduction" nevertheless "adds something new."[12] He lists lithography, photography, film, and sound film as new media that all put pressure on the notion of the original, and the associated concept of "authenticity."[13] In contrast to manual reproduction, which allows "the original [to preserve] all its authority,"[14] technical reproduction doesn't. This is, Benjamin suggests, due to two reasons: technical reproduction "is more independent of the original than manual reproduction"; second, "technical reproduction can put the copy of the original in situations which would be out of reach for the original itself."[15] It can place the copy where the original cannot go.

However, Benjamin famously argues that something is "eliminated" under the conditions of technical reproduction, something that Benjamin calls "aura." The aura is "that [quality of the work of art] which withers in the age of mechanical reproduction."[16] This is the consequence of "a unique existence" being replaced by "a plurality of copies."[17]

Benjamin argues that this has led to "a shattering of tradition,"[18] "tradition" being a word that surely needs to be associated with those outmoded concepts that Benjamin mentions early on in his essay. Again, his Marxism shines through: tradition is shattered by the copy due to the masses' "desire . . . to bring things 'closer' spatially and humanly."[19] It's worth making this resonate with the discussion of touch in the previous chapter, and the quote from Lerner's poetry—which appears in his novel *10:04*—about letting the children touch the painting. Second, tradition is shattered by the copy due to the masses' tendency "[to overcome] the uniqueness of everyday reality by accepting its reproduction."[20] Benjamin notes that art thus becomes disentangled from ritual and—he argues—begins to be based on another practice: "politics." And he has a very specific politics in mind: the fight against fascism. To get rid of creativity, genius, eternity, mystery, tradition, and ritual means to fight against fascism. Clearly, the stakes of post-exceptionalism—a term that's perhaps a bit of a stretch here given Benjamin's insistence on a "real state of exception"—are high.

It should be obvious that Benjamin's "Work of Art" essay is not a nostalgic essay at all. Benjamin is in fact taking it up for the copy, and pointing out its political impact—its importance for the undermining of fascism. Fascism, he famously concludes his essay, aestheticizes politics. To this, Benjamin opposes communism: the project to render aesthetics political.

If much of my discussion of art and damage revolved around an understanding of the avant-garde (which defines itself through an injury that ultimately becomes reappropriated by the system), here too the avant-garde comes into play due to what Rosalind Krauss in a famous essay deemed to be the "One thing only [that] seems to hold fairly constant in the vanguardist discourse and that is the theme of originality."[21] Krauss (who references Benjamin early on in her essay) begins her essay by asking how we are to consider work by the French artist Auguste Rodin that was made more than sixty years after his death? Rodin had given the French state permission to "make bronze editions from [his] estate's plasters."[22] But is the resulting artwork an original, or a fake, as Krauss suggests? Might this be a situation where "multiple copies" of a work exist "in the absence of an original"? Does it even make sense to ask these questions—doesn't it shake the very meaning of the words "copy" and "original"? With the example of Rodin, who died 1918, and specifically of his work *The Gates of Hell*, the first bronze cast of which was made in 1921, we are right around the time of Benjamin's and Schmitt's debates about sovereignty. And Krauss turns to Benjamin to engage the questions that the example of Rodin raises—but only Benjamin's later "Work of Art" essay. Criticizing "the cult of originality" that is obviously at work in debates about an example like Rodin—Krauss notes that Rodin himself invited comparisons of himself and his work to the divine[23]—she also points out the delightful ironies of such an artist giving "his work over to an afterlife of mechanical reproduction."[24] All of this is only the prelude to Krauss' real argument, however, which targets how originality has continued to be a value "in the vanguardist discourse"[25] (the book in which Krauss' essay—originally from 1981—was republished dates from the mid-1980s, so obviously the argument was still valid at that time).

Krauss goes on to show, through an insightful discussion of how in painting, "the grid" keeps being discovered as new throughout modern art history, that such originality in fact depends on "repetition and recurrence";[26] key elements of painting are rediscovered over and over again as if they are somehow new. Originality and repetition, in Krauss' view, become two parts of the same coin once one is capable of seeing "the ever-present reality of the copy as *the underlying condition of the original*."[27] Interestingly, one example she discusses where the singular and the formulaic enter into play is the landscape, whose two logical halves they constitute. If the landscape weren't always in part repetition, it wouldn't be recognized as a landscape; if it weren't always in part singular, it wouldn't be recognized as a landscape either. "What would it look like," Krauss asks at the end of her essay, "not to repress the concept of the copy?"[28] The art of Sherrie Levine, who will return in the next chapter of this book, provides Krauss' answer to that.

Today, however, one would have to note that in spite of the promise that Levine's art posed on this count, the dominance of the copy—the end of the originality system in art—has not arrived. It strikes one, rather, like the promise of the classless society in Marx, or of the end of fascism through the copy and the real state of exception, in Benjamin. As Dario Gamboni in his reference work on vandalism recalls, Nathalie Heinich has in fact turned Benjamin's very thesis around: "far from weakening the 'authenticity' of the 'original,'" Heinich argues,

> multiplication has enhanced by contrast those newly conceived qualities of the work of art . . . [It's precisely in the era of mechanical reproduction that] artists had to defend the specificity of their products against those of industry as well as handicraft, and this was achieved by eliminating from their practice the utilitarian project common to the other two and by stylizing the uniqueness of every work of art into an essential predicate, opposed to the interchangeability of serially produced industrial objects and to the irrelevant variability of handmade artifacts. The art market, followed by the law, entrenched this definition: to be recognized as a work of art, an object had to be "the

> unique product of the undivided labor of a unique creator." The "residual rarity" of ancient objects could be artistically promoted after they had been preserved as culturally significant and defunctionalized; for contemporary production, artistic rarity had to be itself "produced" or "manipulated."[29]

In other words, the era of mechanical reproduction did not so much make the aura wither as produce it.

Indeed, it's far from clear to what extent Benjamin's position can be translated into the present. Even if much of his analysis of the copy in my view still stands—certainly the outmoded concepts that he expected the copy to brush aside are still very much with us—the opposition of the copy (and what in the next chapter we will call the fake) to fascism is not clear. Fascism's cult of originality seems obvious, but in its attempt to produce the same—a purified Aryan race for example—perhaps it is precisely the copy that needs to be associated with fascism? Certainly the mechanical component of the German extinction of the Jewish people does not appear to sit well with Benjamin's analysis. Today, the role that fake news has played in the promotion of fascism would also need to be considered (although one should note, of course, that the fake is not the same as the copy). One can take the fact that Benjamin's essay is still being read and discussed today as evidence of how the political promise he found in the copy has not quite been realized. Indeed, Benjamin's essay has been and is still being rewritten for eras that followed it, as if Valéry's quote about the technical innovations of his time forced it to require continuous updates under perpetually changing—and fast-changing—technical conditions.

Post-Exceptional Images

One such essay that seeks to rewrite Benjamin's "Work of Art" is Hito Steyerl's "In Defense of the Poor Image,"[30] which allows us to transport Benjamin's essay into the digital age and to tie Benjamin's reflections about the copy to the discourse of unexceptionalism—captured, in Steyerl's title, by the very Benjaminian notion of "poverty"—that I have been developing.

What is a poor image? Steyerl opens her essay with a definition:

> The poor image is a copy in motion. Its quality is bad, its resolution substandard. As it accelerates, it deteriorates. It is a ghost of an image, a preview, a thumbnail, an errant idea, an itinerant image distributed for free, squeezed through slow digital connections, compressed, reproduced, ripped, remixed, as well as copied and pasted into other channels of distribution.[31]

She continues by characterizing the poor image as "a rag or a rip":

> It has been uploaded, downloaded, shared, reformatted, and reedited. It transforms quality into accessibility, exhibition value into cult value, films into clips, contemplation into distraction. The image is liberated from the vaults of cinemas and archives and thrust into digital uncertainty, at the expense of its own substance. The poor image tends toward abstraction: it is a visual idea in its very becoming.[32]

We are in the realm of the digital, a realm that Steyerl has elsewhere characterized as "circulationism"[33] and that Byung-Chul Han would associate with the smooth. But that is not what we find in Steyerl: the digital is, precisely, the realm of the *injured* image (if you will), of the image that has given up on the smooth in order to, in its injurious state, become more accessible. This goes against the exceptionalism of the cinema vault and the archive. There is something democratic, even anarchic to this kind of image. In the era of the poor image, under the poor image's technical conditions of reproduction, suddenly "rare prints of militant, experimental, and classical works of cinema as well as video"[34] reappear for everyone (with a computer and internet access) to see.

That Steyerl is theorizing the poor image in part from a political angle becomes obvious when she quotes the Cuban film director and screen writer Julio (Steyerl erroneously has Juan as his first name) García Espinosa, specifically his manifesto "For an Imperfect Cinema."[35] "[P]erfect cinema," Espinosa writes, "technically and artistically masterful—is almost always reactionary cinema."[36] Earlier in her essay, Steyerl had already pointed out how "high-end economies of film production were (and still are) firmly anchored in systems of national culture, capitalist studio production, the cult of mostly male genius, and the original version," adding that they "thus are often conservative in their very structure."[37] We find an echo here of the outmoded notions that Benjamin associates with fascism. Espinosa instead praises "imperfect cinema" as the "cinema of the people": "blurred, amateurish, and full of artifacts."[38] Steyerl embraces, after Espinosa, the poor image's "ethics of remix and appropriation."[39] Espinosa's essay has distinct resonances with Benjamin's "Work of Art" essay, and one understands why Steyerl relies on it in this context. "Perhaps film is the most elitist of all the contemporary arts," Espinosa suggests:

> Film today, no matter where, is made by a small minority for the masses. Perhaps film will be the art form which takes the longest time to reach the hands of the masses, when we understand mass art as popular art, art created by the masses.[40]

One could argue that Espinosa's future, in which film becomes an art of the masses, has in the meantime been realized in part thanks to technical innovations—the introduction of the cellphone that Han associates with the smooth. In that case too, Han's association would be undone: it's precisely through the cellphone that the poor image is realized. In the realm of cinema, the cellphone becomes a tool of post-exceptionalism.

That the adjective "imperfect" in Espinosa's title can be associated with what I am calling post-exceptionalism is clear:

> Imperfect cinema is no longer interested in quality or technique [Espinosa writes] . . . It is not quality which it seeks in an artist's work. The only thing it is interested in is how an artist responds to the following question: What are you doing to overcome the barrier of the "cultured" elite audience which up to now has conditioned the form of your work?[41]

It's Benjamin's Marxist position translated into explicitly post-exceptionalist terms.

It's worth noting that in Espinosa, this also explicitly becomes part of a criticism of a Western, and specifically European, way of thinking about art and making art that he understands to have been dominant. Why, at the time of Espinosa's writing (1969), are the Europeans becoming interested in Latin American cinema? Because, Espinosa provocatively suggests, it is beginning to fit *their* understanding of cinema. He proposes that this should "worry"[42] us. The interest in Latin American cinema that we see coming from Europe marks a form of recognition by the dominant that does not necessarily serve Latin American art well. There is an ethical issue here, as Espinosa notes, but also an aesthetic one—and this relates to Steyerl's point about the poor image as a low-resolution image. Espinosa wants to arrive at a situation where art can be an "uncommitted [desinteresada] activity,"[43] but he notes that this can't be done until the elitism in the arts—a key component of what I call aesthetic exceptionalism—has been done away with. In other words, there is a political vision that is laid out here that assumes a period of committed art before we are able to move into art as an uncommitted activity—and that as such is also an aesthetic vision. Some may read this as Hegel, some as Marx (and Espinosa is certainly indebted to Marx, a European, whom he explicitly references); but when Espinosa writes about how, when Latin American artists look towards Europe, they "wring [their] hands" because "the old culture is totally incapable of providing answers to the problems of art,"[44] one may also overhear a reference to the anti-colonial thinker Frantz Fanon.[45] Why are Europeans getting excited about Latin American art? It's out of nostalgia, Espinosa provocatively suggests: it's because "the European has no other Europe to which to turn" to solve the problems of art.[46] The key issue in Espinosa's text, however, is elitism or what I call exceptionalism: Espinosa praises "the development of science, the social presence of the masses, and the revolutionary potential in the contemporary world" for being "without hierarchical order" and therefore crucial in the process of bringing about uncommitted art.[47] Art should not be limited to specialists. Art schools should stop training specialists. Art should be "democratized";[48] science, the masses, and the revolution have a major role to play in abolishing the elitist film school.

In Steyerl, the influence of Benjamin on this count takes a strange turn, specifically with respect to the notion of aura, because there is a dialectical reversal that happens towards the end of Steyerl's text. "By losing its visual substance," Steyerl writes, the poor image

> recovers some of its political punch and creates a new aura around it. This aura is no longer based on the permanence of the "original" [as it is in Benjamin], but on the transience of the copy.[49]

In other words, if the poor image, as a copy in motion, contributes to the withering of aura that Benjamin diagnosed in his "Work of Art" essay, Steyerl suggests that the poor image, as a copy in motion, also *gains* a new aura that's associated with what she characterizes as the poor image's "political punch." This is anticipated by her counter-intuitive discussion of how the poor image accomplishes a shift from exhibition value to cult value early on in the essay. It's unclear what exactly the poor image's "political punch" consists of—it's not named, although one might expect it to be "communism" based on the title of the book in which Steyerl's essay appeared (*The Wretched of the Screen*, a reference to the Internationale) and also the title of the subsection from which I've just quoted ("Comrade, what is your visual bond today?"). I don't think the answer is quite so easy though, as Steyerl continues the quote above by saying that the poor image "is no longer anchored within a classical public sphere mediated and supported by the frame of the nation-state or corporation, but floats on the surface of temporary and dubious data pools."[50] This hearkens back to her association of the rich image with the nation-state and capitalism earlier on; here, we get something else, though it's not quite clear what: one might think neoliberalism at first, given the disappearance of the nation-state, but then she suggests corporations aren't in the picture either (an odd claim, given for example YouTube's increasingly corporative aspects as a platform for the distribution of poor images). What is clear is that there is something "dubious" about where the poor image "floats," and I will have to come back to this dubious side of post-exceptionalism in a later chapter.

Steyerl's association of the poor image, a copy in motion, with a new kind of aura makes us reconsider the precise effect of the copy on the aura that Benjamin describes in his essay. While the verb "eliminate" sounds rather strong in this context, "to wither" leaves intact, perhaps, the possibility of some kind of remainder—of something that previously shriveled up and was in decay, reflourishing under different conditions or in different ways.

Still, in spite of Steyerl's evocation of a new aura, there is no doubt that her essay operates under the sign of post-exceptionalism. While the poor image is about reality, she concludes, it is not about the reality of the original but about the reality of the circulation of the copy.

Vandalizing Media Art

While Steyerl's own work as a media artist could be an example in this context, I want to focus on a work of media art that appears in Ben Lerner's oeuvre so as to remain within the range of the discussion that I began in Chapter 1. As I've noted previously, media art—and more broadly art that does not take the commodity-form—was suspiciously absent from both Lerner's and Siebers' investigations of art and vandalism. This may have been for a number of reasons, as I suggested. At this point, and building on what I've said previously, we can also suggest that it is media art's association with the copy that may have kept it outside of practices and theories of art vandalism. Much harder to vandalize, and in part immune to the effect of vandalism (since it always already operates in the realm of the copy), media art seems to stand outside of the discourse on art and injury. Byung-Chul Han, who associates the digital with the smooth, may lead one to such a conclusion. Steyerl, however, changes this for us, since she situates the digital image precisely within the realm of injury.

Interestingly, Lerner has made Steyerl's argument in a discussion of the media artwork "The Clock" (2010), by Christian Marclay (a "devotee of Duchamp" who, in the words of one art critic, has "an algorithmic mind"[51]—and I will return to the association of algorithms with post-exceptionalism in my Conclusion). As Lerner writes in *10:04*,

> *The Clock* is a clock: it's a twenty-four-hour montage of thousands of scenes from movies and a few from TV edited together so as to be shown in real time; each scene indicates the time with a shot of a timepiece or its mention in dialogue; time in and outside of the film is synchronized.[52]

In other words: it's an original work of art, made up of copies, that's been called "the ultimate work of appropriation art."[53] Some might go so far as to argue that the work is not original at all but a copy of Christoph Girardet's 2003 work "60 Seconds (Analog)," which shows sixty images of watches taken from films, one for each second of the length of the film. Andy Warhol's "Empire" or Douglas Gordon's "24 Hour Psycho" are other clear antecedents for Marclay's work, as Daniel Zalewski has noted.[54] To complicate matters even further, Marclay himself had already done a previous work also titled "The Clock" in 1990—but that piece was very different from the later "The Clock."[55]

All of that said, Marclay's editing for "The Clock" is original: Marclay insisted on doing it himself, in contrast to artists like Jeff Koons or Damien Hirst, who rely heavily and sometimes even entirely on assistants for the final execution of their work. (Marclay too worked with assistants at the research stage, but not for the final editing.) With Marclay, we are *not* in a situation like the one Rosalind Krauss describes *à propos* of Rodin, or also Cartier-Bresson, "who never printed his own photographs":

> Rodin's relation to the casting of his sculpture could only be called remote. Much of it was done in foundries to which Rodin never went while the production was in progress; he never worked on or retouched the waxes from which the final bronzes were cast, never supervised or regulated either the finishing or the patination, and in the end never checked the pieces before they were crated to be shipped to the client or the dealer who had bought them.[56]

Not so with Marclay. If Krauss brings in this information about Cartier-Bresson and Rodin to undermine the originality of the work of art, Marclay's insistence on being hands-on can be read as the opposite: to maintain the work's originality especially with respect to a work that already thrives in the copy. (And yet, as one reviewer has pointed out, "The Clock" can never quite shake the feeling that it was made by a computer . . . .[57]) In addition, Marclay—who is an experimental musician as well—provides the film with an original score. As far as the editing goes, Marclay's film does not provide a coherent narrative. Instead, the work operates very much within the suggestion of narrative. The viewer wants to tie it all together, but they can't. In Zalewski's rendering: "He [Marclay] wanted to make an expertly edited film that exposed the fakery of editing."[58] "[T]he video, in a way, is one big trick."[59] A copy, then, *and* a fake.

But an interesting thing happens: while Lerner's narrator—called Ben—is watching "The Clock," he checks the time on his phone, a digital watch. This is of course absurd because Marclay's film is not only synchronized with time but also indicates at every moment what time it is. In other words, there is absolutely no need to check the time on your phone: the film relieves its viewers, if you will, from that contemporary tic. But the fact that Ben *does* check the time on his phone leads to an important consequence. While Ben had "heard *The Clock* described as the ultimate collapse of fictional time into real time, a work designed to obliterate the distance between art and life, fantasy and reality"—in other words, while he had heard Marclay's film described as a smooth work of art that overcomes the gap between two orders of reality—in fact Ben realizes when checking his phone that in "The Clock," real time hasn't collapsed into fictional time at all, and the distance between art and life has not been abolished: "while the duration of a real minute and *The Clock*'s minute were mathematically indistinguishable, they were nevertheless minutes from different worlds."[60] "The Clock"'s supposed smoothness collapses, in other words, into injury: into the gap between reality and fiction that no work of art can overcome. The perfect realism that "The Clock" appeared to realize—the coincidence of life and art as evoked by the map Jorge Luis Borges describes in "On Exactitude in

Science"—is not possible. And one should note that this argument about injury is made specifically with respect to a work of media art. Clearly, media art is less smooth than one might think at first sight. It's not quite as removed from injury as one might think.

One wonders, given Marclay's earlier work in music for example, whether "The Clock" was meant to be a smooth work of art. Consider Zalewski's description of Marclay's work in music:

> Marclay, a fixture of the East Village music scene in the eighties, was particularly renowned as an avant-garde dj—in the late seventies, he'd been one of the first people to scratch records in performance, treating the turntable as an instrument. During sets, he sometimes smashed LPs, Frankensteined shards together with tape, and played the hiccupping results.[61]

Wouldn't it make more sense to read the "The Clock" as a continuation of this avant-garde dj practice: as a musical composition full of hiccups? Zalewski notes the film's "intensely musical feel" and suggests that Marclay's "experience as a turntablist is essential"[62] to the work. Perhaps Ben is only discovering here what was present in the work all along; perhaps his association of "The Clock" with the smooth was no more than a red herring.

Steyerl lays out some additional, less philosophical—more practice-based—evidence for this:

> One of the biggest misunderstandings about digital information is that it is replicated identically, without loss or transformation. But anyone who works with such information knows that digital practice is constituted—like perhaps any technology—by malfunction. One has to constantly convert information in order to work with it across different platforms and softwares and on the

> way it is reformatted, translated, compressed or sometimes even blown up, it is enhanced or diminished: it changes. It changes its format or container or outlook or context.[63]

This puts Steyerl in direct tension with Han's association of the digital with the smooth. Steyerl is taking down the idea of an art that could remain outside of unexceptionalism: all art, even media art, is unexceptional, she appears to be saying. And one should note that my use of the term post-exceptionalism, which still carries within itself the notion of the exceptional, allows for Steyerl's admission that a new aura is created around the poor image. It is in other words not because art is post-exceptional that it is no longer art. *Post-exceptionalism is not a relativist position that flattens everything into the same.* In the realm of the poor image, some relief remains.

I've sought to develop a reading of "The Clock" that undermines the smoothness that the work projects and reads the work in the context of Marclay's broader, less than smooth artistic practice; "The Clock" can be understood as a poor image, rather, and one that—via my discussion of Marclay's musical practice—can bring the work in connection to injury. As such, however, the caveats about art's relation to injury—specifically, the way in which this relation has also contributed to art's exceptionalization—that I have raised earlier in this book are valid in this case as well. Indeed, even if Marclay's work is a work of injury that can be read as a poor image, it is worth noting the strict conditions under which Marclay wants the work to exist and be shown: there are only a limited number of copies of the film out there, and they can only be shown as synchronized with real time. When one owner of the work turns out to be showing it in "suboptimal conditions,"[64] Marclay is horrified. In her text on the poor image, Steyerl criticizes this as the reactionary attitude of the master—Marclay is insisting, she would argue, on the rich image.[65] And so, the force of originality and authenticity, indeed the aura of the work of art (its unique presence in space-time), remain strong in "The Clock" which, as a poor image, as a work of injury, nevertheless reigns sovereign—maintains itself as rich. A seemingly exceptional work (projecting the smooth integration of intra- and extra-diegetical time) was shown to tend post-exceptionally (as a poor image), but ultimately turned out to be exceptional all the same (as an original, authentic, and auratic work of art). This is where Espinosa's question about how to *end* the Western tradition of thinking about the work of art returns. While Marclay's work obviously contains elements that move in that direction, ultimately it seems to be the tradition that wins. Where to look for something else?

Looking at China

Walter Benjamin's essay shows that anxiety about the copy is real in the West, because the copy marks the elimination or withering of the original's aura in the age of mechanical reproduction, in the era of what—today—we could call old media. But new media need to be included in Benjamin's argument as well, and my discussion of Steyerl was an attempt to do so. Both Benjamin and Steyerl, however, thought it necessary to *defend* their positions in their essays. In other words, they could not take for granted a culture that would welcome their positions—they were writing, in a sense, against a culture in which the central values were different, a culture in which it was the original rather than the copy, and the rich image rather than the poor image, that was praised. Such is, indeed, by and large the case in the Western culture that forms the background of both Benjamin and Steyerl's arguments. But one other reason why the already discussed work of Byung-Chul Han is interesting is because it draws our attention to another culture that is supposedly not so centrally organized around the notion of originality, and attributes a quite different role to the notion of the copy. That culture can be found, according to Han, in the Far East, and he focuses specifically on its Chinese instantiation.

Let me start by noting that there are different ways of looking outside of the West. With respect to China, we know that one of the major ways in which this has happened—and there is a long tradition of this in contemporary thought—has been called "orientalism." In his landmark book *Orientalism*, which focuses on a different geographical area but proposes conclusions that are relevant in this context as well, Edward Said writes that he is interested in the "interchange between the academic and the more or less imaginative meanings of Orientalism"[66]—between research on the orient and then also what Said refers to as "a style of thought based upon an ontological and epistemological distinction made between 'the Orient' and (most of the time) 'the Occident'" which is the starting point for "elaborate theories, epics, novels, social descriptions, and political accounts concerning the Orient, its peoples, customs, 'mind,' destiny, and so on."[67] What Said refers to as the "traffic" between the two, produces what is in his view "the third meaning of Orientalism," "which is something more historically and materially defined than either of the other two": "Orientalism as a Western style for dominating, restructuring, and having authority over the Orient."[68] Put simply, in the context of a discussion about China, the term orientalism would refer to a practice of construing "China" or "the

Far East" as general categories that are shaped—scholarly and imaginatively, as Said points out—in opposition to "Europe" or "the West." There is a tradition of European philosophers turning to China to find everything that the West is not. Chinese utopias haunt post-Second World War continental philosophy. There is plenty of scholarship on these issues already, and I have dedicated a book chapter to that elsewhere.[69] The U.S.-based critics Lisa Lowe and Eric Hayot for example have already explored these Chinese hallucinations or dreams. Both Hayot and Lowe refer in this context to Gayatri Chakravorty Spivak's article "French Feminism in an International Frame," which points out that "French theorists such as Derrida, Lyotard, Deleuze, and the like, have at one time or another been interested in reaching out to all that is not the West, because they have, in one way or another, questioned the millennially cherished excellences of Western metaphysics: the sovereignty of the subject's intention, the power of predication, and so on."[70] The latter point about sovereignty obviously stands out in this context. In the article, Spivak skewered Julia Kristeva's book *About Chinese Women* for construing the broadest generalizations about China based on very little evidence, and within just a few pages.

To draw out that orientalist tradition and the criticisms it has received obviously does not foreclose the possibility of actually looking at China and finding something there that may diverge from what can be found in Europe; though the more specific one can be about where that particular thing is found, and what the divergence consists in (is it an opposition, or is there another relation that is more appropriate to name it?), the better. Overall, and taking into account the criticisms of orientalism that have been developed, it seems wise to avoid overly general categories such as "the West" or "the Far East," or even "Europe" or "China." Anyone who has traveled in China will be able to testify to the vast differences within the country, even if there are also commonalities. Conversely, while there are obviously structures of thought that are typically found in the West, that does not mean that all Western thought is the same. One could only really "oppose" categories like West and East if they were static, and one thing that's clear is that while Europe or China each have long histories that are both distinguished and troubling, they are hardly names of the past. Instead, these names are still very much in flux—processual and future-oriented rather than comfortably locked in the past. Alive rather than dead. It seems wise, then, too, to avoid a logic of simple opposition whenever they are discussed.

It's with such caveats in mind that I approach Byung-Chul Han's writing about China in his book *Shanzhai: Deconstruction in Chinese*. In a chapter of this book titled "Zhen Ji: Original," Han starts with a discussion of a letter by Sigmund Freud to Wilhelm Fliess in which Freud discusses memory. For Freud, Han concludes,

> [M]emory images are not immutable representations of what has been experienced. Rather, they are products of complex construction by the psychic apparatus, and thus are subject to continual change. New constellations are always arising to alter their appearance. In this the psychic apparatus follows a complex temporal movement, in which later events also reshape earlier ones. Past, present, and future interfuse within the psychic apparatus.[71]

Han references this understanding of memory because he wants to present in his chapter a similar understanding of the work of art.

For that, Han points to the classical Chinese term for "original," "zhen ji." As Han points out, the term literally means "authentic trace," a combination of terms that interests Han because it "deconstructs the idea of [an] original that embodies an unmistakable, immutable, centered presence and identity."[72] After all, when one confronts a trace, it is precisely a sign that whatever made the trace—the authentic original—is always already in some way gone; the trace is, in that sense, a kind of copy and thus a term that at least from the Western point of view can only with some difficulty be tied to the notions of authenticity and originality.

The trace, as Han sees it, can instead be associated with "processuality and differentiality" that "give the trace a deconstructive, centrifugal force."[73] To think of the original artwork as an authentic trace instead means to insert a difference into the original artwork, and Han points out that the artwork's "difference to itself does not allow the artwork to come to a standstill whereby it could achieve its final shape."[74] The trace, in Han's words, "always lets the artwork differ from itself."[75] This leads Han into a thought of "the Chinese idea of the original."[76] Using terms that have been central to my account so far, Han argues that the Chinese idea of the original is

> determined not by a unique act of creation, but by unending process, not by definitive identity but by constant change. Indeed, change does not take place within the *soul* of an artistic subjectivity. The trace effaces the artistic subjectivity, replacing it with a process that allows no essentialist positing.[77]

In contrast to the Western thought of essentialism, soul, definitive identity, and the unique act of creation, "[t]he basic figure in Chinese thought is . . . the multiform, the multilayered process."[78] The artwork thus becomes a kind of palimpsest, comparable in form to Freud's theory of memory with which Han started. The tie to Freud is important because it shows that the kind of thinking Han is after, and that he finds in China, does not exist in China alone: one can find it in as important a thinker for the Western tradition as Sigmund Freud. While Han's approach seems orientalist, then, and seems to operate following the logic of contrast between West and East, his reference to Freud also breaks down such an opposition, and establishes a connection or similarity between Western thought and China.

As Han points out, the understanding of the work of art that he finds in China—but theoretically approaches through Freud—can be said to apply to the oeuvre of an artist as well. For example, Han points out that

> the oeuvre of the famous master Dong Yuan looks different in the Ming dynasty from how it looked during the Song dynasty, with even forgeries or replicas defining a master's image.[79]

In the Chinese tradition, it is "[t]he subsequent or retrospective [that] defines the origin"; "the oeuvre is in large part a lacuna that is always filling up."[80] This obviously leads to a deconstruction of the figure of the "master" and "their" work even if, it should be noticed, it does not entirely do away with it. After all, there still is the figure of the master Dong Yuan.

The case of Emperor Huizong is a great example: while Huizong was known as a great painter and calligrapher, there is little consensus among scholars about which works are truly his. In her discussion of the so-called "Problem of Huizong,"[81] Maggie Bickford notes that "Emperor Huizong painted and that employees made paintings at his behest and some of them in his stead. Moreover, [sources] record that members of the court copied Huizong's paintings and sought his inscriptions, seals or cipher on their copies"[82]—all of which would have muddled the strict distinction between original and copy. "Ghosting" haunts not only writing, but the visual arts as well. The "problem of Huizong" is really a problem of *ghost painting*. Looking at this master's oeuvre, it's possible (as Bickford neatly points out) that *all* of the works in it are by Huizong; that only *some* are; that *some parts of some* are; or that *none* is.[83] Similar issues can of course also be found in the Western tradition, where the actual presence of a master in her or his works is not always established—assistants may be largely responsible for them, as my reference earlier on in the discussion of Marclay to Koons and Hirst (as well as Cartier-Bresson and Rodin) already shows.

While Han builds his arguments starting from concrete historical cases, he quickly moves to present the unstable understanding of the work of art that we can derive from them in more general, philosophical terms—and the writing here begins to fit in what, earlier on, I called orientalism. Starting from Hegel's frustration with the Buddhist notion of "emptiness," Han points out that "emptiness in Chinese Buddhism means the negativity of decreation (*Ent-Schöpfung*) and absence (*Abwesen*). It empties out Being (*Sein*)."[84] In contrast to Western ideas of "essence," ideas that a philosopher like Jacques Derrida has done much to unwork, "Chinese philosophy is deconstructivist from the outset, to the extent that it breaks radically with Being and essence."[85] This orientation may have something to do with "the Chinese awareness of time and history."[86] "For example," Han writes, "transformation takes place not as a series of events or eruptions, but discreetly, imperceptibly, and continually . . . Ruptures or revolutions . . . are alien to the Chinese awareness of time."[87] Chinese thought "does not recognize the kind of identity that is based on a unique event."[88]

But what is, one might ask, "Chinese thought"? Whose thought? When? Where in China? What is "the Chinese awareness of time and history"? Is there only one? Does it make sense to speak in such generalizations? Would it with respect to "the West"? And is this "Chinese thought" really in a relation of simple opposition to "the West"?

Indeed, Han points out that some of what he gathers from looking at Chinese art can be found in the work of Theodor Adorno as well. But whereas Adorno insists on the artwork's "inexhaustible fullness and unfathomable depth," he is quick to continue, "the Chinese artwork is *empty* and *flat*. It is without soul and truth."[89] Again, one might ask: which artwork? All of them? To learn to become an artist in China, one must copy the works of the masters. If one has become such a good student that one's copies are indistinguishable from the master's works, if one has become the master's equal, this is proof of one's own mastership—there is nothing negative associated with that. "Creation," Han points out, "is not a sudden event, but a slow process, one that demands a long and intense engagement with what has been, in order to create from it. In this sense, creation is primarily the act of creating. The construct of the original spirits away what has been, the prior entity from which it is created."[90] The consequences are, from the Western point of view, enormous: "If a forger borrows a painting from a collector, and when returning it hands over a copy unnoticed instead of the original, this is not considered a deception but an act of fairness."[91] Or, as Han concludes: "This is an extraordinary practice from ancient China that would put an end to today's art speculation."[92] If "truth" in the West operates through "exclusion" and "transcendence,"

"Chinese culture uses a different technique that operates using inclusion and immanence."[93] One can only imagine this, he writes, "in a culture that is not committed to revolutionary ruptures and discontinuities, but to continuities and quiet transformations, not to Being and essence, but to process and change."[94] This culture is "China." In the terms I am developing in this book: one can only imagine it outside of aesthetic exceptionalism. While I consider aesthetic exceptionalism to be typical of Western thought, I would not say, however, that it is uniquely Western. And while I can recognize, based on Han's discussion of "China," that elements critical of aesthetic exceptionalism may be found in Chinese thought and art, that does not mean that Chinese aesthetics is entirely free from exceptionalism. Finally, to say that Western thought tends exceptionally does not mean that no traces of post-exceptionalism can be found within it: copying, for example, is certainly part of Western art history as well. When I associate "aesthetic exceptionalism" with the West, this is obviously a broad-stroke generalization that, as I use it here, allows for a much more plural tradition of thought than any such association risks to project.

Han points out that there is something "organicist" to a thought of process and change, since it is "nature" that "provides the model": "The organism also renews itself through continual cell replacement."[95] This applies to the ancient or classical Chinese approach to the master's oeuvre or the art collection, but it is perhaps more clear in the case of a building restoration, where over time all of the parts of the building are replaced, but it is supposedly still the same building (the well-known metaphor of the ship, whose different parts are gradually all replaced *en route*, also comes up in Han's book[96]). "Identity and renewal are not mutually exclusive,"[97] Han writes. In such an approach, modularity is crucial, since it enables reproducibility, which is this approach's central value. This marks the end of the idea of "genius,"[98] as Han points out, an idea that came into being with Leonardo da Vinci and is a cornerstone of Kant's aesthetics.[99] Ultimately, this amounts to an aesthetics of de-creation or *Ent-schöpfung*: the unworking of the figure of the creator who, as both god and the artist, is theological and aesthetic exceptionalism's central figure, with all of its political consequences.[100] While one might disagree with Han's orientalist approach, one senses here, on the side of Western thought, the force of his argument, which targets precisely the aesthetic exceptionalism that I seek to undermine in this book.

Han is certainly not the only thinker to present Chinese thought in this way. Although philosopher François Jullien's entire oeuvre—and the divergence (rather than "difference," as Jullien insists, no doubt because he is aware of orientalism) that it stages between Chinese thought and Western philosophy—applies here, it is perhaps the chapter "Mythology of the Event" from his book *The Silent Transformations* that is the most *à propos*.[101] Jullien takes on there precisely the Western philosophical notion of the event as a representation of "exceptional . . . irruption [and] upheaval,"[102] arguing precisely that it is a "fictive or mythological representation."[103] Instead, and coming from Chinese thought—and it's worth noting that while Jullien too has been accused of orientalism, his work cannot be compared to Han's in the sense that it is carefully grounded in a life-long study of Chinese authors and their texts—Jullien theorizes the event as "a matter of emergence."[104] Where Western philosophy finds the "incomparable, non-integratable event,"[105] Chinese thought offers "a silent maturation of the negative"[106] which, when "conditions are ripe for it"[107] leads the event to emerge.

On the one hand, there is again the question of what is meant here by "Western philosophy" and "Chinese thought." On the other, what Jullien has to say about Western philosophy certainly strikes a chord for those interested in aesthetic exceptionalism. He is putting his finger on precisely that characteristic of Western thought—one that seems undeniable—and tries to think outside of it.

Singling out Alain Badiou's thought as an example of how "the event still continues to fertilize philosophy today,"[108] Jullien considers the "characteristic of Chinese thought" to be "precisely to dissolve the event."[109] Thus, the event enters into an "equality with others, without privileging one moment or excepting it in relation to all moments."[110] Chinese thought, as he puts it, "absorb[s] the prestige of the event."[111] Recalling Richard Wolin's criticism of Schmitt's politics as being too focused on the aesthetic of shock, it's worth noting that according to Jullien's Chinese thought the "brutality of the 'event' [only] amazes us, because we have not known how to distinguish the silent transformation which has imperceptibly led to it."[112] Chinese thought does not know rupture. If Jullien mobilizes such thought here, it is against what he characterizes as the "reign," the "dictatorship" even,[113] of the event, which has discreetly infiltrated all communication. If Han's book risks, at times, to look a little thin, it is Jullien's deep knowledge of Chinese thought that can be brought in to back up the core of Han's shanzhai project. As I've indicated, however, the specter of orientalism remains—even in Jullien's approach.

Some other questions are worth asking. It would be interesting to consider, first of all, the historical location of Han's claims and ask whether they also apply to *contemporary* Chinese art. Han's examples are mostly taken from ancient and classical

Chinese art; Jullien's work mostly draws from ancient and classical Chinese thought and aesthetics. But do those still apply today? What is their relevance in contemporary China? It is true that China's government is keen on projecting a continuity with the past—but is that projection also a fact? How are we to consider that continuity through time? Wouldn't it be more likely that contemporary Chinese art has been fully Westernized; that is, fully folded within the logic of aesthetic exceptionalism, especially because this would also make sense from a capitalist/financial point of view—because it would "open up" Chinese art onto the Western art market? In her book titled *Original Copies*, to which I will turn in Chapter 6, Bianca Bosker addresses this problem after claiming that contemporary experiments in city-making in China can be understood within the context of ancient Chinese thought. Drawing from the work of Jonathan Hay, she argues that such connections across time are possible

> because elements of Chinese belief structures have remained consistent over time, many of the principles that underlie these systems of thought are applicable to modern thinking. According to Hay [Bosker continues], the Chinese tradition has been consistently "reprocessing" itself, giving an elastic quality to its historical evolution. And while historical analysis has revealed these traditional belief systems and narratives of the past to be far more complex than allowed by conventional accounts, certain principles persist and may inform present perspectives. Is it possible that long-standing attitudes about creating simulacrum landscapes have not disappeared but rather have evolved to better suit contemporary pressures and needs? Although Chinese philosophical conceptions have morphed considerably over time, the classical Chinese thinking on landscape re-creation represents a valuable portal for analyzing contemporary events.[114]

In other words, we can have both: continuity and difference. Many of the principles of ancient thought continue, but they have adapted themselves to contemporary pressures and needs. One might quip that it's ancient Chinese thought with contemporary characteristics.

Second, one should also ask, as I already did, whether Western aesthetics has *always* corresponded to the image that Han sketches of it here, or whether that image too is historically located. When it comes to the issue of reproducibility, for example, it seems dubious that it can be used transhistorically to oppose China and the West. In some of his work on aesthetics, the French philosopher Bernard Stiegler recalls for example how in paintings representing the Louvre just a few years after it opened, "one can see that the visitors, who are most definitely almost all artists, mostly reproduce paintings there."[115] At least at that time—the museum opened in 1793—copying appears to have been crucial to Western artistic production. For artists and art *connoisseurs* at the time, it was "impossible to talk about a canvas that one has not copied."[116] In other words, it is through copying that one gets to have intimate knowledge of a painting. "[A] good repetition," as Stiegler appreciatively puts it elsewhere, "will always remain an adventure."[117] Stiegler's position seems to undermine the orientalist opposition between the West and China that Han sets up.

Moreover, when Stiegler considers the shift in Marcel Duchamp's work from the "wet" painting "Nude Descending a Staircase, No. 2" from 1912 and the infamous "Fountain" (from 1917),[118] he is interested in a shift that takes place in between these two works *that concerns the status of copying*. For Stiegler, in other words, copying becomes a key issue in the history of Western art. In between these two works by Duchamp, copying becomes *mechanized* and in Stiegler's view "the readymade is born from the serialized production for mass markets."[119] In other words, it's not so much copying or reproducibility that are the issue here, but precisely *mechanical* reproducibility, and this is why Benjamin's celebrated "The Work of Art" essay is an important resource for Stiegler. Today, with digitization, we are living through a new era of the development that Benjamin was already tracing, and Stiegler is interested in considering the aesthetic consequences of the latter. He marks those as a proletarianization: a loss of the knowledge of (how to copy) a work of art.

There is no doubt, of course that *today* copying has largely disappeared from the museum—even if, occasionally, one will find an artist or a group of art students in a museum gallery copying a famous canvas and even if postcard copies of works will be on sale in the museum gift shop. This may have to be tied to the disappearance not so much of the practice of copying but the practice of drawing, partly as a consequence of how art has developed. It does not make a whole lot of sense to take a group of art students to the museum and ask them to copy a Jackson Pollock—although I will return to the practice of copying Pollock in my Conclusion.[120] Overall then, Han seems correct in his analysis that copying, in the Western art world, has accrued a bad rap and is associated with plagiarism and forgery. The museum is not nearly as open to the copy and to copying as it seems to have been in the late eighteenth century—the institutionalization of artists like Andy Warhol, who turned the copy into a part of their practice, notwithstanding. In this light, "the use of the photocopier as a creative tool" as it was explored in the "Experiments in Electrostatics" exhibition at the Whitney Museum in New York can partly be read as a reaction against these developments.[121] That is so even if this exhibition deals with mechanical reproduction rather than craft-based copying. It is not insignificant, given Stiegler's argument, that this exhibition stopped "at the dawn of the digital era in the 1980s." By and large, however, there appears to have been a progressive institutionalization of art as Art—art with a capital A—that is original and authentic, separate from the "bad" copy (small, very small c). Another indication of this process might be that *if* copying is still allowed in the museum today, *only* dry mediums are allowed. Presumably wet paint is banned because of the risk of interference with the original.[122]

It's worth noting from the political point of view that I am developing in this book that this progression seems to have been set in motion precisely at a time when, as Stiegler in another lecture on aesthetics lays bare, commoners struggled to be recognized as art amateurs against "the practice of the Amateur [amateur with capital A], embodied by persons of noble rank, supposedly endowed with what the ancien régime called the 'natural taste' proper to 'persons of rank.'"[123] As Stiegler puts it in more political terms, it is "monarchical taste" that is being targeted here, and being democratized from the king and the nobility—only those of rank can have taste—to the commoners. A commoner too could copy, and it is because of one's copying skill that one becomes an art amateur—not just because of one's rank.

I would suggest, then, that the three developments we find here need to be read together, in the sense that (1) the democratic birth of the amateur (small a) and (2) their simultaneous proletarianization lead to (3) a kind of monarchization of Art (capital A), because with the proletarianization of the amateur, copying disappeared from the museum, and monarchical

Art prevailed. What *looked like* a democratic moment on the side of the spectator was *actually* a profoundly un-democratic moment on the side of art and the art institution, as marked by the disappearance of the copy. Adam Bosse's Leviathan, the frontispiece of Thomas Hobbes' celebrated work on sovereignty, can thus come to stand in for the work of Art at large, and its sovereign dominance. It is those traces of (1) the democratization of the art amateur plus (2) their proletarianization and (3) the monarchization of Art that one confronts in a discussion of aesthetic exceptionalism. The theological dimension of such a situation is evident and gives new secular-political meaning to Edward Said's observation in *The World, the Text, and the Critic* that "repetition is useful as a way of showing that history and actuality are all about human persistence, and not about divine originality."[124] Indeed, what if "copying is what makes us human—what then?"[125]

Let me close by casting this in even more explicitly political terms. If Plato banned mimesis from his ideal Republic, this was because Western thought tends to have a different view of the original as what Han calls "monomorphic presence," "monoeides" (in Greek, with "*eidos*" marking the Platonic idea or form).[126] However, "the basic figure in Chinese thought is not the monomorphic, unique *Being* but the multiform, multilayered *process*."[127] Chinese thought, by and large, breaks out of a *monological* notion of art. Ultimately, I understand such an aesthetic as political, in the sense of an aesthetic against the monarchic. Although I have used the notion of monarchical art after Stiegler, as a historical understanding of art and specifically the notion of taste (hence aesthetics) as tied to the specific regime of monarchic government, it will have become clear that I also use it in what Stathis Gourgouris remarks is monarchy's literal, Greek-derived meaning: "μονη αρχη—singular authority, unique authority, but also, given the double meaning of archè [as both rule and origin], singular origin, unique origin."[128] By working against such a monological notion of art, Chinese thought also works against a monarchic politics of art or against what I call in more fashionable terms aesthetic exceptionalism.

I am certainly not the only one to have drawn political conclusions from Han's *Shanzhai* book, which begins with a chapter titled "Quan: Law" and includes the words "anarchy" and "democracy" in its final chapter. In a discussion of Han's book, Ursula Anna Frohne notes "the antiauthoritarian movement implied in *Shanzhai*," and ends by arguing that "multiple gestures of repetition in contemporary art . . . challenge art history to face up to the political implications of today's models of creativity."[129] That is, indeed, what drives my own project about unexceptional art. In a review of *Shanzhai*, Mario Wenning begins by noting that "etymologically, the term [shanzhai] refers to the mountain strongholds in which bandits used to hide and thereby evade the official grip of the authorities."[130] If anything, this etymology should put one on the track of a political reading of the copy—even if I don't think this is quite as developed in Han's book as Wenning's review suggests.[131]

In the second half of the *Shanzhai* chapter titled "Zhen Ji: Original," Han begins to discuss forgers and forgeries in this context, both Western forgers like Elmyr de Hory (the central figure in Orson Welles' film *F for Fake*) and Han van Meegeren (the Vermeer forger), and the Chinese[132] forger—and master-painter—Zhang Daqian (all of whom I will discuss in the next chapter). Zhang Daqian, who "was considered the Picasso of China,"[133] was shown to have forged numerous old masterpieces that had been exhibited in the West. Han points out that for

Zhang Daqian, however, "they were anything but forgeries. In any case most of these old pictures were no mere copies, but rather replicas of lost paintings that were known only from written descriptions."[134] They were more something like "original copies" (to recall the title of Bosker's book). Han points out that Zhang Daqian was a passionate collector of art, whose collection "was not a dead archive but a *gathering* of Old Masters, a living place of communication and transformation."[135] Zhang Daqian "was himself a shape-shifting body, an artist of metamorphosis. He slipped effortlessly into the role of past masters and created *a certain kind of original*" (emphasis mine).[136] "His paintings are originals," Han explains further down in the text, "insofar as they carry forward the 'real trace' of the Old Masters and also extend and change their oeuvre retrospectively."[137] In the German original of his text, Han uses the term "Fortschöpfung," rendered as "persisting creation"—I think it would be better to put "ongoing creation," or "continued making" if we want to avoid the exceptionalist associations of the term creation—to capture "this special practice."[138]

Han's term "Fortschöpfung" recalls what Giorgio Agamben has determined to be the methodological principle of his own thought, namely to tap into something that Ludwig Feuerbach called "Entwicklungsfähigkeit"[139] in the books that he is reading: to tap into their "capacity for development." "[I]f we follow this methodological principle all the way," Agamben writes, "we inevitably end up at a point where it is not possible to distinguish between what is ours and what belongs to the author we are reading."[140] This makes Agamben appear as somewhat of a forger—as someone whose work, in its method and its thought, ultimately stands in close proximity to the post-exceptional thought that I pursue. Such a thought is only conceivable, Han suggests, in a culture that is not committed to exceptionalism but to the unexceptional. Following those suggestions, then, I would like to take a closer look in the next part of this book at the picaresque[141] figure of the forger as a key site for thinking through a theory and practice of post-exceptional art.

Notes

1 Byung-Chul Han, *Saving Beauty*, trans. Daniel Steuer (Cambridge: Polity, 2018), p. 35.

2 Tobin Siebers, *Disability Aesthetics* (Ann Arbor: University of Michigan Press, 2010), pp. 83–99, here p. 94.

3 Siebers, *Disability Aesthetics*, p. 93.

4 Walter Benjamin, "Critique of Violence," in: Walter Benjamin, *Selected Writings, Volume 1: 1913–1926*, ed. Marcus Bullock and Michael W. Jennings (Cambridge, MA: Belknap/Harvard University Press, 1996), pp. 236–252.

5 Walter Benjamin, "Zur Kritik der Gewalt," in: Walter Benjamin, *Gesammelte Schriften, Vol. 2.1.* ed. Rolf Tiedemann and Herman Schweppenhäuser (Frankfurt am Main: Suhrkamp, 1997), pp. 179–203.

6 Walter Benjamin, "Theses on the Philosophy of History," in: *Illuminations: Essays and Reflections*, ed. Hannah Arendt, trans. Harry Zohn (New York: Schocken, 1969), p. 257.

7 Walter Benjamin, "The Work of Art in the Era of Mechanical Reproduction," in: Walter Benjamin, *Illuminations: Essays and Reflections*, ed. Hannah Arendt, trans. Harry Zohn (New York: Schocken, 1969), pp. 217–251.

8 See: Arne De Boever, "Poverty's Emergency," *Philosophy Today* 59:4 (2015), pp. 641–655.

9 Valéry qtd. Benjamin, "Work of Art," p. 217.

10 Benjamin, "Work of Art," p. 218.

11 Ibid.

12 Ibid.

13 Ibid., p. 220.

14 Ibid.

15 Ibid.

16 Ibid., p. 221.
17 Ibid.
18 Ibid.
19 Ibid., p. 223.
20 Ibid.
21 Rosalind Krauss, *The Originality of the Avant-Garde and Other Modernist Myths* (Cambridge, MA: The MIT Press, 1985), pp. 151–170, here p. 157.
22 Krauss, *Originality of the Avant-Garde*, p. 151.
23 Ibid., p. 156.
24 Ibid.
25 Ibid., p. 157.
26 Ibid., pp. 157–158.
27 Ibid., p. 162.
28 Ibid., p. 168.
29 Dario Gamboni, *The Destruction of Art: Iconoclasm and Vandalism since the French Revolution* (London: Reaktion Books, 2018), p. 149.
30 Hito Steyerl, "In Defense of the Poor Image," *e-flux* 10 (2009), accessible: https://www.e-flux.com/journal/10/61362/in-defense-of-the-poor-image/
31 Steyerl, "In Defense," p. 32.
32 Ibid.
33 Hito Steyerl, *Duty Free Art: Art in the Age of Planetary Civil War* (New York: Verso, 2017), p. 150.
34 Steyerl, "In Defense," p. 38.
35 Julio García Espinosa, "For an Imperfect Cinema," accessible: https://www.ejumpcut.org/archive/onlinessays/JC20folder/ImperfectCinema.html
36 Espinosa qtd. Steyerl, "In Defense," p. 39.
37 Steyerl, "In Defense," p. 35.
38 Ibid., p. 40.
39 Ibid.
40 Espinosa, "For an Imperfect Cinema."
41 Ibid.
42 Ibid.
43 Ibid.
44 Ibid.
45 See: Frantz Fanon, *The Wretched of the Earth*, trans. Richard Philcox (New York: Grove Press, 2004), in particular p. 236.

46 Espinosa, "For an Imperfect Cinema."
47 Ibid.
48 Ibid.
49 Steyerl, "In Defense," p. 42.
50 Ibid.
51 Daniel Zalewski, "The Hours," *The New Yorker* March 12 (2012), accessible: https://www.newyorker.com/magazine/2012/03/12/the-hours-daniel-zalewski
52 Ben Lerner, *10:04* (New York: Faber and Faber, 2014), p. 52.
53 Roberta Smith qtd. Zalewski, "The Hours."
54 Zalewski, "The Hours."
55 See: https://wexarts.org/press/christian-marclay-s-clock
56 Krauss, *Originality of the Avant-Garde*, p. 153.
57 Roberta Smith, "As In Life, Timing Is Everything in the Movies," *The New York Times* March (2011), accessible: https://www.nytimes.com/2011/02/04/arts/design/04marclay.html
58 Zalewski, "The Hours."
59 Ibid.
60 Lerner, *10:04*, p. 54.
61 Zalewski, "The Hours."
62 Ibid.
63 Daniel Rourke, "Artifacts: A Conversation with Hito Steyerl and Daniel Rourke," *Rhizome* March (2013), available at: https://rhizome.org/editorial/2013/mar/28/artifacts/
64 Zalewski, "The Hours."
65 Steyerl, "In Defense," p. 35.
66 Edward Said, *Orientalism* (New York: Vintage, 1978), p. 3.
67 Said, *Orientalism*, p. 2.
68 Ibid., p. 3.
69 See: Arne De Boever, *François Jullien's Unexceptional Thought: A Critical Introduction* (New York: Rowman & Littlefield, 2020).
70 Gayatri Chakravorty Spivak, "French Feminism in an International Frame," *Yale French Studies* 62 (1981), pp. 154–184, here p. 157.
71 Byung-Chul Han, *Shanzhai: Deconstruction in Chinese*, trans. Philippa Hurd (Boston, MA: The MIT Press, 2017), p. 10.
72 Han, *Shanzhai*, pp. 10–11.
73 Ibid., p. 11.
74 Ibid.
75 Ibid.

76 Ibid.
77 Ibid.
78 Ibid., p. 13.
79 Ibid.
80 Ibid.
81 Maggie Bickford, "Emperor Huizong and the Aesthetic of Agency," *Archives of Asian Art* 53:1 (2002–2003), pp. 71–104.
82 Bickford, "Emperor Huizong," p. 74.
83 Ibid.
84 Han, *Shanzhai*, p. 2.
85 Ibid. Han's phrasing "deconstructivist from the outset" might appear odd given that it projects back into the outset a term, "deconstruction," that was only developed later. However, given Derrida's claim that one does not deconstruct but merely teases out a process of deconstruction that is always already at work, such a retro-projection might be admissible. If anything, it does reveal Han's audience, as he appears to be using the term here to make Chinese thought accessible to the Western philosophical reader, who has come closest to it through deconstruction.
86 Ibid., p. 3.
87 Ibid.
88 Ibid.
89 Ibid., p. 14.
90 Ibid., p. 16.
91 Ibid., pp. 16, 23.
92 Ibid., p. 23. Perhaps Han is a bit naïve here. It is more likely that Chinese artists and art dealers would figure out how to turn this difference into a financial advantage and that the global art market would become Westernized in that sense.
93 Ibid., p. 29.
94 Ibid., p. 31.
95 Ibid., p. 62.
96 See: ibid., n3 p. 83. With this well-known metaphor of the ship being rebuilt while at sea, the risk of conservatism opens up: the metaphor can indeed easily be used to counter proposals of radical change, and indeed change *tout court*. While it will be clear that I am not arguing against change here, it is true that through my criticism of exceptionalism I am countering "radicality" in the sense of a total rupture. That the metaphor of the ship does not necessarily support conservatism may be clear for

example from the use that Maggie Nelson makes of it in her book *The Argonauts* (Minneapolis, MN: Graywolf Press, 2015).

97 Han, *Shanzhai*, p. 62.

98 Ibid., p. 68.

99 See: ibid., n11 p. 84.

100 The notion of "use," and how "use" unexceptionalizes whatever it uses, seems relevant in this context. If "unusability" is a key category of art for Kant (as for example Davide Panagia has discussed: *Ten Theses for an Aesthetics of Politics* [Minneapolis: University of Minnesota Press, 2016]), it should be reread as a trait of aesthetic exceptionalism that "use" seeks to undo. Giorgio Agamben has pursued such a project throughout his oeuvre, but perhaps in particular in his text "In Praise of Profanation." Another name for post-exceptional art could very well be profane art. See: Giorgio Agamben, "In Praise of Profanation," in: Giorgio Agamben, *Profanations*, trans. Jeff Fort (New York: Zone Books, 2007), pp. 73–92.

101 François Jullien, *The Silent Transformations*, trans. Krzysztof Fijalkowski and Michael Richardson (London: Seagull Books, 2011), pp. 116–135.

102 Jullien, *Silent*, p. 116.

103 Ibid., p. 117.

104 Ibid., p. 126.

105 Ibid., p. 122.

106 Ibid., p. 121.

107 Ibid., p. 119.

108 Ibid., p. 122.

109 Ibid., p. 126.

110 Ibid., pp. 126–127.

111 Ibid., p. 127.

112 Ibid., pp. 129–130.

113 Ibid., p. 130.

114 Bianca Bosker, *Original Copies: Architectural Mimicry in Contemporary China* (Honolulu: University of Hawai'i Press, 2013), p. 22.

115 Bernard Stiegler, "The Proletarianization of Sensibility," trans. Arne De Boever, *boundary 2* 44:1 (2017), pp. 5–18, here p. 6.

116 Stiegler, "Proletarianization," p. 6.

117 Bernard Stiegler, *Symbolic Misery, Vol. 2: The Katastrophe of the Sensible*, trans. Barnaby Norman (Cambridge: Polity, 2015), p. 109.

118 Duchamp of course has to be a lodestar in any thinking about unexceptional art and I turn to his work on multiple counts in this book.

119 Stiegler, "Proletarianization," p. 5.

120 I would like to thank Alex Robbins for these points about drawing.

121 The quoted text is lifted from the exhibition's webpage: https://whitney.org/Exhibitions/ExperimentsInElectrostatics. I would like to thank Martin Woessner for bringing this exhibition to my attention, and for underlining the importance of Warhol in this context.

122 Think here of Duchamp's little-known work "Pharmacie," which "consists of a mass-produced poster-sized print of a 'winter landscape,' available to painting novices as an example of a composition they might attempt." Duchamp's "readymade 'intervention'" was to "sign the piece . . . but he also adds a tiny dab of red and green paint to the landscape's far horizon" (Stephen Barker, "Unwork and the Duchampian Contemporary," *boundary 2* 44:1 (2017), pp. 53–78, here p. 63). Duchamp quite literally uses wet paint to interfere—but within the mass-produced print. The mass-produced print is supposed to be the original, which painting novices are supposed to copy—but of course the original is already a copy. Duchamp intervenes in this chain of copies by adding original elements to the original copy. This doesn't quite render the original copy into an original, but it does intensify its exceptionalist element. Some confusion is produced by Duchamp's project, similar to the confusion produced by the signature "R. Mutt" that marks "Fountain": Does it exceptionalize, or unexceptionalize? I will return to this later.

123 Bernard Stiegler, "The Quarrel of the Amateurs," trans. Robert Hughes, *boundary 2* 44:1 (2017), pp. 35–52, here p. 38.

124 Edward Said, *The World, the Text, and the Critic* (Cambridge, MA: Harvard University Press, 1983), p. 113.

125 Marcus Boon, *In Praise of Copying* (Cambridge, MA: Harvard University Press, 2010), p. 2.

126 Han, *Shanzhai*, 11.

127 Ibid., p. 13.

128 Stathis Gourgouris, *The Perils of the One* (New York: Columbia University Press, 2019), p. 63.

129 Georg Baselitz, Christian Katti, Kirk Ambrose, Elizabeth Edwards, Ursula Anna Frohne, Cordula Grewe, Daniel Heller-Roazen, Ian McLean, Saloni Mathur, Lisa Pon, and Iain Boyd White, *Notes from the Field: Appropriation: Back Then, In Between, and Today*, *The Art Bulletin* 94:2 (2012), pp. 166–186, here pp. 173 and 174.

130 Mario Wenning, rev. Byung-Chul Han, *Shanzhai: Dekonstruktion auf Chinesisch*, *Philosophy East & West* 64:1 (2014), pp. 264–266, here p. 264.

131 It is more correct, I think, to speak about Han's "relative distance to politics," as Jeremy Bell does: "Against Surfing," rev. Byung-Chul Han, *The Transparency Society* and *The Burnout Society*, *Cultural Politics* 13:1 (2017), pp. 129–131, here p. 131.

132 It would probably be more correct to refer to Zhang Daqian as a "Chinese diasporic" artist, since he spent significant parts of his life abroad, including in Northern California. In that sense his paintings really were between China and the West.

133 Han, *Shanzhai*, p. 29.

134 Ibid., p. 30.

135 Ibid.

136 Ibid.

137 Ibid. The practice of copying, then, was for Zhang Daqian a way to study the old masters and continue their tradition.

138 Ibid.

139 Giorgio Agamben, *Signatura Rerum: Sur la Méthode*, trans. Joël Gayraud (Paris: Vrin, 2008), p. 8; Giorgio Agamben, *Creation and Anarchy: The Work of Art and the Religion of Capitalism*, trans. Adam Kotsko (Stanford, CA: Stanford University Press, 2019), p. 14.

140 Agamben, *Creation and Anarchy*, p. 15.

141 Sándor Radnóti has noted the proximity of the forger to the picaro, and has more specifically identified the genre of the forgery anecdote as picaresque. Radnóti writes of "picaresque aesthetics" in this context. Sándor Radnóti, *The Fake: Forgery and Its Place in Art*, trans. Ervin Dunai (Lanham, MD: Rowman & Littlefield Publishers, Inc., 1999), here pp. 1, 10. I should add that I also read this figure through a neoliberal lens, as not unrelated to the figure of the freelancer, which Hito Steyerl has traced back to "the medieval term for a mercenary soldier, a 'free lance,' that is, a soldier who is not attached to any particular master or government and can be hired for a specific task" (Hito Steyerl, "Freedom from Everything: Freelancers and Mercenaries," *e-flux* journal 41 (2013), accessible: https://www.e-flux.com/journal/41/60229/freedom-from-everything-freelancers-and-mercenaries/). In other words, while the picaro undermines the economic and political regime that I have characterized as exceptionalist, it is also a figure who, in the present time, ought to be read as a product of neoliberalism's unexceptionalizing tendencies.

Part II

The Forger

3

Post-Exceptional Fakes

E for Exceptionalism

What to make of a sequence, early on in Orson Welles' video-essay *F for Fake* (Planfilm/Specialty Films, 1973), featuring what the voice-over narration (by Welles) calls "the fine outdoor sport of . . . girl-watching"? It features Welles' girlfriend, the Croatian actress Oja Kodar, walking the streets in a close-fitting, short dress and turning men's heads. Watching the sequence today, it probably makes many (if not most?) viewers cringe—even those who believe that Kodar herself suggested the scene for feminist reasons (as she has claimed).

Welles' purpose with the scene is unclear. He mentions that it was made as part of another film, and the scene does indeed appear to be out of place in *F for Fake*. Is Welles' reference to girl-watching ironic? After all, he does indicate that Oja operates in the sequence as "bait," delivering a performance that is in fact meant to trigger another performance: that of the men, who are caught with their pants down. (This could connect with Oja's reasons for doing the scene, which exposes the men and implicates the viewer.) The sequence arguably plays some narrative role, since Welles announces that he will return to Oja later, thus creating an anticipation in the viewer that helps hold *F for Fake* together. The viewer is perhaps more willing to let the disorienting madness of the film happen when given the promise of it all coming full circle. That is not what happens though: when Oja returns some twenty minutes before the film's ending, it's as Picasso's lover and muse, the supposed subject of some twenty portraits that the master made of her. Again, and in a clear echo of the film's beginning, she is shown walking the streets, near naked this time, now turning Picasso's head.[1] There is also a sequence of nude shots, featuring Oja (or a stand-in?), at a painter's studio, creating the impression that the anticipation that is fulfilled at the end of the film is that of the gaze (Welles', or any other) that wanted to see Oja naked. Certainly, if "truth" is what the viewer was expecting at the end of this tale about fakes, the second Oja sequence does not deliver: Welles suggests, in fact, that it was entirely fake—that it was the only fake part of the film which otherwise was true (whatever that can still mean in this context).

One might conclude from this, uncharitably, that *F for Fake*'s drive is pornographic. Some might counter that "pornographic" is an overstatement given how Oja's naked body (someone else's?) is shown late in the film; "erotic," or even "aesthetic" may be more appropriate to characterize the representation. This may lead one to reformulate the question about the Oja sequences outside of their plotting purpose: what might be their *aesthetic* role in this film about fakes? One would then need to suspend one's judgment of those sequences for a moment to consider the role of the nude in the film's overall problematic of authenticity/originality and fakery.

That is the path I want to pursue by critically considering the role that the nude has played in Western art as a figure of exceptionalism. This role is immediately evident from the subtitle of Kenneth Clark's famous book on the nude: "A Study In Ideal Form."[2] As such, the nude is connected to Western art's obsession with the authentic, original work of art and it is no surprise that it would have some place in a film like Welles', which undermines our exceptionalist attachment to the original. The nude is indeed one of the sites where that exceptionalism was most feverishly maintained. Anyone interested in the fake would have to at some point consider the nude in relation to their project.

There are other such connections within exceptionalism that Welles establishes in the film that I consider less convincing: his engagement with the fake rehearses his work on *War of the Worlds*, a radio-play that managed to convince many of its listeners that the Martians had landed. But fake news is hardly the same as fake art: news that is fake isn't news. Fake art can still be art. In other words: art—this is at least my position—is not in the last instance determined by the quality of the fake in the way that news is. Forgery may be art in the space of deceit, but that does not mean that fake news is fact in the space of the fake—a contradiction in terms. Facts *are* facts; but art *is not* art. Indeed, after Marcel Duchamp, all art becomes fake art. Or at least Duchamp introduces the suspicion that it might be—that it might not truly be art, whatever that is.

F for Fake mostly considers the economic repercussions of any decision made about the authenticity/originality of a work of art. Art and value, and the exceptionalism which structures the art market, are at the center of Welles' film. In the previous chapter, I looked at this as well, but I placed my focus elsewhere: on politics. When the Hungarian (if he is indeed Hungarian) forger Elmyr de Hory (if that is indeed his name), around whom

Welles' film revolves, exclaims that "it should not exist that one single person makes a decision about what's good or what's bad"—the reference here being "art"—the pronouncement resonates politically, in relation to a political decisionism that is (in a tradition of political thought including the controversial German legal scholar Carl Schmitt) associated with the figure of the sovereign. The fake is, indeed, the sovereign's nightmare, if the faker is considered the figure who undermines the sovereign decision.

From another point of view, one can consider the fake to be the sovereign's condition of possibility: for it is because there is such a thing as the fake that a sovereign decision becomes necessary. It is precisely when a situation cannot be decided that the sovereign's decision is needed. Certainly, sovereigns have been known to make use of the fake: of doubles, or also of minted coins worth less the amount of precious metal that they represent. Whatever the case may be, one senses in de Hory's criticism of expertise, of crooked art dealers who seek to make money by selling fakes, a criticism of political authority—and a defense of a more anarchic approach to art.

That does not mean that all verticality goes out the window: de Hory roams through Welles' film in great relief, as "the twentieth-century's *greatest* [emphasis mine] art forger." Welles, *F for Fake*'s most pronounced verticality, identifies with de Hory, presenting himself as a magician who will use every trick in the film-maker's book to push his tales of fakery onto the viewer. Still, "greatness" in *F for Fake*, and the power that comes with it, are shown to always be somewhat of a trick. Sovereign power, real as it may be in its effects, is always somewhat of an optical illusion, as Giorgio Agamben's extended reading of the frontispiece of Thomas Hobbes' *Leviathan* allows us to conclude.[3]

The nude, operative in *F for Fake*'s sequences with Oja, ought to be read along similar lines, as something like an optical illusion—an ideal form as which no body exists. (To summarize this, as Kenneth Clark does, by saying that "on the whole there are more women whose bodies look like a potato [he is partly referring back to what earlier on in the same chapter he calls "the Vegetable Nude" from Prehistoric art] than like the *Knidian Aphrodite*,"[4] is to perpetuate the problem. Needless to say, you will find no such line in his chapter about the male nude.) Abandoning the exceptionalist attachment to the nude, and letting it go in an overall exploration of the fake, does not only have aesthetic consequences; it may, in the end, be a political project as well.

F for Fake does not realize that project—Welles' gaze is too complicit for that. But how might it nevertheless put us on such a project's tracks?

In the first part of this chapter, I consider how in his book *Shanzhai*, Byung-Chul Han develops a critique of what he understands to be the Western approach to the work of art, starting from a discussion of art forgers and art forgeries. Criticizing Han's orientalist framework, which opposes on this count the Western and Chinese approaches to the work of art and the forgery, in part through a discussion of Wen Fong's work on forgery in Chinese painting (one of Han's sources), I focus on the role of Walter Benjamin in Han's argument, and specifically on how the presence of China in Benjamin's work becomes relevant as part of a conversation about what I have presented in this book as "aesthetic exceptionalism"—*both* in the West *and* in China.

In a second part, I turn to the Chinese master-painter and forger Zhang Daqian and the authenticity issues related to the work “Riverbank,” a Chinese landscape painting that is now generally considered to be an early painting attributed to Dong Yuan but was also thought to have been a masterful forgery by Zhang Daqian. Teasing out the role of aesthetic exceptionalism in James Cahill’s argument that “Riverbank” is a forgery (Cahill and Wen Fong famously disagreed about “Riverbank”’s status), my central question is: how does Cahill’s writing about “Riverbank” reveal what Jonathan Hay describes as forgery’s uncomfortable place in art history as “art in the space of deceit”?[5] I focus not so much on whether “Riverbank” is an original or a forgery but on the criteria that Cahill and others rely on to settle this question. What are the forms of evidence that are brought in, and how do they apply in other, later cases where the issue of forgery, or more broadly copying, was at stake? Do those forms of evidence continue to strike us as relevant, or might cases of forgery—like Han van Meegeren’s forgeries of Vermeer paintings—make us reconsider, precisely, the centrality of the original in our conception of the artwork, the architecture of the art market, and art’s politics?

Returning finally to Orson Welles’ video-essay *F for Fake*, I end by considering the importance of the nude for such debates in Western art history. Not a landscape, the nude is the aesthetic materialization of the Western idea of ideal form. Developing a critical reading of Kenneth Clark’s landmark study of the nude that lays bare the nude as a figure of what I call aesthetic exceptionalism, I consider its role in Welles’ video-essay to be critical in that Welles’ interest in the fake in his video-essay undermines not only our attachment to the original, but also our attachment to the nude as a figure of such an ideal notion. The nude then becomes aligned with the original as a potentially fascistic notion, an alignment that is supported by Tobin Siebers' work in disability studies and the critique it has developed (with reference to fascist aesthetics) of the idealized nude. In the next chapter, I will turn to the genre of the landscape in Chinese art history and specifically the close relation of the ancient Chinese thought of daoism to such painting, as sites from where a critique of aesthetic exceptionalism can begin to develop. Importantly, and in contrast to Han's orientalist framework, that discussion of Chinese landscape painting will not be laid out in opposition to the Western art historical tradition but in full recognition of the fact that what one might call the "Dao" of Chinese landscape painting is present in Western art history and contemporary arts practices as well, even if it is not the dominant way in which in the West the work of art has been theorized. It all depends on where you look. My approach, then, is crucially not orientalist but seeks to uncover, rather, traces of exceptionalism and post-exceptionalism in both Western and Chinese art history and arts practice.

Overall, this chapter continues my critical consideration of the connections between the figure of the artist and the figure of the sovereign, this time by triangulating those two figures with the figure of the forger—the one who makes works in the name of someone else. As Daniel Kehlmann writes in his novel *F*:

> I often think about the artists of the Middle Ages. They didn't sign things, they were craftsmen who belonged to guilds, they were spared the disease we call ambition. Can it still be done that way, can you still do the work without taking yourself seriously—can you still paint without being 'a painter'? Anonymity is no help, it's merely a clever hiding place, another form of vanity. *But painting in the name of someone else is a possibility; it works* (emphasis mine).[6]

Kehlmann's novel hints at what I explore in this chapter: the ways in which the forger is a key figure for a theory and practice of post-exceptional art.

Risk of Orientalism

As a way into an extended line of thinking about the fake that would give a central place to the nude, let me return to the end of Han's chapter "Zhen Ji: Original," and the discussion of forgers and forgeries that opens up there. Elmyr de Hory from Orson Welles' video-essay is one of the figures Han mentions; he also considers Han van Meegeren, the Vermeer forger. Han recalls how "[a]fter the war, when Reichsmarshall Hermann Göring's collection of paintings was being inspected, a hitherto unknown Vermeer, *Christ and the Adulteress*, was discovered."[7] However, "[d]uring the search for the Dutchmen who had sold the Vermeer to the Nazis, Han van Meegeren was arrested and put in prison."[8] "At first," Han continues, "no one believed his claim that *Christ and the Adulteress* was a forgery."[9]

> So, under supervision, he painted his last Vermeer, *Jesus Among the Doctors*. During the trial he was reported as saying: "Yesterday this picture was worth millions. Experts and art lovers from all over the world came to see it. Today it's worth nothing and nobody would even cross the road to see it for free. But the picture hasn't changed. What's different?"[10]

Working within the Western tradition, Han points out that "[i]f Elmyr and van Meegeren had been born during the Renaissance they would undoubtedly have enjoyed more recognition" because "[t]he idea of artistic genius was only in its infancy."[11] Han notes that at this time

> the artist still generally remained in the background behind the work. What counted was artistic skill alone, which could be proven by producing forgeries of masterpieces that ideally were indistinguishable from the latter. If a forger painted as well as a master, then he was indeed a master and not a forger.[12]

Han's observation draws out a point that others have made as well, namely that the exceptionalist understanding of the artist as genius was one that has been constructed over time. As for example Giorgio Agamben has pointed out in his book *Creation and Anarchy*, before such an understanding of the artist was in place—and Agamben has specifically dated this "before" to the time before St. Thomas Aquinas[13]—the artist was a much more banal figure, a mere technician who found their self-realization in the work they produced rather than in their creative activity. In other words, before Aquinas the artist was a much more unexceptional figure, even if that does not mean people did not appreciate the difference between a shoemaker and a sculptor,[14] as Agamben points out. Nevertheless, the two figures of the craftsman and the artist were much more closely related.

Here's Agamben challenging the understanding of the artist as a creative figure in an essay titled "What Is the Act of Creation?":

> I have to begin by saying that I am rather uneasy about the use of the term "creation" with respect to artistic practices, which is unfortunately very common today. While I was investigating the genealogy of this use, I discovered to my surprise that architects are partly responsible for it. When medieval theologians had to explain the creation of the world, they drew on an example that had already been given by the Stoics. Thomas Aquinas writes that just as a house preexists in the mind of the architect, so too did God create the world while looking at the model he

> had in his mind. Naturally, Aquinas still distinguished between *creare ex nihilo* (creation out of nothing), which defines divine creation, and *facere de materia* (making from material), which defines human making. At any rate, the comparison between the act of the architect and that of God already contains the seed of the transposition of the paradigm of creation onto the activity of the artist.[15]

"For this reason," he continues, "I prefer to speak instead of the poetic act."[16] *Poièsis*, the Greek word for "doing," is brought in here as an unexceptionalizing gesture, to unwork the exceptionalism of the artist as a creative figure. It is in part Agamben's insistence on the figure of the artist as a hinge in the process of the artist's exceptionalization that will justify my discussion of architecture in Chapter 6 of this book.

Interestingly, it's on the above grounds that Han in his book characterizes Michelangelo—a master who was also a known forger—as "one of the last Chinese of the Renaissance."[17] The West's pre-Renaissance openness to the copy allows Han to characterize it in his book as "Chinese." But what does Han mean by Chinese? In the following chapter of his book, titled "Xian Zhan: Seals of Leisure," Han expands his thought in a productive though also problematic new direction. Focusing on so-called seals of leisure, the seal stamps on old Chinese paintings, Han points out that those are very different from the signatures used in European paintings:[18]

> Instead, most seal stamps come from the connoisseurs or collectors who inscribe themselves into the picture not only through their seals but also through their commentaries. Here art is a communicative, interactive practice that constantly changes even the artwork's appearance.[19]

No Western art collector would even think about making their seal part of a Western painting in the same way.

To capture this difference, Han then situates the reader between two works, Jan van Eyck's "Arnolfini Portrait" (from 1434) and a landscape painting by Wang Fu (1362–1416). Han reads the Arnolfini portrait as an "image of presence,"[20] specifically the painter's presence. Van Eyck's signature is centrally located in the image, painting emerges here as an individual act. Wang Fu's landscape, by contrast, is presented as an "image of absence": it contains no such "authorial, authoritative presence."[21] Instead, seals and poems are added to the painting, in the large empty space that landscape paintings typically contain. Painting becomes instead a communal act. Whereas the signature in a Western painting has an "exclusive, executive effect," the seal in a Chinese painting is instead "inclusive and communicative."[22] Read next to each other, these works by van Eyck and Wang Fu mark a shift from the understanding of the artwork as event (the authentic original) to an understanding of the artwork as process (copy, palimpsest). Process, in this shift, is closely associated to nature; it needs to be contrasted to genius.[23] This shift in our understanding of the artwork is closely related to a shift in our understanding of the artist: from the artist as genius (subject, actor) to the artist as a highly-skilled copier or technician paying tribute to a master—or even less than this: an understanding of the artist as one who disappears in the work.

Han's approach of contrasting a Chinese work of art to a Western work of art, and drawing from that conclusions about Chinese approaches to art in general, can be characterized as orientalist in that it construes "China" and "the West" in opposition to each other. As such, it is problematic, as critics of orientalism allow one to point out, first because Han generalizes conclusions about a single work of art into speculations about art at large (something that all theory is, to a certain extent, guilty of); second, because it allows conclusions about a single Chinese work of art to stand in for speculations about "the Chinese" in general (this is more problematic than the first element, in my view); and finally because the theories about "the Chinese" and "Chinese art" that it develops are construed in opposition to the West, following a logic of difference (this is a key component of orientalism—one does not get the sense from reading Han's book that what it has to say about "the Chinese" and "Chinese art" is based on a deep and varied understanding of Chinese art history and arts practice).

In addition, one might add that Han's view of Western art is limited as well. Staying with the references that I already discussed in Chapter 1, could one not consider in this context Andy Warhol's "Piss Paintings" as examples within the Western tradition of precisely the kind of communal act of painting that Han finds in "China"? For these works, Warhol urinated—and asked his guests to urinate—on large canvases covered in metallic paint that were then allowed to oxidize. This created in the words of Rosalind Krauss "whorls and halations of what can often resemble the action painter's gesture"[24] and has been read specifically as a queer pastiche of the machismo of Jackson Pollock's work. It's worth evoking the affinity between these works and Chinese landscape painting as well, both in terms of their aesthetic—"whorl" and "halation" (a term that also evokes Benjamin's notion of "aura") are definitely words that apply to Chinese landscape painting, both traditional work and contemporary continuations of it for example in the work of Zhang Daqian—and as far as the communal act of their generation goes. Not only, then, do Han's generalizations about China not hold; neither do his generalizations about Western art.

It's worth noting that Han closes this chapter with the idea of the artist disappearing in the work, something that—very interestingly—he finds in Walter Benjamin's *Berlin Childhood around 1900*:

> The story comes from China [Benjamin writes], and tells of an old painter who invited friends to see his newest picture. This picture showed a park and a narrow footpath that ran along a stream and through a grove of trees, culminating at the door of a little cottage in the background. When the painter's friends, however, looked around for the painter, they saw that he was gone—that he was in the picture. There, he followed the little path that led to the door, paused before it quite still, turned, smiled, and disappeared through the narrow opening.[25]

This story, rendered within the Western tradition of continental philosophy and more specifically Western aesthetics, marks the end of the exceptionalist figure of the sovereign artist as the creating genius. It's an end that is paired in Han's analysis with the exceptionalist understanding of the original, authentic work of art—but as such, and because of the remark about the story's provenance, it also becomes emblematic of "China" in Han's thought.

Benjamin's reference to China is in itself interesting, and it hardly constitutes an exceptional moment in his oeuvre. Andrea Pinotti among others has discussed the multiple references to China in Benjamin's collected works and offers a good account of how the particular story that Han quotes ends up in Benjamin's *Berlin Childhood*. Pinotti points out that it can be found "in a very synthesized form" in Benjamin's "Work of Art" essay as well (the reference is specifically to paragraph 18 of the 1935–1936 typescript of the essay[26]).[27] Based on much of the same evidence that Pinotti is looking at, Graeme Gilloch and Jaeho Kang go so far as to suggest in an essay titled "'Ink-Play': Walter Benjamin's Chinese Curios" that:

> The very concept of "aura" itself, Benjamin's key category developed in [the "Work of Art" essay], is described in terms that are suggestive or reminiscent of the simplicity and tranquility characteristic of the masterpieces of East Asian landscape painting. Here Benjamin writes: "To follow with the eye—while resting on a summer afternoon—a mountain range on the horizon or a branch that casts its shadow on the beholder is to breathe the aura of those mountains, of that branch."[28]

The suggestion is provocative, because it brings the notion of aura, central to Western aesthetics, in line with the East Asian landscape. This suggestion is in part enabled by the fact that when Benjamin is discussing aura in his essay, he is not only talking about the aura of the original work of art, *but also* about the aura of the natural landscape—which goes lost in any representation of it. While these two arguments are combined in Benjamin's essay, they are in fact not the same. According to the former, an original work of art—an original landscape painting, for example—would have an aura, but a mechanical copy of that painting wouldn't, or a photograph of that same landscape wouldn't (because it is mechanically reproducible; no matter that it may be an original photograph of which only one print exists). According to the latter argument, *only* the natural landscape has aura—and even an original painting of that landscape would have to be considered a copy in which the aura of the original withers. Neither Killoch and Kang nor Pinotti pursue these consequences.

Moreover, it's worth noting that the East Asian landscape seeks to maintain the vibrancy and vitality of the natural landscape, and such a project would immediately trouble Benjamin's analytical distinctions: for a good landscape painting would precisely be one that is able to preserve nature's aura. If the term aura can indeed be applied, as Gilloch and Kang suggest, to East Asian landscapes, then some of the meaning of the notion in Benjamin's essay would necessarily be lost. In fact, in the rest of this book I pursue the suggestion that traditional Chinese landscape painting, "monumental" as it may be, contains traces of the unmonumental in the central place it accords to water, clouds, mist, and fog—all parts of nature that require a painting style that effaces or even does not paint, as much as or even more so than it traces or paints. The traditional Chinese landscape painting, auratic and exceptional as it may be, incorporates significant signs of the unworking of exceptionalism and the aura, to such an extent that, I want to suggest, either Benjamin was wrong to draw aura from Chinese landscape painting or we have generally misunderstood what Benjamin meant by aura. If the focus of discussions about aura in Benjamin's text strike an exceptionalist chord overall, in other words emphasize aura's connection to the unique presence in time-space of a natural landscape or the original work of art, and then of course consider the blow that the copy deals to aura understood in that way, perhaps it is rather the figure of *the withered aura*—not entirely gone, but transformed somehow in the era of mechanical reproducibility—that is the more interesting one to pursue as what persists in the era of post-exceptionalism. It is not that the aura is entirely gone; it is, rather, that the aura with its potentially fascistic applications has been transformed into something more open, more democratic, in which the forgery and the copy might also participate. Such an understanding of aura would have no problems with acknowledging "art in the space of deceit," to recall Jonathan Hay's phrase. Hito Steyerl may have been on the track of this when she recognized, towards the end of her essay "In Defense of the Poor Image," the new kind of aura that the poor image has.

Again, while I develop a focus on Chinese landscape painting to lay out such an argument, I do not do so within a framework that would oppose Chinese landscape painting to Western landscape painting, and more generally "the West" to "China." Whenever such analyses of the West in relation to China of the kind that we find in Han are at work, one should beware of orientalism, and the approaches—familiar to us thanks to Edward Said's already discussed work on this issue—that all too easily construe China in opposition to the West rather than considering Chinese thought as a thought that has its own coherence, one that is no doubt partly different from the West but most likely also has some similarities to it given that humans are involved on both counts and that the human brain tends to think in certain ways (Edward Slingerland has insisted on this in his work, which develops precisely as a criticism of orientalism[29]).

As an example of how this can be done, consider Wen Fong's article "The Problem of Forgeries in Chinese Painting," which is one of the texts on which Han for his own orientalist approach relies. Fong in fact begins by noting—and it's worth highlighting the deconstructive thrust of the claim—that "Bona fide copying in ancient China, *as in ancient Rome* [emphasis mine], was not only an honorable but also a vitally necessary form of art."[30] Later, Fong also brings nuance to Han's discussion by distinguishing between "four methods of forging" in Chinese landscape painting: "*mu*, to trace; *lin*, to copy; *fang*, to imitate; *tsao*, to invent."[31] Han himself distinguishes in his book between "fangzhipin," or "imitations where the difference from the original is obvious," and "fuzhipin," or "exact reproductions of the original, which, for the Chinese, are of equal value to the original."[32] "The term fuzhipin" has, in Han's assessment, "no negative connotations."[33] Alexander Stille has noted this distinction between "fangzhipin" and "fuzhipin" as well.[34] Following Fong's non-orientalist presentation of the issue, it's worth adding that in the West, too, there are many different terms for a "copy": in discussions about copies, for example, my interlocutors will regularly use the terms "version," "rendering," "borrowing," "imitation," "translation," "appropriation," or phrasings such as "made after" or "inspired by" with reference to a "copy."

Still, Fong points out that

> It should be noted that art forgery in China has never carried such dark connotations as it does in the West. Since the aim of studying art has always been either aesthetic cultivation or pure enjoyment, rather than scientific knowledge, the acquisition of a genuine masterpiece—and by the same token, the ability to create a perfect forgery—was a matter of virtuosity and pride. The legal or ethical problems of an "honest business transaction" never entered into the picture. As a matter of fact, it was precisely for very good reasons of ethics and even better ones of tact, that the owner of a forgery was usually protected, as far as possible, from knowing the truth. Scientific truth certainly had no immediate bearing on art appreciation.[35]

While this does not mean that the difference between a forgery and an original is entirely denied or even unappreciated—Fong's paragraph ends with the line: "If someone is gullible enough to buy as well as derive pleasure from forgeries, why spoil the poor man's illusions?"[36]—it still confirms some of what Han also draws out in a much less careful way. In short, it does not seem that Han is wrong in his overall characterization of the copy in Chinese thought, even if much nuance needs to be brought to his notion of the copy and the various forms it takes, and even if his denomination of that understanding as "Chinese" ought to be resisted.

"A Certain Kind of Original"

At the end of the last chapter, I briefly mentioned the Chinese master-painter—and forger[37]—Zhang Daqian, and I would like to look now at one possible forgery in which Zhang may have been involved: the landscape painting titled "Riverbank." The work is possibly a forgery by Zhang Daqian, but this very question is the topic of a book titled *Issues of Authenticity in Chinese Painting*,[38] published by the Museum of Metropolitan Art in New York (the MET) in 1999 (and co-edited by Wen Fong), which counts "Riverbank" among its collection. In the question and answer session following an event about Asian art that was held during Summer 2020, Joseph Scheier-Dolberg, assistant curator in the Department of Asian Art at the MET, notes that today there is general agreement that "Riverbank" is an early painting attributed to Dong Yuan. As with the Toporovski affair that I discussed in my Introduction, I am not interested in determining whether this work is an original by Dong Yuan (something that Scheier-Dolberg acknowledges would in any case be impossible to do) or a forgery by Zhang Daqian. Rather, I want to focus on how this case was discussed so as to tease out the ways in which the discourse of aesthetic exceptionalism is operative there. What are the forms of evidence that are brought in to argue for "Riverbank"'s status as an original or a forgery, and to what extent do they still apply today? What can the answers to those questions tell us about what we consider to be an original work of art?

In *Issues of Authenticity in Chinese Painting*, the renowned U.S.-based art historian James Cahill—the West Coast counterpart of Wen Fong, who was based at Princeton—makes the case that "Riverbank" is a forgery by Zhang. Cahill lays out what his title describes as "an Indictment in Fourteen Counts." A number of those counts focus on elements internal to "Riverbank": the fact that the work does not fit its historical period (Cahill focuses on the upper part of "Riverbank," specifically how the clouds hide the tops of the mountains); what he considers to be "fatal, structural flaws"[39] in the painting; the fact that the work does fit with other Zhang Daqian works from the late 1960s; brushwork; composition; light; human figures in the painting; and of course the signature and the seals. I mention all of these elements because if they are brought in to determine that "Riverbank" is a forgery, they are evidently also considered to be essential, identifying components of a work. In short, looking at these elements is interesting because it makes us think about what makes a certain work *that* work, about what determines the originality and authenticity of a work. It also draws attention to all of the elements that are involved in a copy, from general composition to brushwork and light. Could an accusation of forgery be built around brushwork alone? Light? Composition?

The last two were important elements in the accusation of plagiarism against the Belgian painter Luc Tuymans, who was convicted for copying the artfully framed and lighted work of a newspaper photographer, Katrijn Van Giel, as a painting—and without giving credit to or asking permission from the photographer. Evidently, in the eyes of the law, the similarity in light and composition was enough to convict Tuymans of plagiarism—or the transformation of the photograph into painting was not enough to free him of the charge. The accusation is troubling, given how often painters work with existing photographs. The walls of many a painter's studio are filled with pictures cut out from magazines, newspapers, and other sources (even library books sometimes!), and many painters take inspiration precisely from such images, and without crediting them in the titles of their own paintings. In the case of Tuymans' painting "A Belgian Politician," however, the proximity of the painting to the photograph was deemed to be too close. Tuymans' defense, which argued that Tuymans' appropriation of the image was "parodic," did not stick.

The defense's argument may have been inspired (I avoid the word "copied") by Jeff Koons' defense in a plagiarism case that was brought against him in 1992. As Elizabeth Cropper reports in the Coda to her book *The Domenichino Affair*, "a Court of Appeals in New York City upheld a previous decision that in his *String of Puppies* the artist Jeff Koons had illegally appropriated the work of Art Rogers, a photographer."[40] Koons had for his "Banality" show in 1988 "commissioned four identical sculptures in wood from Italian artisans, to be based on Rogers's photograph of 1980 entitled *Puppies*," a photograph that (Cropper adds) "had been widely distributed commercially in the form of a notecard bearing Rogers's copyright."[41] Koons' defense took "recourse to the parodic quality" of Koons' work—but without success (so clearly it was not a good strategy to imitate, if that is what Tuymans' lawyers were doing). Cropper concludes: "In judging the fair use aspect of the case, the judge considered that, in order for Koons's critique of the image to be effective, the public should have been informed that the work was based on an original by a different artist, who should have been given credit."[42] The fact that Koons only copied "factual information from his source, not the expression"[43] was not enough to save him.

Koons *was* saved later though: in another plagiarism case from 2006, for his use of a fashion photograph in his painting *Niagara*, the judge did not convict him. Koons was thought to have reinterpreted and transformed in his work an image that was available for appropriation. By then, as Peter Jaszi has suggested,[44] Koons may have had postmodernism on his side.

What is it, exactly, that makes a work someone's work? What is the particular element in the work that *makes* the work, and makes it *their* work? The question is almost as gnarly as asking what it is that makes you *you*. Cahill's list of evidence internal to "Riverbank" gives one a clue as to what to look for—at least when it comes to a painting.

Tuymans or Koons are certainly not the only cases that can be productively considered in this context: one can think of Elaine Sturtevant's reproductions of paintings and objects made by artists of her time (the early 1960s). One other obvious example would be Sherrie Levine's photographed reproductions of well-known photographs,[45] or works of appropriation by others in the so-called Pictures Generation—Cindy Sherman or Richard Prince. Douglas Crimp and Craig Owens among other critics found in those works a subversion of originality and authorship.[46] When copying becomes appropriation, other dynamics enter into play, especially today: gender (Levine's intervention focused on this), or race (think of Dana Schutz's or Sam Durant's appropriations in their art—"Open Casket" and "Scaffold," respectively—of a historical and personal trauma that is not theirs);[47] status may be another concern, as when an established artist appropriates the work of a less established one—as in the Richard Prince/ Audrey Wollen controversy, for example, about an established, male artist (Prince) appropriating (without giving credit) the work of a younger, female artist in his work.

In an interview about her work, Wollen usefully identifies the problem as she sees it:

> I think a lot of people mistake Prince's work as purely an issue of appropriation—like, if you condemn Prince, you condemn appropriation on principle. That's not the point: Appropriation is chill, as long as the person doing the appropriating is not the person in power. What Prince is doing is colonizing and profiting off a territory of the internet that was created by a community of young girls, who, needless to say, do not have the cultural space Prince has. Selecting specific bodies from a sea of images, amputating them from their context, and then naming yourself the owner of those bodies: that isn't just boring art, that verges on predatory and violent behavior.[48]

Interestingly, Wollen is not against appropriation as such. It's the ethics and politics of specific appropriations with which she takes issue. She is against appropriation *from above*.

And what about reenactments of performances? For example, Chris Burden's "Shoot," which was recently reenacted—re-performed by Eva and Franco Mattes—on Second Life?[49] What are the criteria for those?

The legal term "plagiarism" is part of this conversation as well: used especially with respect to the literary arts, it marks the moment when forgery becomes theft—when someone's writing or ideas are stolen, and claimed by someone else as their own. In the literary arts too, one will find the Sherrie Levines (I am thinking of David Shields) and Cindy Shermans and Richard Princes and Dana Schutzes and Sam Durants (Kenneth Goldsmith, Vanessa Place)—the conversation is similar to that in the visual and performing arts. So the issues and debates cut across the arts and reach far outside of that, into other kinds of writing (criticism, for example), the news (fake news), architecture (see my Chapter 6), technology, and design.

In his article on forgeries, Wen Fong draws attention to a system that was developed by Chinese critics, to "['authenticate'] paintings."[50] The existence of such a system clearly shows that authentication was a concern in China as well, regardless of some differences in its cultural attitude to the copy. That system involved criteria very much like those that Fong's colleague James Cahill lays out in his text about "Riverbank": "the material (silk or paper) of the painting"; "the artist's inscriptions, signature and seals"; "previous collectors' seals"; and any other elements internal to the painting.[51] To those, Fong adds what one might call "external" criteria, even if the first remains partly internal to the painting itself: "colophons written by critics of preceding periods, which are found either on the painting proper, on some attached papers, or on the mounting"; "records of the painting in ancient catalogues, if available."[52] Cahill, too, summons such external evidence. He points out that there are no references to "Riverbank" in old catalogues or other texts, and no paintings from the Yuan period or later that are based on "Riverbank."

Here, the evidence takes an interesting turn: it's precisely because there are no copies of "Riverbank," Cahill suggests, that "Riverbank" cannot possibly have existed in its time. The lack of copies is brought to argue "Riverbank" is a copy. "Riverbank," like the Russian avant-garde works in the Museum voor Schone

Kunsten (MSK; Museum of Fine Arts) in Ghent, is a case of a work that is "too good to be true,"[53] Cahill argues. He goes on to provide an alternative recent history for "Riverbank" that draws out how this work came to hold the place that it does.

As with the works from the Toporovski collection that I discussed at the beginning of this book, I am not interested in determining whether "Riverbank" is by Dong Yuan or by Zhang Daqian. I don't have the expertise to do so, and making these kinds of discriminations is not my main concern when looking at a work of art. Having considered the criteria by which works are deemed original or fake with respect to both a Chinese case and several Western cases, I remain fascinated, however, by the discourse that Cahill develops as he is laying out his case against "Riverbank" as a work by Yuan. This is because that discourse is strangely torn between (on the one hand) acknowledging "Riverbank" as an exceptional work and (on the other) criticizing the work as flawed.

Consider how this schizophrenic split presents itself in Cahill's text. At first, Cahill writes about "Riverbank" very positively, and even in explicitly exceptionalist terms. He points out, for example, that as a forgery "Riverbank" "stands very high in [Zhang Daqian's] oeuvre as a whole" and he refers to it as "an exceptionally fine Zhang Daqian, perhaps his finest."[54] This is high praise. We should give Zhang Daqian, Cahill remarks, "the credit he deserves."[55] "Riverbank" is an exceptional work of art.

Very quickly, however, the negative terms begin to accumulate when it comes to assessing "Riverbank" as a forgery, in other words: as a work that merely claims to be one by Dong Yuan. Suddenly, everything shifts: Cahill characterizes parts of the work or even the entire work as "unreadable," "inconsistent," "incoherent," "confused," "ambiguous," et cetera. Clearly, Cahill is torn between praising the work as an original (exceptional) and condemning it as an unexceptional copy (flawed). "Riverbank" is a certain kind of original, perhaps something like what one could call (to return to Bianca Bosker's term that I already mobilized in the previous chapter) an "original copy," but doing so creates real difficulties for an art historian like Cahill, who then comes to assess the work both as an "original" (exceptional) and as a "copy" ("fatally flawed"). We would do well to recall here the question that the Vermeer forger van Meegeren is supposed to have asked at his trial, and after a supposedly original Vermeer was revealed to have been painted by van Meegeren:

> Yesterday this picture was worth millions. Today it's worth nothing and nobody would even cross the road to see it for free. But the picture hasn't changed. What's different?[56]

Cahill's text is torn between "yesterday" (his assessment of the original) and "today" (his condemnation of the copy). But what's different? It is worth comparing this situation to the appeal that the real *Mona Lisa* had on the public, *even after it had been stolen* in 1911: Darian Leader reports that "during the time the image was absent from the museum, huge crowds flocked to see, not the painting, but the space upon the wall where Leonardo's work once hung."[57] Even the absence of a real work is more valuable than a fake work—that is how powerful a pull the original has on us.

In spite of the great expertise of Chinese art that it lays bare, Cahill's text emerges, then, as a typical product of exceptionalist thinking about art. One has to look elsewhere if one wants to understand anything about why Zhang Daqian may have painted "Riverbank." I like better the conclusion that Alfred Lessing draws in his discussion of Han van Meegeren's Vermeer forgery even if it, too, drips with exceptionalism: "*The Disciples at Emmaus* is as much a monument to the artistic genius of Vermeer as are Vermeer's own paintings."[58] Van Meegeren's copies are brought in to support the exceptionalist notion of Vermeer's genius. Lessing's conclusion is one way to allow for the copy within the realm of art, to allow for art in the space of deceit: because the deceitful work ultimately confirms the genius of the original. But that does not undermine, of course, the powerful status of the original itself, the way in which it continues to structure aesthetic discourse and the art market. Ultimately, and in view of the Schmittian concept of sovereignty that I have shown to circulate in contemporary arts discourse, I am interested in what this powerful pull of the original tells us about the politics of art. Walter Benjamin suggests that the notion of the original may have fascistic tendencies. What are we to do with that suggestion given the continued dominance of originality as a value of avant-garde art today, some fifty years after the height of postmodernism?

F for Fascism

With respect to politics, and specifically Benjamin's association of fascism with the original, it is worth noting that one of the forgers that I have discussed so far has a specific tie to the history of fascist totalitarianism in Europe: Han van Meegeren, the Vermeer forger. Byung-Chul Han's account of van Meegeren's fake Vermeers leaves out a number of interesting elements on this count. First of all, it's interesting that van Meegeren was able to pass off so many of his copies as authentic Vermeers in part due to the success of his most famous Vermeer forgery, *The Disciples at Emmaus*. As John Brewer reports in *The American Leonardo*, this forgery (from 1937) received "an ecstatic appraisal" from "the leading Vermeer scholar in Holland, the ageing Abraham Bredius."[59] Experts recognized the forger's hand in subsequent, lesser forgeries—but because *Disciples at Emmaus* had been deemed an original, so were the later forgeries.

Second, and here is where we get to political history, van Meegeren's forgery was only exposed because the sale of a Vermeer to Göring was traced back to van Meegeren, who then confessed to the forgery because he did not want to be accused of having sold a national treasure to the occupier.[60] Brewer explains that at first, no one believed van Meegeren—which led him to confess many more of his forgeries. Still, he was not believed; and so they asked him to "'copy' a Vermeer from memory." Brewer continues:

> Van Meegeren was scornful—he would never make a copy, but he would paint an original Vermeer. Watched by officials of the court, and by journalists and photographers, over the course of two months he produced his last Vermeer, a version of *The Young Christ Teaching in the Temple*. The charges of collaboration were dropped to be replaced by those of forgery, but there were still eminent experts, notably the Belgian art historian Jean Decoen and [Dirk] Hannema, who were convinced that *The Disciples at Emmaus* remained a genuine Vermeer.[61]

Brewer goes on to note, however, that "once he was exposed as a forger rather than a traitor," the public perception of van Meegeren "was remarkably positive":

> The fact that Göring had paid for his fake Vermeer by returning a large number of Dutch works of art to their homeland rather than in cash transformed van Meegeren from a possible

> Nazi sympathizer into a patriotic hero who had outwitted the Reichsmarshall. A number of intellectuals and writers lauded his genius, taking the view of the popular writer Godfried Bomans in an Amsterdam newspaper that, "It is not the Vermeers, but the experts who authenticated them that are the fakes!"[62]

In other words, the case turned into a trial of the art *connoisseurs.*

This is quite literally a situation in which the copy was perceived by the general public, correctly or not, to have been *a weapon in the fight against fascism*—and where it ends up being those who authenticate works of art that become the people's target. While the latter are not necessarily associated with fascism, Benjamin does allow us to make that connection and I don't think it is a stretch to say that the same picaresque attitude that rejoices at a Vermeer forger outwitting the Nazis is in play also in the more general public—and popular, even populist—appreciation for the forger outwitting the art connoisseur. Even if that does not lead to the conclusion that the art connoisseur is a fascistic figure, such a connection does become worth considering in this context and confronts us yet again with the problem of decision—the question of who decides whether a work is original or fake—that is central to the concept of sovereignty as it was defined by Carl Schmitt. Sovereign is he who decides on the exception. In this case, the sovereign is the art connoisseur, who decides on the originality of the work of art; and to fool the art connoisseur meant, in this case, to fool the fascists as well. From my point of view, it becomes possible to read this conflation of elements as an accidental but insightful commentary on the politics of an aesthetic that attributes central value to the original.

I am certainly not the only one to have drawn such conclusions. Indeed, John Brewer does so as well in *The American*

Leonardo. Consider how, in Brewer's book, connoisseurship becomes the critical focus, specifically the tension between a knowledge of art based on the expertise acquired through many years of "looking at paintings" to one that's rooted in "scientific evidence"[63]—material-technical analyses done in laboratories. Brewer recalls a time (1929) when, while in the eyes of the general public art connoisseurship appeared to be something like "charlatanism" or even "black magic,"[64] it was defended in *The New York Times* by comparing it to "business acumen" (specifically, "bond-trading").[65] But Brewer points out that this is already confusing the issues, for when asked to attribute a painting one is asked to state a fact; whereas deciding to invest in a bond means making "a prediction about the potential value of a stock," which is "an informed guess about investor confidence."[66] To compare the one (determining originality) to the other (value and future value) means to already reveal the confusion between science and economics, between art history and the art market.

Even more interestingly for my purposes, Brewer explicitly notes the "anti-democratic aura"[67]—and we should emphasize the use of the term "aura"—of art connoisseurship, the way in which it claims an expertise *beyond science* (a point that recalls my brief discussion of the role of science in Julio García Espinosa's "For an Imperfect Cinema" in the previous chapter) acquired only after many years of study, that truly does sound something like magic—"inaccessible"[68] to the non-initiated, and even then hotly disputed (with the experts often disagreeing with each other, or changing their mind over time). In short, *there is no* "'science' of connoisseurship,"[69] and it is precisely this that constitutes the exceptionalism of the connoisseur that Elmyr de Hory and his fellow forgers relentlessly expose.[70]

Moreover, and tying this conclusion back to the previous chapter, this attack on expertise is also central to the figure of the vandal, and specifically the figure of the artist-as-vandal after Marcel Duchamp. Consider, for example, the Los Angeles-based artist Edward Kienholz, who "used to drive a truck with the legend 'ED KIENHOLZ-EXPERT' painted on the door."[71] On the one hand, the story refers to Kienholz working as a handyman to pay the bills—the unexceptional work that, to this day, artists are often doing to support their practice. But the skills that Kienholz's specific story evokes also "speak to the expanded domain of the post-medium artist, where expertise in art as such is not bound to specific materials, skills, traditions, or content":[72] it is, rather, expertise *in general*, something that from a certain point of view also makes *no sense*. Ryan Bishop and John Beck have tied such a "generic," post-medium sense of expertise to the post-Duchamp era, in which "expertise is what the expert says it is."[73] If that maxim has already been played out in this book in relation to Duchamp-the-art-vandal, it is returning in this chapter in the context of our study of the related figure of the forger.

The Fake vs. The Nude

Let me loop back now, in closing, to the question of the nude as it was raised for us in Welles' *F for Fake*, so as to consider in a bit more detail the tense relation between the fake and the nude. Why the nude in Welles' film on the fake? What is the nude's relation to the debates about originality that I engaged with in this chapter, and in this book at large?

In his classic *The Nude*, Kenneth Clark observes that "the body is not one of those subjects which can be made into art by direct transcription."[74] "[A]nyone who has frequented art schools and seen the shapeless, pitiful models that the students are industriously drawing will know," Clark notes (with obvious disdain for the bodies of those models), that the widespread supposition "that the naked human body is in itself an object upon which the eye dwells with pleasure and which we are glad to see depicted" is "an illusion."[75] In that, the naked body is "unlike a tiger or a snowy landscape," Clark adds. Clark reads the nude instead as the "artist's view of what the naked body *should* be";[76] painting a nude is about turning "the unfortunate body in the nude."[77] In contrast to what he deems to be the shapeless, pitiful bodies of the models, the nude seeks to capture "pure form."[78] Hence, the subtitle of his book: "A Study in Ideal Form."

Clark's book, problematic as it is, nevertheless offers a richly illustrated history and theory of the nude, ranging from the male nude that was dominant in the Western tradition until the seventeenth century as well as the female nude (which had become dominant by the nineteenth century). His book convincingly lays out the argument that the nude marks Western art's pursuit of the mathematically proportioned ideal form, and notes the important role that the classics (Greek and Roman sculpture) have played in this project.

Importantly, however, math is not *all* there is to it: Clark in fact navigates continuously between "math" and "nature" in his approach of what makes a nude a nude ("the idea of the nude does not depend on analyzable proportions alone";[79] perhaps it is indeed some "strangeness in the proportion" that, as Francis Bacon proposed, renders a nude beautiful[80]). The nude is not a purely architectural thing, even if much of what we appreciate about it seems to be architectural ("And yet when we look at the splendidly schematized bodies of Greek sculpture, we cannot resist the conviction that some system did exist"[81]). His book constantly negotiates this tension between a "formula" for the nude's ideal form, and then a certain *je ne sais quoi* "natural" element in the nude that precisely makes the nude a nude and allows Clark to posit, at the end of his first chapter, that the nude "reconciles several contrary states."[82] Still, mathematics comes through very strongly as a determining element of the nude.

It's worth noting (as many others have done) that the kind of nude Clark studies and theorizes is absent from Far Eastern art history (mentioned by Clark late in his book as part of an argument that we should not take the nude for granted[83]); there, one can find naked bodies but no nudes similar to those that have become dominant in the West, as Clark notes:[84] "The idea of offering a body for its own sake, as a serious subject of contemplation, simply did not occur to the Chinese or Japanese mind."[85] The one example that Clark mentions in this context is not taken from China, but Japan: in Japanese prints, naked bodies are "part of *ukioye*, the passing show of life,"[86] which includes naked bodies that would otherwise not be shown in art. In her discussion of the poor image, Hito Steyerl has referred to this as well when she indicates that the poor image, while associated with contemporary digital culture, is in fact much older than today, and is arguably already realized in the kinds of Japanese prints that Clark too discusses.[87] Clark, of course, is emphatically *not* interested in *bodies* and *poor images*; he is interested in the *rich image* of the Western *nude*.

The nude, then, is an idea, an idea of an ideal that is very similar to the philosophical idea and ideal of truth. Clark succinctly states that "the nude is not the subject of art, but a form of art,"[88] and one must surely read his use of the term "form" in a philosophical way, in relation not so much to the Greek term "*morphè*" (form) but to "*eidos*" (also form), the Platonic "idea" (a little later, Clark has "pure form,"[89] which renders this notion more precisely; indeed, the nude "was an idea"[90]). To pursue the nude, aesthetically, is a project that is thus similar to the pursuit of the truth in philosophy. "[E]very time we criticize a figure," Clark writes, "saying that a neck is too long, hips are too wide or breasts are too small, we are admitting, in quite concrete terms, the existence of ideal beauty."[91] In philosophical terms, Clark's statement shows how the nude is caught up in Western metaphysics, a kind of thought that posits that there is an idea and ideal of beauty hiding behind everyday appearances of what is considered beautiful (or not). Clark offers us the typical, dualist split of Western thought that operates within a distinction between the beauty of what appears and an idea and ideal of beauty hiding behind that.

Interestingly, given the role that the figure of the architect has played in the construction of the artist as a creative, exceptionalist figure related to God, Clark points out that one will often find architectural analogies here: "Like a building," he writes, "the nude represents a balance between an ideal scheme and functional necessities."[92] Da Vinci's Vitruvian Man can illustrate this. Clark makes the relation to sovereignty—both secular and divine—explicit a few pages later in this account, when he indicates that the ideal body has "something regal"[93] to it, and needs to be understood, in fact, as a theological figure in which "the Word was made flesh."[94] The ties to the Western idea of sovereignty are obvious.

I began by suggesting how Welles' film *F for Fake* might put us on the tracks of a non-exceptionalist politics through its engagement with the nude. How so? Such a reading would revolve around the fact that while Welles ends his film by showing us a fairly traditional nude, *F for Fake* supposedly culminates in twenty-two works by Picasso, a painter who is known in part for destroying the nude (he is also known, as Clark points out, for painting it[95]—in Picasso both the ideal form and its destruction came together; but it is the destructive element that Welles emphasizes, by cutting images from Picasso's cubist work into the film). In his discussion of Picasso's *Demoiselles d'Avignon*, Clark seems to come close to regretting this painting, which he characterizes as "a triumph of hate":[96] it shows "a totally un-Hellenized stylization of the body"[97] that, while still recognizably a nude, nevertheless "dismembers" it, if not quite "monstrously" displacing it (that dubious accomplishment he ascribes to a later Picasso, "Woman in an Armchair").[98] For all of that, Picasso was indebted "to the Congo."[99] And while Picasso will reappreciate classical values after a visit to Rome, Naples and Pompei, Clark writes, there were more "savage distortions"[100] to follow, distortions that Clark compares to the work of "the naughty child": "'Look what I've made, Mummy; it's a man. Yes, it *is* a man.'"[101] It might not be fascism, but it certainly is racism, and Tobin Siebers' work in disability studies about degenerate art has drawn out the relevance of art historical representations of the body, including the naked body, in this context.[102] The nude too, then, tends fascistically—at least in its typical, idealized representation. Certainly it is not an image of democracy.

It perhaps does not do full justice to Siebers' work to evoke it on this count. In an article titled "The Tyranny of the Aesthetic," Siebers has questioned the association of "the artistic personality" with fascism, specifically the claim that "it is in the nature of aesthetics to collaborate with power and money but especially with power."[103] "Whenever anyone tries to think about politics in a way that links it to aesthetic creativity, the argument rises up that the aestheticization of politics leads to only one place: National Socialism."[104] Siebers references Terry Eagleton on this count, but the association of fascism with the aestheticization of politics obviously leads back to Benjamin's "Work of Art" essay that I discussed in Chapter 2. While I agree with the criticism that Siebers lays out, I still find it difficult to ignore art's association with power and money, or the echoes of fascist thought in the exceptionalist ways in which art and artists have been understood. Recognizing those associations or echoes does not mean essentializing the aesthetic as fascistic. I take it as an impetus to unwork potentially fascistic elements in the aesthetic so as to ultimately also unwork them in politics. It seems there will be a problem as long as we continue to celebrate aesthetically what is politically problematic. If changes are difficult to accomplish politically, then perhaps it makes sense to effect them aesthetically—to put them out there as latent or manifest signals—in the hopes that politics will eventually follow suit.

My conclusion about the role of the nude in Welles' film would be this: while the second Oja sequence may look like it's showing a traditional nude, in fact what it evokes—and what the film's violent, emphatic cutting from a nude model to fragments from Picasso's paintings evokes—is a *hatred of the (ideal) nude* that in *F for Fake* is praised, and aligned with a hatred of the sovereign original. This is the precise constellation within which the role of the nude in Welles' film, and in my inquiry into exceptionalist aesthetics and politics, needs to be read: Picasso, who paints the nudes for which Oja is a model, is a destroyer of ideal form. A vandal of the avant-garde, he represents a break in Western thought and its related aesthetic tradition by quite literally breaking up the ideal body that is the figure of ideal form. Welles responds to the exceptionalist lure by which Picasso's vandalism is all too easily reappropriated by Picasso's stature—by the ideal form of Picasso himself—by adding a twist to the tale: Oja allowed Picasso to paint her on the condition that she would own the paintings afterwards. She returns with the paintings to Paris, has her forger grandfather repaint them (or paint new paintings in the style of Picasso's portraits of her? the film does not quite clarify) and then puts the works up for sale, as works by Picasso. The works receive rave reviews. Picasso shows up at the gallery enraged, only to find that none of the paintings on show is actually his. When he asks Oja what she has done with the originals, she replies that she burnt them. We are not entirely outside of the art market here, but whatever "value" these Picasso's have accrued, they have accrued as "fakes." If Picasso already destroyed the ideal form of the nude, here the ideal form of Picasso himself is destroyed as well.

If Clark's book is in part problematic because of the obvious disdain it voices for bodies that are less than ideal—a disdain that is occasionally expressed in his book in gendered and raced terms—the root of this occasional racism and sexism is the notion of an ideal form itself, and it is that very notion of the ideal (associated with the nude) that I have targeted. Welles' film helps us understand the important role that the fake plays in such targeting. With Welles and Clark and the nude as a figure of the ideal form, we have pursued this targeting within the Western tradition where exceptionalism is particularly strong. I have drawn out, in the opening section of this chapter, some of the political consequences of such a project: how it undermines, for example, what Elmyr de Hory deems to be a single person's decision on what is good and bad art. My discussion of the case of "Riverbank," attributed to Dong Yuan but possibly a forgery by Zhang Daqian, was of course meant to continue my discussion of the fake from the previous chapter, and to extend it in relation to the figure of the nude.

But it's worth noting also that what is shown in "Riverbank," in this painting that is at the center of an intense debate about its originality and more largely about "issues of authenticity in Chinese painting" (as the title of the MET book published in relation to this work has it), is not a nude but a landscape. Indeed, and as I will continue to explore in the next chapter, landscape—present in Western art history but central to Far Eastern art history in the same way that the nude is central to Western art history—has been understood as a counterpart of the Western nude, as an unexceptionalizing topos in relation to the nude's exceptionalism. The Chinese term for "landscape," "mountain(s)-water(s)" (shan shui [山水]), a term that combines both the vertical, tall peaks of the mountains with the horizontal flow of water, arguably already points in this direction, since it unworks the verticality of the exceptional mountain into the horizontality of the unexceptional water. It is, to be sure, around the figure of water—difficult to paint, like the clouds, fog, or mist that are a key part of Chinese landscape painting (as in the top section of "Riverbank," for example)—that, in Part III of this book, some of my considerations of the importance of daoism for unexceptional thought will come together.

Notes

1 This part of the film recalls The Modern Lovers' song "Pablo Picasso" recorded just one year prior to the release of Welles' film but released only in 1976. It includes the lines: "Well . . . Some people try to pick up

girls / and get called "asshole!" / This never happened to / Pablo Picasso He could walk down your street / And girls could not resist his stare and so / Pablo Picasso was never called an asshole." The track can be found on: The Modern Lovers, *The Modern Lovers* [music album] (Beserkley, 1976).

2 Kenneth Clark, *The Nude: A Study in Ideal Form* (Princeton, NJ: Princeton University Press, 1972).

3 See: Giorgio Agamben, Stasis*: Civil War as a Political Paradigm* (*Homo Sacer II, 2*), trans. Nicholas Heron (Edinburgh: Edinburgh University Press, 2015).

4 Clark, *The Nude*, p. 93.

5 Jonathan Hay, "Editorial: The Value of Forgery," *Anthropology and Aesthetics* 53/54 (2008), pp. 5–14, here p. 6. Hay's full thought is worth quoting: "The forgery: classically, an artwork that fraudulently passes itself off as genuine. Forgery: deceit in the space of art. Art history has never been comfortable, though, with the corollary of the second proposition—that forgery is art in the space of deceit."

6 Daniel Kehlmann, *F*, trans. Carol Brown Janeway (New York: Vintage, 2015), pp. 189–190.

7 Byung-Chul Han, *Shanzhai: Deconstruction in Chinese*, trans. Philippa Hurd (Boston, MA: The MIT Press, 2017), p. 24.

8 Han, *Shanzhai*, p. 24.

9 Ibid., p. 24.

10 Ibid.

11 Ibid., p. 29.

12 Ibid.

13 Giorgio Agamben, *Creation and Anarchy: The Work of Art and the Religion of Capitalism*, trans. Adam Kotsko (Stanford, CA: Stanford University Press, 2019), p. 8.

14 Ibid., p. 6.

15 Ibid., p. 15.

16 Ibid.

17 Ibid.

18 Based on the research I have done on seals, I am inclined to read this as an overstatement. In an article about Emperor Huizong, for example, Maggie Bickford points out that "Huizong insistently claimed these pictures by applying to them multiple inscribed and impressed formulae"—and by claimed she means "claimed as his work." So the seal was evidently used here in a signature-like way: Maggie Bickford, "Emperor Huizong

and the Aesthetic of Agency," *Archives of Asian Art* 53:1 (2002–2003), pp. 71–104, here p. 76.

19 Han, *Shanzhai*, p. 34.

20 Ibid., p. 52.

21 Ibid.

22 Ibid.

23 See: Ibid., p. 68.

24 Yve-Alain Bois and Rosalind Krauss, *Formless: A User's Guide* (New York: Zone Books, 1999), p. 102.

25 Benjamin qtd. ibid., p. 56.

26 Andrea Pinotti, "The Painter Through the Fourth Wall of China: Benjamin and the Threshold of the Image," in: Daniel Weidner and Sigrid Weigel, eds., *Benjamin-Studien 3* (Paderborn: Wilhelm Fink, 2014), pp. 133–149, here p. 139.

27 Pinotti, "The Painter Through the Fourth Wall of China," p. 139.

28 Graeme Gilloch and Jaeho Kang, "'Ink-Play': Walter Benjamin's Chinese Curios," *Sociétés* 31 131:1 (2016), pp. 119–130, here p. 121.

29 See: Edward Slingerland, *Mind and Body in Early China: Beyond Orientalism and the Myth of Holism* (Oxford: Oxford University Press, 2019). In this context, I have commented on Slingerland's reading of François Jullien, a philosopher I rely on in this book, elsewhere. See: Arne De Boever, *François Jullien's Unexceptional Thought: A Critical* Introduction (New York: Rowman & Littlefield, 2020), in particular chapter 1.

30 Wen Fong, "The Problem of Forgeries in Chinese Painting: Part One," *Artibus Asiae* 25:2/3 (1962), pp. 95–119 and pp. 121–140, here p. 95.

31 Fong, "The Problem of Forgeries in Chinese Painting," p. 103.

32 Ibid., p. 60.

33 Ibid.

34 Stille qtd. Bianca Bosker, *Original Copies: Architectural Mimicry in Contemporary China* (Honolulu: University of Hawai'i Press/Hong Kong University Press, 2013), p. 25.

35 Fong, "The Problem of Forgeries in Chinese Painting," p. 99.

36 Ibid., p. 90.

37 The scope of Zhang Daqian's forgery is disputed, as for example the catalogue of Zhang Daqian's recent exhibition *Chang Dai-Chien: Painting from Heart to Hand* at the Asian Art Museum in San Francisco makes clear (Mark Dean Johnson and Fan Jeremy Zhang, *Chang Dai-Chien: Painting from Heart to Hand* [San Francisco: Asian Art Museum,

2019]). In this catalogue, for example, Mark Dean Johnson rejects the "accusation" that Zhang Daqian is a "master forger," but assessing this statement poses some difficulty given the ties between Daqian, Johnson, and the museum—ties that the catalogue also makes clear. I in any case do not refer to Zhang Daqian as a forger to accuse him; it's precisely the accusatory mode that then forces Johnson into a rejection. Rather, it is the attitude towards forgery that needs to be changed, coming from a deeper appreciation of the role of copying in Zhang Daqian's practice and beyond that a sharper understanding of the art world's exceptionalism.

38 Judith G. Smith and Wen C. Fong, *Issues of Authenticity in Chinese* Painting (New York: The Metropolitan Museum of Art, 1999).

39 James Cahill, "The Case Against *Riverbank*," in: Judith G. Smith and Wen C. Fong, eds., *Issues of Authenticity in Chinese* Painting (New York: The Metropolitan Museum of Art, 1999), pp. 13–63, here p. 17.

40 Elizabeth Cropper, *The Domenichino Affair: Novelty, Imitation, and Theft in Seventeenth-Century Rome* (New Haven, CT: Yale University Press, 2005), p. 203.

41 Ibid.

42 Ibid.

43 Ibid.

44 Peter Jaszi, "Is There Such a Thing as Postmodern Copyright?," in: Mario Biagioli, Peter Jaszi, and Martha Woodmansee, eds., *Making and Unmaking Intellectual Property* (Chicago, IL: University of Chicago Press, 2011), pp. 413–427.

45 Krauss has suggested these should not be understood as copies. Writing about Levine's reproductions of photographs by Edward Weston specifically, she understands them rather as copies of works that already weren't strictly speaking "originals"—copies of copies. Interestingly, Krauss relies on Roland Barthes' understanding of realism, as developed in *S/Z*, to make this point: Rosalind Krauss, *The Originality of the Avant-Garde and Other Modernist Myths* (Cambridge, MA: The MIT Press, 1985), pp. 151–170, here p. 168. Along related lines, Stephen Bann provocatively inscribes Walter Benjamin's essay "The Work of Art in the Era of Mechanical Reproduction" into the "grand narrative of the progress of realism" (Stephen Bann, "Ingres in Reproduction," *Art History* 23:5 [2000], pp. 706–725, here p. 706). From such a point of view, this book on post-exceptionalism can be read as an extension of my interest in realism, which I have developed elsewhere (see: Arne De Boever, *Finance*

Fictions: Realism and Psychosis in a Time of Economic Crisis [New York: Fordham University Press, 2018]).

46 For a brief art-historical framing of appropriation art with a focus on China and Japan in particular, see: Christoph Zuschlag, "Appropriation Art aus China und Japan?," in: Guido Isekenmeier, ed., *Interpiktorialität: Theorie und Geschichte der Bild-Bild-Bezüge* (Bielefeld: transcript, 2013), pp. 205–217.

47 Indigenous art has also played an important role in these conversations. See for example: Fred Myers, "Ontologies of the image and economies of exchange," *American Ethnologist* 31:1 (2004), pp. 5–20.

48 Benjamin Barron, "Richard Prince, Audrey Wollen, and Sad Girl Theory," *i-D* (*Vice*) November 12 (2014), accessible: https://i-d.vice.com/en_us/article/nebn3d/richard-prince-audrey-wollen-and-the-sad-girl-theory

49 I thank my former graduate student Allie Smith for bringing this case to my attention.

50 Fong, "The Problem of Forgeries in Chinese Painting," p. 97.

51 Ibid., p. 98.

52 Ibid.

53 Cahill, "The Case Against *Riverbank*," p. 46.

54 Ibid., p. 15.

55 Ibid.

56 Han, *Shanzhai*, p. 24.

57 Ronan Deazley, *Rethinking Copyright: History, Theory, Language* (Cheltenham: Edward Elgar, 2006), p. 101.

58 Alfred Lessing, "What Is Wrong with a Forgery?," in: Dennis Dutton, ed., *The Forger's Art: Forgery and the Philosophy of Art* (Berkeley: University of California Press, 1983), pp. 58–76, here p. 76.

59 John Brewer, *The American Leonardo: A Tale of Obsession, Art and Money* (New York: Oxford University Press, 2009) (Ebook), p. 111.

60 In his account of the van Meegeren case, Frank Arnau notes that this triggered the suspicion that van Meegeren faked his forgeries; in other words: invented the forgeries to avoid being accused of collaboration (Frank Arnau, *The Art of the Faker: Three Thousand Years of Deception*, trans. Maxwell Brownjohn [Boston, MA: Little, Brown, and Company, 1959], p. 315). This suspicion persisted even after van Meegeren's death.

61 Brewer, *The American Leonardo*, p. 111.

62 Ibid., p. 112.

63 Ibid., p. 97.

64 Ibid.

65 Ibid., pp. 97–98.
66 Ibid., p. 98.
67 Ibid., p. 106.
68 Ibid.
69 Ibid., p. 100.
70 Brewer's name for this is the "aristocratic" values of the art world and recalls my discussion of Kiefer's use of this term in my Introduction. Ibid., p. 113.
71 John Beck and Ryan Bishop, *Technocrats of the Imagination: Art, Technology, and the Military-Industrial Avant-Garde* (Durham, NC: Duke University Press, 2020), p. 107.
72 Beck and Bishop, *Technocrats*, p. 107.
73 Ibid.
74 Clark, *The Nude*, p. 5.
75 Ibid., p. 5.
76 Ibid., p. 7.
77 Ibid., p. 10.
78 Ibid., p. 8.
79 Ibid., p. 20.
80 Bacon qtd. ibid., p. 19. Alain de Botton has characterized this as the difference between a Platonic and a Kantian concept of beauty: Alain de Botton, *Essays in Love: A Novel* (London: Picador, 1993), chapter 9.
81 Ibid.
82 Ibid., p. 25.
83 See: ibid., p. 358.
84 Ibid., p. 9.
85 Ibid., p. 10.
86 Ibid., p. 9.
87 Daniel Rourke, "Artifacts: A Conversation with Hito Steyerl and Daniel Rourke," *Rhizome* (March 2013), available at: https://rhizome.org/editorial/2013/mar/28/artifacts/
88 Clark, *The Nude*, p. 5.
89 Ibid., p. 8.
90 Ibid., p. 12.
91 Ibid., p. 13.
92 Ibid., p. 20.
93 Ibid., p. 25.
94 Ibid., p. 29.
95 Ibid., pp. 3–4.

96 Ibid., p. 361.

97 Ibid., p. 363.

98 Ibid.

99 Ibid.

100 Ibid., p. 365.

101 Ibid.

102 Tobin Siebers, *Disability Aesthetics* (Ann Arbor: University of Michigan Press, 2013), here pp. 8–9.

103 Tobin Siebers, "Hitler and the Tyranny of the Aesthetic," *Philosophy and Literature* 24 (2000), pp. 96–110, here p. 97.

104 Siebers, "Hitler and the Tyranny of the Aesthetic," p. 97.

4

Turning Towards Landscape

Disability Art (Part Two)

With reference to the work of Tobin Siebers (which I already discussed in my first chapter) one might suggest that through its criticism of the original, Orson Welles' film *F for Fake* invites us to "disable" the idealist nude: to break out of the ableist aesthetic of the ideal body into what Siebers—in part with reference to the work of Pablo Picasso, which is prominently present in Welles' film—calls a "disability aesthetics." In its undermining of the idealist nude, such an aesthetics is, as Siebers work makes abundantly clear, a disability *politics* as well in that it foregrounds aesthetically those bodies that are often less visible politically.

In the Introduction to *Disability Aesthetics*, Siebers points out that:

> Works of art engaged with the body serve to critique the assumptions of idealist aesthetics, but they also have an unanticipated effect . . . Whether or not we interpret these works as aesthetic, they summon images of disability. Most frequently, they register as wounded or disabled bodies, representations of irrationality or cognitive disability, or effects of warfare, disease, or accidents.[1]

"Disability aesthetics," in his view, "embraces beauty that seems by traditional standards to be broken."[2] Siebers' project in his book is to make the influence of disability in art obvious: as he shows, disability—far from being ignored—is in fact everywhere in modern and contemporary art. (This is Siebers' version of poet, critic, and novelist Ben Lerner's claim, discussed in Chapter 1, that the history of twentieth-century art is the history of acts of vandalism.) It might require some shift in perspective to consider the *Venus de Milo* as a beautiful sculpture of a double amputee, but the artist René Magritte already realized such a change in his work *Menottes de Cuivre*, in which he turns Venus' arms into bloody stumps. Siebers also mentions Andy Warhol's *Car Crash* as a work that highlights both the mangled human body and that of a car. Compare and contrast Warhol's car, the philosopher Byung-Chul Han might suggest, to the smoothness of the Citroën DS that the French thinker Roland Barthes writes about in *Mythologies*. Juxtaposing images of what the National-Socialists considered "degenerate art" to medical photographs of facial deformities—one of which is pictured on the cover of Siebers' book—Siebers draws out how omnipresent, and ultimately appreciated, such faces actually are in modern and contemporary art. Siebers ends his introduction with a discussion of work by Paul McCarthy, an able artist whose performances are often described as "sick," and work by Judith Scott, a disabled artist whose intricate sculptures will be familiar to those who have read Eve Sedgwick's *Touching Feeling*, in order to ask about the role of disability in our conception of the artist as well.

All of the above examples are about breaking down idealist conceptions of the artist and especially the work of art: its ideal form, made visible—Siebers would enable us to argue—in the figure of the nude. It's important to point out that while Siebers was himself disabled (he had polio) and thus could make a personal claim to the disability aesthetics he was theorizing, he pointed out that "[n]either disabled artists nor disabled subjects are central to my argument"; "What is central is how specific artists and works force us to reconsider fundamental aesthetic assumptions and to embrace another aesthetics."[3] As I will explore in this chapter, such a reconsideration is closely tied to the breaking down of the philosophical idea of truth, whose pursuit has dominated Western thought. Siebers guides the reader, rather, in another direction: that of a thinking about disabled artists and disabled works, one that is very close to the thinking I have developed in this book about the copy and the fake (through my discussions of Walter Benjamin, Rosalind Krauss, Welles, and Han [specifically his book *Shanzhai: Deconstruction in Chinese*]), the poor image (Hito Steyerl, Julio García Espinosa), and of course already discussed work by Han (*Saving Beauty*), Lerner, and Siebers himself. With respect to the philosophical pursuit of the idea of truth, this will mean moving away from the ontological attempt to think being, or the metaphysical attempt to find the truth behind appearances.

While such a move will turn out to have much to do with an unworking of the nude that is central in Western art, in the previous chapter it also became associated with a thinking about landscape in Chinese art. In this chapter, I work in between those genres—"I paint landscapes, and I paint nudes / I contain multitudes," as Bob Dylan has it[4]—to give some more depth to that framework. As in the previous chapter, I want to draw attention to the risk of orientalism in this context, and this chapter will do much to unwork a comparative approach that would follow the logic of difference, and simply construe "the West" in opposition to "China" or "the Far East," and vice versa. Instead, I will seek to foreground how what some find in "China" or "the Far East" as undermining the Western tradition of the nude and the philosophical pursuit of truth (as ideal form/idea that is closely linked to the nude), is in fact already operative in "the West" as well. This is so even if I will show daoism—and specifically chapter 41 from Lao Zi's philosophical classic *Dao De Jing*—to be a particularly fruitful site for developing a thought that would undermine the Western philosophical pursuit of truth as captured in the ideal form of the nude.

For such a project I am going to rely, first, on the work of the French sinologist François Jullien, who has developed the divergence of the Western nude from the Chinese landscape in some detail in his work. Jullien has frequently been accused of orientalism in this context, and part of my goal in this chapter will be to show how the particular relation Jullien develops between "the West" and "China" in his work is precisely not one of opposition. Drawing out the influences of daoism in Jullien's aesthetic thought, I will discuss (first) the work of the Beijing-based contemporary artist Song Dong—specifically his water works—as an example of the daoism-influenced art that I am interested in. Such art, however, and the thinking that is associated with it can hardly be said to be the monopoly of "China." Indeed, in an influential article from 2009 the art critic Raphael Rubinstein coined the notion of "provisional painting" to name a group of Western contemporary painters who privilege the unfinished rather than the ideal form in their work. While in the press statement for a group exhibition titled "Provisional Painting" that he curated at Modern Art in London a few years later, Rubinstein associated this kind of painting with daoism (and specifically the excerpts from the

Dao De Jing that I discuss in this chapter), Jullien's work in fact allows us to see that a preference for the provisional is very much present within Western art history beyond the contemporary as well—even if, for a long time, it may have been overlooked. While this chapter continues my focus on the forger by further developing the references to "China" and "the Far East" that we encountered in the previous chapter, with the turn to both landscape and daoism this chapter goes a long way towards introducing the figure of the sage that will take center stage in the third part of this book.

With the Western philosophical figures of truth and ideal form/the idea, the figure of the sovereign remains prominently present in this chapter as well. Rubinstein's thought about the provisional in painting, Jullien's reflections on the unfinished and in particular the sketch in art, and more broadly the considerations about Chinese landscape painting that will be laid out in this chapter arguably introduce precisely the zone of indeterminacy—the border area—upon which the sovereign, in Carl Schmitt's conception, needs to take a decision. As such, however, they also bring a challenge to that sovereign decision, because they insist on their indeterminacy as a state—or more precisely, a process—to be maintained, arguing moreover that the greatest accomplishment in art is the presentation of such indeterminacy, of something that in the West has often been considered to be the opposite of greatness. If this, rather than Schmittian sovereignty, is what art delivers—and if that payoff can in fact be presented in a sharp tension with Schmittian sovereignty—then the question becomes what politics might be associated with such an understanding of art. While this question will be broached here, it will only be discussed in detail in the next chapter.

Landscape and the Nude

In his book *The Impossible Nude: Chinese Art and Western Aesthetics*, François Jullien seeks to lay out the philosophical reasons why he considers the nude, at least the nude as we know it in the West, to be impossible in Chinese art. Jullien is certainly not the only one to have commented on this absence of the nude in Chinese art—you'll even find this absence noted in the Wikipedia entry for the "Nude" in art. But Jullien's work goes further than noting this absence: it seeks to lay out the philosophical reasons why the nude is in fact *impossible* in Chinese art. This is so, Jullien proposes, because "[t]he nude is a paradigm of what the 'West' consists of in cultural terms, and brings to light the stances that originally underpinned our [by which he means Western] philosophy."[5] Jullien provocatively associates the nude with Western philosophy's obsession with "[t]he question of essence, of the 'thing itself,'"[6] in other words with ontology and metaphysics. The nude is exceptional: it "surg[es] out," it is "stunning"; Jullien characterizes it as an "event, offered like a miracle for contemplation."[7] As such, he contrasts it to nakedness, which always "implies a diminished state."[8] The nude, on the other hand, "tends toward the Ideal and serves as the 'image' (eikon) for the [Platonic] Idea."[9] Explicitly using the language of the miracle, Jullien notes that it "turns toward the 'divine'"[10]—not at all towards the oblique and the discreet that, under the header of "blandness," he considers characteristic of Chinese thought.[11] Indeed, if Western thought is all about exceptionality, Chinese thought is associated in Jullien's work with the unexceptional—and this becomes visible, aesthetically, in the centrality of the nude to Western art and its absence in Chinese art (absence at least as a Western nude—Jullien is obviously not saying there are no naked bodies in Chinese art; rather his point is that they are not rendered in the exceptionalist way that nudes are in the West).

Although Jullien does not present his thinking about the nude in explicitly political terms, its references to the nude as a figure of the divine, and specifically the miracle make it resonate with the work of Carl Schmitt. One can consider, for example, Schmitt's book *Political Theology* (already discussed in my Introduction), and Schmitt's claim that, like other major concepts in the modern theory of the state, the state of exception is a secularized theological concept, specifically a political concept that results from the secularization of the theological notion of the miracle. The state of exception, then, and the sovereign's close relation to it—the sovereign creates the exception, and the exception creates the sovereign, as I discussed in my Introduction—have something of the miracle to it, and in that, their being resonates with how Jullien characterizes the nude. This is not so much a tale of the emperor not having any clothes, which is a tale of nakedness; it is a tale of the sovereign as a Western nude, something that according to Jullien would be impossible in Chinese thought. Like the nude, sovereignty and its decision on the state of exception are something like a stunning event that surges out; in its decisionist force, sovereignty is nothing like the bland. If Western sovereignty, like the nude, is exceptional, Jullien presents Chinese thought in his work as unexceptional—as offering a mindset that makes the kind of exceptionality one finds in the nude and Western sovereignty impossible.

Here too, one ought to be weary of the risk of orientalism, something of which Jullien has been frequently accused. If we can perhaps accept, given that it appears to be the scholarly consensus, that the nude is impossible in Chinese art history (something that further appears to be borne out by accounts I have received from young artists who engage with the nude in their work but are finding it difficult to exhibit in contemporary China even today[12]), that does not necessarily lead to the conclusion that there is no exceptionalism in China, or that there is no sovereignty in Chinese political history. Indeed, looking at Chinese political history, it often seems as if sovereignty is the only game around; and even when looking at the work of the sages, in particular the daoist sages, which is Jullien's foundation for his argument about the lack of exceptionalist Western thinking in China, one would have to note that the very figure of the sage may strike one as elitist; that is, as a figure of the very exceptionalism that Jullien deems to be absent in China. This would be particularly relevant given that political rulers were supposed to model themselves after the sages.

And what about so-called monumental landscape painting that dominates Chinese art history? Couldn't that, in its monumentality, be read as an example of exceptionalism in art? Note, for example, Wen Fong's discussion of the distinction between figure painting and landscape painting in China. Whereas the former, as a kind of professional painting, was considered a "lowly skill" closer to "craftsmanship," the latter—landscape painting—"was quite free from utilitarian stigma."[13] Fong notes that "gentleman-painters, who were interested in painting as a fine art, had managed to lift it to the same exalted level with other noble intellectual pursuits such as poetry and calligraphy."[14] As such, the pursuit of landscape painting was supposed to be an amateurish one (amateurish in contrast with professional figure painting/craftsmanship). Moreover, and pushing this discussion towards politics, haven't the monumental mountains in those paintings been connected to the figure of the emperor, with scholars comparing the composition of a monumental landscape painting to portraits of the emperor made in the same era?[15] Clearly, it will not do to create a strict opposition of "the West" to "China" on this count. Indeed, if exceptionalism—philosophical, political, aesthetic—can be shown to be present in China, the other side of this deconstructive move is to show (as I will do later in this chapter) that unexceptionalism can certainly be present in Western philosophy, politics, aesthetics as well.

One thing ought to be clear: Jullien is very critical of Western exceptionalism and how it has played out in aesthetics—and it would be difficult to deny that he is onto something here. In the chapter titled "The Cult of the Beautiful" in Jullien's book *This Strange Idea of the Beautiful*, Jullien writes that in the West, the beautiful is sacralized and works of art collectively share, in his words, the "charter of exception."[16] (He adds, again reinforcing the potentially problematic comparative framework from which he also seeks to distance himself, that he is "unaware of any functional equivalent in China or in other countries of the far east."[17] There works of art are not "erected as totalitarian symbols of beauty."[18]) In the West, as Jullien sees it, the veneration of art has come close to the veneration of the "divine" and art has become the object of a "cult,"[19] a term that recalls my discussion of "cult value" in Walter Benjamin's "Work of Art" essay in Chapter 2. If Benjamin in the era of mechanical reproduction saw exhibition value on the rise, Jullien might counter by saying that cult value eventually reemerged victorious.[20] Jullien explicitly characterizes this as the cult of "*exceptional* beauty" (emphasis mine).[21] The beautiful has become isolated and promoted as "the only divine thing left which does not compromise, but is compatible with, science and even very ably counterbalances it, and into which the religious consequently can flow back without difficulty."[22] The museum is "the modern temple";[23] "it offers the immense, even unique, advantage of a profane sacred."[24] The beautiful "is the final messianism left to us."[25] This is not, in my view, a bad description of art in the West, specifically of the way of thinking about art that reveres genius and originality and that in Benjamin's view tends fascistically because of that.

In another book titled *The Silent Transformations*, Jullien associates ontology and metaphysics with philosophies of the event. Here we find most explicitly Jullien's argument *against* exceptionalist philosophies of "'sudden' shattering,"[26] the "resonant thunderclaps of Revolutions,"[27] "spectacular bombshells, shocks and political after-effects,"[28] "rupture."[29] In a chapter entitled "Mythology of the Event," Jullien takes on the Western philosophical notion of the event—which includes Carl Schmitt as a major voice—as a representation of "exceptional . . . irruption [and] upheaval," arguing that it is a "fictive or mythological representation."[30] Instead, and coming from Chinese thought, Jullien theorizes the event as "a matter of emergence."[31] Where Western philosophy finds the "incomparable, non-integratable event,"[32] Chinese thought offers "a silent maturation of the negative"[33] which, when "conditions are ripe for it"[34] leads the event to emerge. Singling out Alain Badiou's thought (already mentioned in my Introduction, and put in conversation there with Schmitt's work) as an example of how "the event still continues to fertilize philosophy today,"[35] Jullien considers the "characteristic of Chinese thought" to be "precisely to dissolve the event."[36]

To be sure, if all of this seems to get something right about both Western thinking and Chinese thinking, the opposition it stages between the two remains dubious because of the high degree of generalization on which it relies. Jullien himself would not describe the framework that is developed here as comparative: he claims, no doubt in response to accusations that his work is orientalist, that he does not compare, specifically that his work does not follow the logic of difference which construes one identity in opposition to another. Instead, Jullien develops a dynamic of divergence ("écart") where he works across a gap between two historically and geographically removed living thoughts that are constantly transforming and can therefore not be confined to an oppositional, comparative logic of identity. His thought is quite close in that sense to that of postcolonial thinkers like the Moroccan poet and theorist Abdelkebir Khatibi (very interested in daoism, as indicated by his long poem from 1976 *Class Warrior—Taoist Style*[37]) and the Martiniquan writer and theorist Édouard Glissant.[38] Jullien's terminology of divergence and the gap, which mark an important nuance of thought, is supposed to save him from orientalism—but reading his work (and writing about it) it is hard to escape the orientalist logic of opposition, which seems prominently present. The least one can say is that in its stated purpose, Jullien's work as an orientalist operates critically within this discipline, often rejecting what he refers to as those "Chinese utopias" so common in French thought (and associated with the journal *Tel Quel* in the 1970s—Roland Barthes was part of a group of Telquelians who traveled to China in 1974—but going back to long before then). Jullien emphatically distinguishes his own study of China from those utopian approaches. Elsewhere, I have done extensive work on both Chinese utopias in French thought and Jullien's connections to postcolonial thought,[39] and I won't repeat that here. Let me just point out that if the nude is perhaps most at risk of exoticization and orientalization—exoticist and orientalist nudes are precisely very common, no doubt because such exoticism and orientalism are practiced by Westerners who have been shaped by tradition of thought that produces the nude—it's worth noting that Jullien situates and thinks through the nude *on the side of the West*, as if to preempt precisely such a move. His is *an occidentalist theory of the nude*, and a critical one at that. This may in fact help to explain why the nude is an exoticist and orientalist commonplace: because it is one of the aesthetic strongholds of the West, one among many means through which the other is colonized—a process that, as decolonial thinkers well know, marks not merely an aesthetic appropriation but also an appropriation into a mode of thought. Following Jullien, one might describe this as the violence of making the nude possible in aesthetic traditions and traditions of thought where it could not be found.

I want to return now, after this discussion of the nude as the aesthetic outcome of a Western thought focused on the sovereignty of ideal form, being, and truth, to a question I raised earlier on: What about so-called monumental landscape painting that dominates Chinese art history? Couldn't that, in its monumentality, be read as an example of exceptionalism in art? Although Jullien notes the presence of landscape painting in both Western and Chinese art history, it is fair to say that his work develops a thought on Chinese landscape painting that diverges from his thinking about the Western nude; in other words, there is a way in which, in Jullien's work, Chinese landscape paintings become the focus of a thought—specifically, a wisdom—that diverges from Western philosophy and its exceptionalist traits. In Jullien's work, the Chinese landscape, then, arguably becomes a figure of the post-exceptional, and as such it comes to operate in a tension with the Western nude. Once more, the risk of orientalism looms, because one constantly risks to fall in an all-too-easy opposition of Chinese landscape painting to the Western nude. Still, and again in a roughly analytical way, Jullien seems to get something right about the Chinese landscape that allows it to figure in Jullien's work in this way.

Although landscape is present throughout Jullien's work, his books *Living off Landscape* and also *The Great Image Has No Form* are good places to look for those interested in the post-exceptionalism of landscape in Jullien's thought. It's where Jullien writes about so-called "ink and wash" landscape paintings of the "literati," the Southern school of landscape painting. Let me return here to the two terms, ontology and metaphysics, that (apart from theology) Jullien associates with the Western tradition (and that he considers the Chinese tradition, in its divergence with the West, to target). Ontology refers to the logic of being, which understands the world in terms of unitary essence and identity. Even if variety within such a logic is possible, it is the variety of what Jullien dismissively calls "comparison," which merely confirms unitary essence and identity. The Chinese mode of "comprehension of things stands apart from ontology,"[40] Jullien writes in *Living Off Landscape*. It can "be understood only by correlation,"[41] by which Jullien means the relations between everything. (He frequently points out, for example, that "thing" in Chinese is rendered as "east-west,"[42] that is, as a correlation rather than as being.) Chinese thought explores thinking as de-ontology. Driving such thought is not the Platonic question of the "what is?"—the celebrated "*ti esti*" that is at the core of the Platonic dialogues.[43] Dong Yuan's paintings—Dong Yuan is the master to whom, let's recall from my Chapter 3, "Riverbank" is now attributed—are praised instead, Jullien writes in *The Great Image*, for their "as-if-there-were-as-if-there-were-not"-quality.[44] The Western principle of non-contradiction has no reign in such a thought: "there is thus no self-identical entity to erect into an essence or from which to constitute an object."[45] In fact, Jullien clarifies that in *The Great Image*, his "object is the nonobject: [that which] is too hazy-indistinct-diffuse-evanescent-con-fused to keep still and isolated."[46] Chinese thought—and by extension, in Jullien's analysis, Chinese landscape painting—escapes not only subjectification but also objectification.[47] It is interested not just in mountains, but in mountains in clouds, haze, penumbra; waters; mist, fog. The human form is only interesting when it is moving, which is why it is shown with undulating garments.[48] Chinese thought is interested in floating and melting. "To melt," Jullien writes in *This Strange Idea*, "thus speaks of the transition where the physical (the opaque) dissolves and opens out, makes itself indistinct and becomes expansive. And opens itself up to the imperceptible and the unlimited—to 'melt' is the anti-dualist word par excellence."[49]

As Jullien sees it, ontology is quite simply set aside here. Interested in the foundation-fount of all things, their ground and source, Chinese thought sought to paint, then, the "Without-form."[50] Such a "Without-form" "cannot enjoy an ontological status"; because it is without form, "it does not give rise to the determination of essence, or *eidos*."[51] "At the same time," Jullien adds, "it cannot be considered *chaos*."[52] There is certainly coherence here, but it is not the coherence of ontology. The daoist "Without-form" therefore should not be understood simply as a negative; "it is not of the order of nonbeing or nothingness."[53] In that, it differs from the nothingness of Buddhism, which arrives in China from India and is still ontological.[54] It is, quite the contrary, the ground or source from where "'there is' can come about by becoming distinct—just as a line can ap-pear, a form ex-ist."[55] Hence Jullien's interest in the first stroke that opens up a canvas. Any ontologically determining discourse "on" the Dao or the way should be avoided.[56] As per the *Laozi*: "Each utterance does not picture but *de*-picts. The *de*- here signifies not completion but the reverse: effacement, undoing."[57]

Apart from the fact that Jullien considers this perspective to lie at the origin of the Western split between philosophy (determining) and literature (indistinct), he also points out the challenges it poses to Chinese painting, which is non-mimetic (non-representational) through and through. For how to paint within this kind of thought? How to paint the Dao? "It is not," Jullien writes, following authors like Li Rihua and Bu Yantu,

> that [painters] gave up the ink and brush, but that they used a wash so diluted, so close to the dry-pale end of the spectrum, that it approximates the white of the paper. It is so dim that it almost fades away altogether. Hence the painter pictures while de-picting: in using that "inkless ink" and that "brushless brush," that ink grown pale and that barely-painting brush, he paints between form and without-form and renders the evanescence of the foundational."[58]

If ontology "rests essentially on a gesture of assigning," Chinese painting is interested in for example "the wind" (present throughout Chinese thought, across different schools), which is unassignable.[59] Hence the importance of the sketch, in Chinese painting—but not only in Chinese painting. Much of Jullien's chapter titled "Theory of the Sketch" in *The Great Image* in fact focuses on Western art history and Western artists and lays bare how, there, the sketch has had a subterranean importance that risks to put the West's appreciation of the finished, completed work on shaky ground.

In both *The Great Image* and *Living Off Landscape*, the other name (in addition to ontology) that is most frequently given to Western thought is metaphysics. Consider Jullien's definition of it in *This Strange Idea*:

> If things are judged beautiful [in the Western tradition], it is because there exists "the beautiful" which renders them beautiful. In "the beautiful" as substantive, what is beautiful is no longer seen as related to anything other but is withdrawn into what becomes its substance . . . From what "is beautiful" to "the beautiful"—(European) philosophy was born from this added article and is promoted in its displacement.[60]

China, however, "projects no metaphysical 'beyond,' because it does not split the world (in the Platonic way) such that the intelligible (Being) in-forms the sensible, and such that the sensible amounts to a mere reflection of the intelligible."[61] Again and again, we are reminded that in Chinese thought, there is no metaphysical split.[62] Chinese thought sets metaphysics aside.[63] Consider what the metaphysical notion of the beautiful "obliterates": "process," "vital interactions."[64] It replaces those by an "Elsewhere,"[65] a metaphysically instigated "Ideal."[66] By focusing on the process of things, Chinese thought follows a completely different path: immanent, certainly, but not without spirituality. Metaphysics is the reason why, as Jullien puts it at the very beginning of *Silent Transformations*, "all that tirelessly occurs in front of us, that functions in such an effective way and is also obvious, remains unseen."[67] "Subject" needs to be replaced by "process."[68] This means we need to pass from the metaphysical and the ontological to the "taoique,"[69] as the translators somewhat awkwardly copy the French (why not taoic, as the translator of *The Great Image* suggests?[70]). Chinese landscape painting captures this approach and in that it needs to be considered in its divergence with Western art's obsession with the nude.

But what are the politics of this? Seen from the Western point of view, it seems that the post-exceptionalism of Chinese landscape painting begins to undermine not just the exceptionalism of Western thought but also the exceptionalism of its politics, specifically the exceptionalist concept of sovereignty that I have introduced in this study through the work of Carl Schmitt and that remains dominant in Western aesthetics even after postmodernism which declared the death of the author and celebrated the copy. But does that mean Chinese landscape painting is critical of sovereignty? As I've pointed out earlier, scholars have argued that the mountains in so-called monumental landscape painting in fact symbolize the emperor and their power. Jullien, of course, does not so much focus on the mountains but on the clouds, the mist, the fog that surrounds them—on the water, shui (水), that, in the Chinese word for landscape painting, shan shui (山水), is in fact combined with the character for mountain, shan (山), to name the full range of the paintings that Jullien studies. It is, indeed, from the element of water and its varied presence in Chinese landscape painting that Jullien draws his unexceptional reading of those works. Still, this does not fully remove us from the association with sovereignty: given in fact that when it comes to politics, sovereignty seems to have been in ancient China the only political game in town, it is difficult to accept that an entire philosophical thought and aesthetic tradition would have remained at odds with political reality. It seems much more likely, rather, that there was some continuity between philosophy, aesthetics, and politics.

That continuity, however, may not necessarily need to pass via the figure of the mountain as a symbol of sovereignty that can fairly easily be brought in line with the concept of sovereignty as it exists in the West; it may, indeed, also pass via the figure of water—and its related instantiations as clouds, mist, fog—in landscape painting.[71] This would entail thinking a sovereignty that operates otherwise, not in the exceptionalist, monumental ways that we may associate with the West and also with the mountain in Chinese landscape painting, but post-exceptionally, in the ways that water, given time, will undo any mountain. Water, indeed, is something like "the unmonumental," a term that already came up in my Chapter 1 and will return in my argument here from within the Western art historical tradition. Should the sovereign want to be like a mountain, or like water, one might ask (with a faint echo of Bruce Lee)? What different forms of power do these different figures—mountain, water—name? Rather than finding a simple comparative opposition then between the West and China, it is more likely that we are encountering diverging views of sovereignty here, and debates within both Western and Chinese painting whose complexity cannot be reduced to simply opposition.

Daoist Influences

While Jullien often claims to be speaking for "Chinese thought" at large—it's a generalization for which he has been criticized—one has to point out that in the books I have discussed in the previous sections, it is mostly daoism—the Ancient Chinese thought associated with Lao Zi and the text of the *Dao De Jing*—that is central to Jullien's thinking. It's worth noting from the get-go that while this text is ascribed to Lao Zi, literally "old master," it's unlikely that such an author ever existed. The name is probably a humorous reference to old master Kong—Kong Zi, also known as Confucius—to whose thought daoism related critically. The wisdoms collected in the *Dao De Jing* likely have multiple authors, a multiplicity that works well with how the thought collected in the book—adding up to a mere 5,000 words—seeks to go beyond exceptionalism. That is, at least, the argument that Jullien enables us to make about the text and about daoism at large, even if as I've already pointed out the ancient Chinese sages have also been associated with elitism.

An entire book could be written about the influence of daoism in Jullien's thought, but for reasons that will become clear later in this chapter as well as the remainder of this book, I focus only on the *Dao De Jing*'s chapter 41, from where Jullien takes the title of *The Great Image Has No Form*. It is this chapter that has been very influential in Jullien's thought, but also in some of the critical and creative work that I discuss in what follows. To give the reader unfamiliar with ancient Chinese philosophy a sense of its style, I reproduce the chapter in its entirety, in the translation by Roger Ames and David Hall (adding the Chinese characters whenever they are relevant for the discussion below):

> When the very best students learn of way-making (*dao*) [道]
> They are just barely able to keep to its center.
> When mediocre students learn of way-making
> They are sporadically on it and off it.
> When the very worst students learn of way-making
> They guffaw at the very idea.
> Were they not to guffaw at it
> It would be something less than way-making.

It is for this reason that in the *Established Sayings* we find it said:

> Radiant way-making seems obscured,
> Advancing way-making seems to be receding,
> Smooth way-making seems to have bumps,
> The highest character (*de*) [德] seems like a deep gorge,
> The most brilliant white seems sullied,
> The most broadminded character seems deficient,
> The most steadfast character seems dubious,
> The most pristine and authentic seems defiled.
> The greatest square has no corners,
> The greatest vessel is last to be attended to,
> The greatest sound is ever so faint,
> The greatest image has no shape [大象無形].

Way-making is so profuse as to be nameless (*wuming*) [無名],
It is only way-making that is as efficacious in the beginning of things
As it is in their completion.[72]

The first part of this chapter leads with the notion of dao, translated as "way-making." The translators' choice for the "-ing" form to translate dao instead of "path" or "course" nicely highlights the process-character and indeterminacy of dao (translators and scholars have indeed suggested that because of the importance of process here, it would be a mistake to speak of dao as "the" dao; for this reason, as this very chapter also shows, it does not make a lot of sense to ask what the dao "is"). Like much ancient Chinese writing, the first part of the chapter repeats a parallel structure, introducing three kinds of students ranked from best to worst, and it describes their experiences when learning of dao. The text dedicates the most lines to the worst students, although it's worth noting that in those lines the perspective shifts: from the students back to way-making ("it would be something less than way-making"). The focus therefore remains on Dao—not the students. If all of this seems to tease the question of what way-making is, again, one would have to point out that this is the wrong question.

This then leads into a second part, taken from the *Established Sayings* (it is unclear, as translators Ames and Hall explain in a footnote, whether this refers to an actual book that is no longer extant or whether this phrase should just be rendered as "wisdom sayings" in general, in other words not as the title of a book that once existed), which includes a series of what appear to be paradoxical formulations culminating in the famous line "the greatest image has no shape"—which Jullien, in a slightly different translation, uses for the title of his book. Here, too, important shifts occur in the English translation: from the use of the verb "seems" to the more affirmative "has," "is," "is" and "has." If at first, it seems the sayings combine terms that are clearly opposed—"most brilliant white" and "sullied," for example—by the end the opposition does not appear to be so clear (how are "image" and "no shape" opposed?).

The slight difference between Jullien's title and the Ames and Hall translation is worth noting because it avoids the (exceptionalist) superlative and instead opts for "great" (not "greatest," as Ames and Hall have it). That distinction is not marked in Chinese; it is a dimension—comparison—that is added by Ames and Hall. Jullien's translation makes one wonder about the validity of that addition, especially because it is not marked in the Chinese and especially because of the philosophical and political importance of the exceptionalism/post-exceptionalism problematic in Chinese thought. Dao, precisely, cannot be captured in a comparative or superlative. Some of chapter 41's formulations stand out specifically in the context of the materials that have been covered in this book: "Smooth way-making," the chapter recalls, "seems to have bumps";[73] "the most pristine and authentic seems defiled."[74] All of these formulations pull back an exceptional positive into a negative, unwork the exceptionalism of the positive into something a little less radiant, advancing, smooth, high, white, broadminded, et cetera. They un-monumentalize. The chapter ends by summarizing all of those formulations in the idea that dao is nameless or "wuming," a term that should be read as the culmination of the other negations that precede it. "Wuming" is one of the so-called "wu-forms" that are central to daoist thought (I will discuss another such wu-form, "wu wei," in the next chapter). Wu-forms are phrases, verbal or nominal, that combine the character "wu" (無), which marks a negation, with another character, for example "ming" (名), "name." If daoism is full of such wu-forms, it is because it is particularly fond of the no.[75] The daoist text known as the *Zhuangzi* is probably the most pronounced expression of that. A political consequence of this is that the dao does not operate according to the logic of the one. As Jullien puts it, "'great' means that which is open to both one and the other, that which does not exclude."[76]

The last four lines that are quoted in chapter 41 from the *Established Sayings* focus on a square, a vessel, sound, and image. They take the daoist wisdom to geometry (or architecture? they are not unrelated . . .) and the visual and performing arts, specifically sculpture, music, and painting. It seems that what is evoked here is a square so great that its corners would disappear. But great how? Large? Or great as in somehow superior? Is the great square's greatness merely a matter of size, or of some other quality—or perhaps better: capacity? If the latter, ought we to revisit the claim that I just made, namely that Jullien's use of "great" removes us from the exceptionalism of the superlative "the greatest"? Perhaps it is precisely the notion of "great" as being outside of classification altogether that names such exceptionalism. In that case, it would be reminiscent of Anselm Kiefer's claim, as discussed in my Introduction, that he is not an artist-as-aristocrat, because the word aristocrat refers to the idea of being "the best," and as an artist Kiefer considers himself rather to be outside of classification altogether. Indeed, Ames and Hall in their commentary on chapter 41 point out the "cultural elitism" of daoism.[77] Greatness appears to be thought in relation to infinity here—with the greatest vessel being the last one to be filled (because the infinite vessel cannot be filled?). A truly great sound—one that is everywhere?—is perhaps no longer heard. The greatest image, then, the one that somehow holds infinity within it, has no shape. Its shape does not determine infinity.

Jullien's question in his thinking about Chinese aesthetics was how to render daoist wisdom into painting, in other words, how to paint an image that has no shape. How to paint with the negative, if you will. The literati's brushwork, and their focus on clouds, fog, mist, or water took him in that direction. This is the direction of the undifferentiated, of what lies upstream from all actualization into separate identities. It is the direction of the hazy and the evanescent. Jullien associates this with determination rather than determination: it is the de-termination that renders the "term" in "determination"—a word associated with "sovereign power,"[78] Jullien notes—indistinct. What is great about the great square is that it

> cannot be restricted or compelled by what constitutes the particularity of its form. The square's form becomes emancipated from form instead of allowing the specifying-objectifying

> character of form to operate. We might ordinarily think that a square by virtue of its straight and prominent corners, rather than being completely rounded off, is of a nature to "cut sharply." But Wang Bi comments laconically, "square but not sharp. That is why it is without corners."[79]

Due to its interest in the indistinct, landscape painting becomes Jullien's central example in *The Great Image Has No Form* and elsewhere.

But one certainly does not need to stay limited to traditional painting to consider influences of daoist thought in Chinese art. One contemporary artist who has claimed to be influenced by daoism, and specifically the line "the greatest image is formless" is the Beijing-based artist Song Dong. In a short text about Song's work that was published on the occasion of the exhibition "The Allure of Matter" (shown at the Los Angeles County Museum of Art from 2019 until 2020), Nancy P. Lin starts with Song's "early fascination with the *Dao De Jing*" before quickly turning to the water-based works that Song started to develop around 1992. For Song, Lin notes,

> The transparent, formless and ephemeral qualities of water instantiate these Daoist notions of the ineffable; water's naturally occurring transitions between solid, liquid, vapor thus provide opportunities for artistic reflections on presence, absence, action, trace, and impermanence.[80]

It's worth emphasizing, as Lin does, that the water works all develop "at the intersection of performance, video, and conceptual art,"[81] because some of these elements will enter into a tension with the material of water and the daoist qualities that Song ascribes to it.

Consider, for example, "Stir-Fry Water," in which Song tries to stir-fry water: "Lasting only one minute and forty seconds, the video documentation is the only evidence of the work's existence."[82] Song's attempt "to treat water as a bounded concrete object"[83] obviously appeared futile—the work it produced is barely even there. Yet one should point out, as Lin does, that the video documentation operates as "a counterweight to the fugitive nature of water,"[84] and this is something that returns in Song's work. In "Water Diary," for example, Song records "his most intimate thoughts on a stone slab"[85] practicing calligraphy that uses clear water. "Song's brushstrokes leave only a brief trace," Lin writes, "quickly evaporating like an invisible ink that betrays none of the writer's secrets."[86] Yet here, too, there is documentation that adds a permanence that stands in tension with the work's absence.

Even more interesting for us is a work called "A Pot of Boiling Water." For it, "Song walked along an alleyway pouring a pot of boiling water":[87] "The water trail temporarily marked the artist's passage and later dissipated just as the artist himself disappeared from view."[88] Although this work might recall earlier, Western works like Edward Ruscha's series of paintings titled "Liquid Words" or Robert Smithson's "Asphalt Rundown" or "Glue Pour" (both from 1969), it's worth noting the very different effect of Song pouring hot, evaporating water, and for example of Smithson pouring asphalt or glue. Both Smithson's works and Song's work thrive in the formless, but Song's choice for the disappearing element of water delivers something much more ephemeral, much less exceptionalist, than Smithson's rather grand gestures of formlessness. That difference can also be marked by the ways in which landscape has figured in both artists' work. Smithson's work evidently leaves a trace on the landscape and that is, in a work of land art like "Spiral Jetty" for example, very much the point. Entropy may be the principle of Smithson's work, but Smithson did not want to condemn his work to "entropic destruction"—that would have defeated the purpose of making entropy visible.[89] In one of his other projects Song, by contrast, is stamping the water in a performance whose documentation—more specifically, whose staging as a landscape painting—evokes, rather, the ephemerality of the artist's gesture and highlights the unexceptionality that others have also found in landscape painting.

In "Pot of Boiling Water," Song's work and its documentation recalls the story that (as I discussed in the previous chapter) Byung-Chul Han found in Walter Benjamin, and that Benjamin himself claims to have found in China, about a painter who disappeared in his own work. Evidently, Song's interest in water is not only undermining the exceptionalism of the artwork but also of the artist himself. The contrast with Karl Ove Knausgaard's profile of Anselm Kiefer, or the attachment to the original work of art that enabled the Toporovski scandal at the Museum for Fine Arts in Ghent (both of which I discussed in my Introduction), is stark.

Now, as part of the continued critique of orientalism that I have been developing, specifically of a comparative approach that would construe "China" or "the Far East" in a simple opposition to each other, it's worth pointing out that in Jullien's work, the approach to art that is theorized there as "daoist" is very much represented in the history of Western art as well. In the titular chapter of his book *The Great Image Has No Form*, for example, Jullien in fact writes about *both* Chinese landscape painting *and* Western modern art. Guo Xi's point that when looking up towards a mountain, one does not see a single mountain, but that "the mountain seen from up close is 'so'; seen from farther away 'a different so'; and from a greater distance, 'yet another so.' As we move away, each 'so' is different and 'the form of the mountain alters with every step,'"[90] is anticipated earlier in the chapter in a discussion of how Picasso paints glasses: "Picasso, it appears, paints drinking glasses, even paints them exhaustively, without losing anything of them. He displays them from various angles: from the front and the side, from above and below, all at once."[91] "Why should this 'so,' emerging from the brush," Jullien asks in the sentence immediately preceding the one I just quoted, "come about only at the expense of other 'so's'? Why can it exist only by relegating all the others to the void?"[92] This is the issue that Jullien places at the center of Picasso's painting—but it is central to Chinese landscape painting as well. As he puts it in more philosophical terms at the beginning of the chapter: "How to conceive of and produce an image that is not limited by the individual (or better, individuating) character of form? Of any form, whatever it might be."[93] Clearly, these are not uniquely "Chinese" questions; indeed, they inform some of the most interesting works of modern art and approaches in Western thought (for example, the work of Gilbert Simondon).

At various points in the chapter "The Great Image Has No Form," Jullien offers the image of a stream to clarify the unexceptional approach to art that he seeks to put forward. Daoism invites us to move upstream in the conversation about form, to a situation where the difference that comes with individuation has not yet occurred. It's along those lines that one must appreciate the notion of "greatness" evoked in "the great image":

> "Great" means that which is open to both one and the other, that which does not exclude. This term interminably expresses

> the coexistence upstream from what, in coming into actuality, undergoes differentiation and comes to stand opposed to itself. "Great," in short, expresses the plenitude of compossibility. It is when "the great way" is "lost" that one begins to separate and specify [. . .].[94]

While Chinese landscape painting brings us close to such "greatness," in the chapter immediately following "The Great Image Has No Form," Jullien offers "the sketch" as an example of it as well. There, too, many of his examples are from the Western tradition: Picasso is quoted as criticizing the idea that any painting could ever be complete,[95] Van Gogh for rejecting paintings that are "overdone" as bad paintings—"true painters" instead might not finish their paintings.[96]

In a beautiful passage that ties this back to the Chinese tradition, one actually begins to sense connections between Jullien's "theory of the sketch"[97] and Edward Said's development of the notion of "late style"[98] after Theodor Adorno:

> Note that, as when the Chinese evoke the training painters undergo, it is the latest works attributed to the old masters that are at issue. After completing so many finished works that brought them renown, these masters declare their freedom and cast aside perfection and workshop norms. Now doing as they like, they paint only to paint, that is, to put the powers of painting to work once again, wishing each time that these powers will be even more radical. They do not paint to paint well, with everything that "well" implies in terms of the intolerable strictures imposed by diligent work. Having reached the pinnacle of his art, the painter confines himself to blotches or inventive, inchoative brushstrokes, ridding himself of all the extras: he will be careless about filling in. As Pliny says of Apelles: he knows how to "lift his hand from the painting." Did not Leonardo, who surpassed everyone else in the art of representation, also

> leave room for the *non finito* and for the *sfumato*, left indistinct? Even his *Mona Lisa* is unfinished.[99]

The sketch, which comes before the finished work that ends up in the gallery or the museum, thus reveals its affinity with a master's late works, the works bearing the mark of their late style, liberated from the "intolerable strictures" of "painting well." My discussion of this passage here as part of a critique of the continued dominance of the concept of sovereignty in Western art theory also invites us to consider the notion of late style within the framework of the criticism of sovereignty that Said's work—including for example his engagement with Jean Genet in *Late Style*, a chapter that is not so much focused on late style but on Genet's politics of betrayal in relation to the nation-state—develops. If, as Bruce Robbins has argued,[100] Said's notion of the secular needs to be read in tension with the political theology of the nation-state and in line with Said's criticism of nationalism, one can extend this argument to Said's notion of late style and consider how it too, like the notion of the unfinished in ancient Chinese painting and thought, needs to be understood as a secular concept critical of sovereignty: "I'd like to explore the experience of late style that involves the nonharmonious," as Said writes, "nonserene tension, and above all, a sort of deliberately unproductive productiveness going *against* . . . ."[101] Late style, in Said's paradoxical formulation that recalls my discussion of Laozi, is about "artistic lateness not as harmony and resolution but as intransigence, difficulty, and unresolved contradiction."[102] If that's articulated here as part of a style, it is also legible as a politics.

Moreover, while this applies at the level of Said's critique of the nation-state, it's worth pointing out that more fundamentally, the notion of the individual and its identity—the sovereignty of the individual and its identity, if you will—are in question here as well. Said's chapter about Genet which is situated in the center of his *Late Style* book even if it never mentions the notion of late style is focused entirely on identity and undermines imperialism as "the export of identity"[103]—even if it also acknowledges the identifications that were at work in Genet's critique of identity, for example his identification with the Algerians and the Palestinians as part of his struggle against French imperialism.[104]

Recall two examples from Jullien's chapter "The Great Image Has No Form" that I mentioned earlier on. When Picasso paints a glass, Jullien writes at the beginning of that chapter, he does not have to decide for any single perspective on the glass. Instead, Picasso paints drinking glasses "exhaustively, without losing any of them": "He displays them from various angles: from the front and the side, from above and below, all at once."[105] Jullien returns to this idea at the end of his chapter, where he discusses the claim by Guo Xi that when looking up at a mountain from up close, from farther away, and then again from a greater distance, you actually see different "so's" of a mountain—you see the mountain like this, like that, and like that. And with each perspective, indeed with each step, "the form of the mountain alters."[106] "'To paint the great image of the mountain is to deploy all these many so's,' without any excluding any other,"[107] Jullien writes following Guo. As a consequence, it is not possible to say that there is an individual mountain here; indeed, in Jullien's reading both Guo and Picasso go against the Western philosophical notion of the individual, of the sovereignty of the individual and its identity. Instead, the tao requires one to situate oneself before individuation has occurred, before the individual that is the result of individuation; it is not so much concerned with identity but with what comes before it.

If in Jullien's thought this is arguably a product of French universalism (although here we would have to acknowledge Jullien's own understanding of the universal as precisely not the uniform as which, these days, it is often cast), it is attributed here to ancient Chinese philosophy, specifically daoism. Such a critique of individualism can be found in other schools of ancient Chinese thought as well: Henry Rosemont Jr. for example has provided a study of Confucianism that is titled *Against Individualism*, in which this scholar of ancient China lays out a theory of the Confucian "relational person" to argue "that the belief in an essential individual self residing in each of us is an ontological fiction; a psychologically comforting (and/or frightening) fiction perhaps (like the belief in an immortal soul); but a fiction nevertheless."[108]

> At a very simple level we are tempted to think we each have something about us, something essential that makes us who we are and not anyone else. But attempting a description of that unique essence proves to be extremely difficult so long as we ignore the relatedness of human beings and think only of their purported aloneness. We encounter similar difficulties when we attempt to establish criteria in a social vacuum of what makes others uniquely what they are, even though we are almost always capable of doing so in specific cases.[109]

A little further in his book that leads to the following conclusion, tying such a Confucian theory of the individual (aspects of which are represented in Western thought as well, as Rosemont Jr. shows) back to the problematic of the sovereignty of the nation-state: "The political dimensions of a Confucianism . . . would be those of local community, not of the state"[110]—and

Rosemont Jr. is actually quoting Alasdair MacIntyre's take on Confucianism here.

In short, ancient Chinese philosophy makes not only the Western idea of the sovereign individual, but also the idea of the sovereign nation-state impossible. Moreover, it is incompatible with the ideology of capitalism which, as Rosemont Jr. points out,[111] is inextricably connected with the sovereign nation-state and the sovereign individual. The effects, then, of daoist wisdom, and by extension Said's notion of late style which resonates with daoist thought, are profound, reaching down from the sovereignty of the nation-state into the sovereignty of individual identity and capitalist economics.

The Not-So-Fine Arts and their Politics

Jullien may find an inclination towards the unfinished in Da Vinci, Van Gogh, and Picasso, but it is arguably prominently present in contemporary painting as well. Indeed, Rosalind Krauss—whose work I discussed previously in this book—and Yve-Alain Bois have perhaps most exhaustively documented this inclination in contemporary art (ranging, roughly from 1920 until the 1970s) in an exhibition inspired by George Bataille, and titled *Formless*.[112] However, and as with Benjamin's essay on the copy, it's as if this work never quite arrived, and so—in an ironic confirmation of Krauss' own point about the originality of the avant-garde—its main insights continue to be repeated, updated, and expanded, into the contemporary era.

Some years ago for example, Raphael Rubinstein published a noteworthy essay titled "Provisional Painting,"[113] in which he argued that there is a provisionality that characterizes the work of many contemporary painters—artists who have "made works that look casual, dashed-off, tentative, unfinished or self-cancelling." "In different ways, they all deliberately turn away from 'strong' painting for something that seems to constantly risk inconsequence or collapse." (Raoul De Keyser, Albert Oehlen, and Michael Krebber are his initial examples—but he has many more to back up his case.) Tracing such an attitude back to well-known figures in Western modern painting—Cézanne (one of Jullien's examples as well), Giacometti, Polke—as well as literary figures like Valéry (a poem is "never finished, only abandoned"; Giorgio Agamben, whose work I discussed earlier in this book, is very fond of this line as well and uses it in reference to his *Homo Sacer* series[114]) and Artaud ("no more masterpieces"), he also connects it to more contemporary phenomena like punk (Rubinstein mentions "punk's knowing embrace of the amateurish and fucked-up"). Richard Tuttle, Noël Dolla, Robert Rauschenberg, David Salle, and Martin Kippenberger are part of provisional art's genealogy: their work needs to be understood in part as "a struggle with a medium that can seem too invested in permanence and virtuosity, in carefully planned out compositions and layered meanings, in artistic authority and creative strength, in all the qualities that make the arts 'fine.'" The not-so-fine-arts, then: that is what provisional painters are interested in.

It's worth noting the ethical and political overtones of some of Rubinstein's descriptions. De Keyser's paintings "[forfeit] 'heroic' ambitions even before the first mark is made"; Rubinstein points out "he works in a manner so low-key that even sympathetic critics can be unsure how to evaluate his paintings": we are somewhere between "deliberation and indecision" (according to Roberta Smith, whom Rubinstein quotes); with respect to these paintings, "The sense of doubt never quite goes away" (Barry Schwabsky). These are, then, explicitly *non-sovereign* paintings, where the very mastery of the painter is in question. The works are not smooth, to recall the terminology of my earlier chapters; one critic compares De Keyser's paintings to "stuttering," as Rubinstein notes. It's a reference that recalls the work of Gilles Deleuze and it sets up Rubinstein's theoretical framing of provisional painting at the very end of his text through the lens of Deleuze and Felix Guattari's work on minor literature. Provisional painting is painting in the minor mode. Unexceptional, as I would have it.

At one point in Rubinstein's text, "Chinese ink painting" comes up, but the reference is not developed. It's merely used to characterize Michael Krebber's paintings, which demonstrate a hastiness that according to Rubinstein "seems closer to a prostitute's hurried coupling than to the rapid elegance of a Chinese ink painting." Still, the reference is interesting, because its context indicates that we are not in some post-critical universe here: Rubinstein clearly distinguishes between different kinds of hasty work—some bad, some good (Rubinstein ends his piece, by the way, with a discussion of how "At times, provisional painting overlaps with 'bad painting,' a mode with roots in the 1970s that continues to offer artists means of engaging the medium without having to take on all of its unwanted trappings"; in addition, there is painting that is, quite simply, bad, in other words: that does not even rise to the established mode of "bad painting"). Noting that Krebber's 2004 show at Dépendance gallery in Brussels was titled "Unfinished Too Soon," Rubinstein eventually ties Krebber's attitude to a few lines from Marianne Moore: "I, too, dislike it, / Reading it, however, with a perfect contempt for it, / One discovers in / It, after all, a place for the genuine." This too projects us back into earlier parts of this book: Moore's line "I, too, dislike it" happens to be the leitmotiv of Ben Lerner's *The Hatred of Poetry*,[115] a book that suggests poetry is hated because it cannot live up to the poetic idea/ideal that any poetry inevitably betrays as it is written down. Indeed, we are not too far removed here from some of the concerns that drive Lerner's work on art vandalism: actually existing poetry always does violence to the virtual ideal of poetry. Thus, Lerner distinguishes—after Allen Grossman (after Gilles Deleuze after G. W. F. Hegel)—between the "'virtual' poem'—what we might call poetry with a capital 'P,' the abstract potential of the medium as felt by the poet when called upon to sing" and "'the actual poem,' which necessarily betrays that impulse when it joins the world of representation."[116]

Moreover, we seem to find exactly the same idea in the second chapter of the *Zhuangzi*, when the text references "Mr. Zhao" both playing and not playing the lute. As translator Burton Watson in a note explains, tying this idea to the problematic of injury that was central to the first part of this book as well: "Zhao Wen was a famous lute (qin) player. But the best music he could play (i.e., complete) was only a pale and partial reflection of the ideal music, which was thereby injured and impaired."[117] Provisional painting, then, is painting that is aware of the injury that it brings to the ideal. It's important to observe, however, that I am referencing here a note by Burton Watson, and that I am not quoting from the original text: one might, for that reason, want to cast some suspicion on the distinction that Watson introduces between "the music that Zhao Wen can play" and "ideal music"—a metaphysical distinction that, within the framework of Jullien's thought, might strike one as very Western. Indeed, when Brook Ziporyn translates the very same passage that, in Watson, is about Zhao playing and not playing the lute, Ziporyn instead foregrounds the process in both playing and not playing the lute, where not playing silently transforms into playing and vice versa:

> What set the Course to waning was exactly what brought the cherishing of one thing over another to its fullness.
>
> But is there really any waning versus fullness? Or is there really no such thing as waning versus fullness? In a certain sense, there exists waning versus fullness. In that sense, we can say that the Zhaos are zither players. But in a certain sense, there is no such thing as waning versus fullness. In that sense, we can say, on the contrary, that the Zhaos are no zither players.[118]

Here the point is not so much to distinguish between actual and virtual, or music one can play and ideal music, but to break down the contrast between playing and not playing and focus on how the one is constantly emerging from the other. This seems closer to Chinese thought. It's not so much that injury wounds the ideal—a thinking about injury that would work within a metaphysical split between real and ideal—but that the imperfect and the perfect, the empty and the full, are constantly turning into each other, with injury becoming ideal and vice versa; and this would be an interesting way to restate Lerner's problematic of the actual poem versus the virtual poem as well, moving away from this Western metaphysical split towards a "Chinese" conception of poetry.

To draw out further the connections to ancient Chinese thought in Rubinstein's text, it's worth noting that through a reference to Miró's "rejection of the idea of a finished, durable work"—Rubinstein includes the painter's confession that "after completing a painting he had his dealer take it away as quickly as possible," a confession that recalls an anecdote about Noah

Davis, the painter I mentioned in my first chapter, overpainting new work more quickly than his friends were able to come see it—Rubinstein even embarks on a discussion of "greatness" in his essay. Rubinstein asks in particular: "what makes 'great' painting impossible?" While this question makes sense within the Western tradition, the issue can be reflected differently from the Chinese side as a question about how to maintain that impossibility in painting. In other words, seen from the Chinese side, great painting is painting that paints this impossibility.

Rubinstein seems to have realized as much in his later work on provisional painting, which culminated in an exhibition titled "Provisional Painting" at Modern Art in London in 2011.[119] Summarizing his curatorial vision there, Rubinstein ends up quoting the *Dao De Jing*: "The greatest straightness looks like crookedness. The greatest skill appears clumsy. The greatest eloquence sounds like stammering." Provisional painting, then, becomes a way of asserting within the Western tradition, through contemporary painting, a wisdom that was at the heart of Chinese thought and painting in the sixth century BC—and this is one crucial expansion that Rubinstein brings to Krauss' and Bois' Western framework. This connection to Chinese thought and painting is further confirmed in Rubinstein's follow-up essay, published in 2012, where the connection to Chinese thought is again explicitly made (he references and quotes from François Cheng's book *Empty and Full*).[120] "How curious," Rubinstein writes in this second piece, "that the prospect of leaving a work intentionally unfinished remained controversial in Western aesthetics some 10 centuries after its virtues had been recognized in Chinese painting, and some four centuries after Michelangelo's ambiguous embrace of the non finite." I could not agree more.

This point about "the new" has been put in sharp relief by Leah Kalmanson, who focuses on connections between the work of Steven Shaviro and Jane Bennett and the Chinese tradition (which remains unacknowledged in these thinkers' books). Kalmanson does not only do important philosophical work in her article but also intervenes politically by arguing against "academic practices that continue to define the 'new' on Eurocentric models alone."[121] Art history can certainly be included in the charge. "In picking her way through the thicket of materialism and vitalism in Western thought," Kalmanson writes, "Bennett has unknowingly veered close to strands of Ruism [the Chinese scholarly tradition] whose roots are in China's Song dynasty and whose branches extend throughout East Asia."[122] No one can, of course, be a specialist of everything; but Kalmanson's criticism is that when such work in the Western tradition characterizes itself or gets characterized as "new," the "new" only applies within a Western perspective, and holds up only within a Eurocentric model of thought.

Kalmanson argues, for example, that the critical engagement with Kant's philosophy in speculative materialism/realism is entirely anticipated in a Chinese tradition of thinking that far predates the work of those major new names associated with that development in European thought. When Shaviro writes that the "speculative aesthetics" he is interested in "is still to be constructed,"[123] Kalmanson points out that it can already be found "fully developed" in "Song-Ming Ruism";[124] in other words, that Shaviro's claim about such an aesthetic "still [needing to] be constructed" only applies in a Western context. It is perhaps the role of Alfred North Whitehead's work and process philosophy in general in some of the work associated with speculative realism/materialism that provides the most obvious grounds for this suspicion, since there is a well-developed body of scholarship on the connections between Whitehead and Chinese thought that is worth pursuing.[125] In this book, we've thus seen amply illustrated a perceptive observation already made by Jonathan Hay: that Western art's thinking about the fake is determined by its Eurocentrism.[126] All the more reason, then, to decenter that thought.

Foregrounding the provisional, or what with the already discussed Julio García Espinosa we may call the imperfect, is key to such a project. Although scholars like Edward Said or Hito Steyerl may need to do a lot of work to foreground—or, in Steyerl's language, "defend"—notions like "late style" or "the poor image" within the framework of Western thought, one thing that the focus on daoism in this chapter has made clear is that the Chinese tradition of thought has been much closer to such notions. To say this, once again, does not mean to oppose those traditions of thought following a logic of difference. Following Jullien, I am merely foregrounding diverging tendencies not just between those traditions but also within them, based on a variety of sources that I have consulted in each. To say this also does not mean that the Chinese tradition of thought realizes, for example, the full aspirations of a project like Steyerl's, or Said's, or Espinosa's. I have mentioned for example how Chinese wisdom, and the sages, have been criticized for being "elitist"—but elitism is of course precisely what Espinosa's emphasis on imperfect cinema targets. Espinosa's essay is relentless in its targeting of the elitism of film schools, film-makers, and films, and Steyerl continues that in her own project. Said could be criticized, perhaps, for developing his notion of late style through what is by and large an elitist and predominantly European canon—even if a figure like Jean Genet, part of Said's work on late style, of course falls outside of that. In all of these references, however, we find what one might call a reservation about the Western philosophical, aesthetic, and political framework that expresses itself as a practice of "poverty," "lateness," or "imperfection."

If the commitment to provisionality that is shared here, across these Western references but also with ancient Chinese thought, poses a challenge to the Western concept of sovereignty, as I have suggested, it is worth asking how it can have coexisted, in ancient China, with a concept of sovereignty that has remained dominant in China until today. In other words, if the discussion of ancient Chinese thought that I have provided here somehow found elements in that thought that undermined the Western concept of sovereignty, why is it that those elements did not make the concept of sovereignty *impossible* in China, in the same way that according to Jullien ancient Chinese thought made the emergence of the nude in Chinese art history *impossible*? Given the exceptionalism of Western thought, it is perhaps no wonder that the central concept of Western politics is exceptionalist as well—how could it have been otherwise? But if we then find post-exceptionalism in Chinese thought, and note for example its force in aesthetics (given the absence of the nude), why is it that it has not had the same force in politics? How has the concept of sovereignty been able to coexist with it? Those questions, which I already began to articulate elsewhere, will be central to the third and final part of this book, which will continue my investigation of the vandal and the forger through a focus on the figure of the sage and its related politics.

Notes

1 Tobin Siebers, *Disability Aesthetics* (Ann Arbor: University of Michigan Press, 2010), p. 2.
2 Siebers, *Disability Aesthetics*, p. 3.
3 Ibid.
4 Bob Dylan, *Rough and Rowdy Ways* [music album] (Columbia Records, 2020).
5 François Jullien, *The Impossible Nude: Chinese Art and Western Aesthetics*, trans. Maev de la Guardia (Chicago, IL: The University of Chicago Press, 2007), p. vii.
6 Jullien, *Impossible Nude*, p. vii.
7 Ibid., p. 36.
8 Ibid., p. 4.
9 Ibid., p. 7.
10 Ibid.
11 Jullien critically appropriates this association of blandness with China from Roland Barthes. See: François Jullien, *In Praise of Blandness: Proceeding from Chinese Thought and Aesthetics*, trans. Paula Varsano (New York: Zone Books, 2008).
12 I am thinking in particular of Becky Kolsrud, whose work I discussed at length in: *Against Aesthetic Exceptionalism* (Minneapolis: University of Minnesota Press, 2019).
13 Wen Fong, "The Problem of Forgeries in Chinese Painting: Part One," *Artibus Asiae* 25:2/3 (1962), pp. 95–119, pp. 121–140, here p. 104.
14 Fong, "Problem of Forgeries," p. 104.
15 I thank my former graduate student and research assistant Ling Tiong for drawing my attention to this. Ling's own work about the politics of the clouds in Chinese landscape painting will have much to say about this point.
16 François Jullien, *This Strange Idea of the Beautiful*, trans. Krzystof Fijalkowski and Michael Richardson (London: Seagull, 2016), p. 219.
17 Jullien, *This Strange Idea*, p. 219.
18 Ibid.
19 Ibid.
20 Hito Steyerl, too, is onto this when at the end of her text on the poor image, she notes the return of a different kind of "aura" in relation to the political community that the poor image creates (Hito Steyerl, "In

Defense of the Poor Image," *e-flux* 10 [2009], p. 42, accessible: https://www.e-flux.com/journal/10/61362/in-defense-of-the-poor-image/). This might explain Steyerl's seemingly erroneous use of the terms cult value and exhibition value in the opening paragraphs of her text. There, Steyerl suggests that with the poor image, cult value takes over from exhibition value, but within the logic of terms that she lays out there—a logic that clearly preferences terms associated with Benjamin's theory of the copy over the original—such a preference for cult value makes no sense. *Unless* Steyerl means to evoke here the new cult value that the poor image creates . . . . This would be a subtle point, to be sure, for the very attentive reader.

21 Jullien, *This Strange Idea*, p. 220.
22 Ibid., p. 221.
23 Ibid.
24 Ibid.
25 Ibid.
26 François Jullien, *The Silent Transformations*, trans. Krzystof Fijalkowski and Michael Richardson (London: Seagull, 2011), p. 62.
27 Jullien, *Silent Transformations*, p. 65.
28 Ibid., p. 67.
29 Ibid., p. 95.
30 Ibid., p. 116.
31 Ibid., p. 126.
32 Ibid., p. 122.
33 Ibid., p. 121.
34 Ibid., p. 119.
35 Ibid., p. 122.
36 Ibid., p. 126.
37 Abdelkebir Khatibi, *Class Warrior—Taoist Style*, trans. Matt Reeck (Middletown, CT: Wesleyan University Press, 2017).
38 Sam Coombs has in his book on Glissant explored the Jullien/Glissant connection: Sam Coombs, *Édouard Glissant* (London: Bloomsbury, 2018).
39 Arne De Boever, *François Jullien's Unexceptional Thought: A Critical Introduction* (New York: Rowman & Littlefield, 2020). See chapter 1.
40 François Jullien, *Living Off Landscape or the Unthought-of in Reason*, trans. Pedro Rodriguez (London: Rowman & Littlefield, 2018), p. 32.
41 Jullien, *Living Off Landscape*, p. 32.
42 Jullien, *This Strange Idea*, p. 35.

43 François Jullien, *The Great Image Has No Form, or On the Nonobject through Painting*, trans. Jane Marie Todd (Chicago, IL: University of Chicago Press, 2009), p. 7.
44 Jullien, *The Great Image*, p. 3.
45 Ibid.
46 Ibid., p. xv.
47 Ibid., p. 10.
48 Jullien, *Impossible Nude*, pp. 36, 61.
49 Jullien, *This Strange Idea*, p. 60.
50 Jullien, *The Great Image*, p. 18.
51 Ibid., p. 19.
52 Ibid.
53 Ibid., p. 21.
54 François Jullien, *L'écart et l'entre* (Paris: Galilée, 2012), p. 52.
55 Jullien, *The Great Image*, p. 21.
56 Ibid., p. 32.
57 Ibid., p. 33.
58 Ibid., p. 35.
59 Ibid., p. 41.
60 Jullien, *This Strange Idea*, p. 9.
61 Jullien, *Living Off Landscape*, p. 31.
62 See ibid., p. 71.
63 See Jullien, *The Great Image*, p. 13.
64 Jullien, *This Strange Idea*, p. 35.
65 Ibid., p. 43.
66 Ibid., p. 47.
67 Jullien, *Silent Transformations*, p. 1.
68 Ibid., p. 6.
69 Ibid., p. 34.
70 Jullien, *The Great Image*, p. 23.
71 This is the intuition that informs my former student Ling Tiong's work.
72 Roger Ames and David Hall, eds., *Dao De Jing: "Making This Life Significant" (A Philosophical Translation)*, trans. Roger Ames and David Hall (New York: Ballantine Books, 2003), pp. 140–141.
73 Ames and Hall, *Dao De Jing*, p. 140.
74 Ibid., p. 141.
75 If the term "post-exceptionalism" were to be rendered into Chinese, it may need to be through a wu-form. Jullien himself has captured much of

what I am interested in with the notion of the post-exceptional through his focus on the term "bland," *dan* [淡].

76 Jullien, *The Great Image*, p. 51.
77 Ames and Hall, *Dao De Jing*, p. 141.
78 Jullien, *The Great Image*, p. 63.
79 Ibid., p. 48.
80 Nancy P. Lin, "Song Dong: Water," in: Wu Hung, ed., *The Allure of Matter: Material Art from China* (Chicago, IL: Smart Museum, 2019), pp. 187–191, here p. 187.
81 Lin, "Song Dong," p. 187.
82 Ibid.
83 Ibid.
84 Ibid.
85 Ibid., p. 188.
86 Ibid.
87 Ibid.
88 Ibid.
89 Yve-Alain Bois and Rosalind Krauss, *Formless: A User's Guide* (New York: Zone Books, 1999), p. 188.
90 Jullien, *The Great Image*, p. 55.
91 Ibid., p. 44.
92 Ibid.
93 Ibid., p. 43.
94 Ibid., p. 51.
95 Ibid., p. 59.
96 Ibid., p. 62.
97 Ibid., p. 61.
98 Edward Said, *On Late Style: Music and Literature Against the Grain* (New York: Pantheon, 2006).
99 Jullien, *The Great Image*, p. 62. This description of the old masters is confirmed, for example, in: Jerome Silbergeld, "Chinese Concepts of Old Age and Their Role in Chinese Painting. Painting Theory and Criticism," *Art Journal* 46:2 (1987), pp. 103–144.
100 See: Bruce Robbins, *Feeling Global: Internationalism In Distress* (New York: New York University Press, 1999).
101 Said, *Late Style*, p. 7.
102 Ibid.
103 Ibid., p. 85.
104 Ibid., p. 86.

105 Jullien, *The Great Image*, p. 44.
106 Ibid., p. 55.
107 Ibid.
108 Henry Rosemont Jr., *Against Individualism: A Confucian Rethinking of the Foundations of Morality, Politics, Family, and Religion* (New York: Lexington Books, 2015), p. 50.
109 Rosemont Jr., *Against Individualism*, p. 50.
110 Ibid., p. 62.
111 Ibid., p. 72.
112 Bois and Krauss, *Formless*.
113 Raphael Rubinstein, "Provisional Painting," *Art in America* May 1 (2009), accessible: https://www.artnews.com/art-in-america/features/provisional-painting-raphael-rubinstein-62792/
114 Giorgio Agamben, *The Use of* Bodies, trans. Adam Kotsko (Stanford, CA: Stanford University Press, 2014).
115 Ben Lerner, *The Hatred of Poetry* (New York: Farrar, Straus, and Giroux, 2016).
116 Lerner, *Hatred*, p. 9.
117 Zhuangzi, *The Complete Works of Zhuangzi*, trans. Burton Watson (New York: Columbia University Press, 2013), n8 p. 12.
118 Zhuangzi, *The Essential Writings*, trans. Brook Ziporyn (Indianapolis, IN: Hackett, 2009), p. 15.
119 Raphael Rubinstein, "Provisional Painting Part Two: To Rest Lightly On Earth," *Art in America* February 3 (2012), accessible: https://www.artnews.com/art-in-america/features/provisional-painting-part-2-62924/
120 See: https://contemporaryartdaily.com/2011/05/provisional-painting-at-modern-art/
121 Leah Kalmanson, "Speculation as Transformation in Chinese Philosophy: On Speculative Realism, 'New' Materialism, and the Study of Li and Qi," *Journal of World Philosophies* 3 (Summer 2018), pp. 17–30, here p. 17.
122 Kalmanson, "Speculation as Transformations," p. 21.
123 Shaviro qtd. Kalmanson, "Speculation as Transformation," p. 23.
124 Ibid., p. 23.
125 See, for example: Fan Meijun and Wang Zhihe. "Toward a Complementary Consciousness and Mutual Flourishing of Chinese and Western Cultures: The Contributions of Process Philosophers," *Philosophy East & West* 65:1 (2015), pp. 276–297. But there are many other articles.
126 Jonathan Hay, "Editorial: The Value of Forgery," *Anthropology and Aesthetics* 53/54 (2008), pp. 5–14.

Part III

The Sage

5

Post-Exceptionalism as Political Formalism

Critique of the Sage

After the vandal and the forger, we have now arrived at the third figure that structures this book: the Chinese sage. Presented here specifically in its tension with the Western "philosopher,"[1] as the representative of a thought—ancient Chinese thought—that stands in tension with Western—Greek—philosophy, the sage marks a coherent thinking that is nevertheless not Western. I have suggested, here and elsewhere, that this "not," or the "tension" between the sage's thought and that of the Western philosopher, can be captured as the tension between post-exceptional thought and Western exceptionalism. The sage's thought, and in particular the daoist sage's thought which I have focused on, revolves around process and the provisional; Western thought, by and large, is about the event and the sovereignty of the finished. I write "by and large" because Western thought is of course haunted by figures who have challenged those core features: Gilbert Simondon, for example, insisted upon the process of individuation against the sovereign figure of the individual.[2] Byung-Chul Han has characterized Jacques Derrida's deconstructive thought as "Chinese."[3] The phenomenologist

Maurice Merleau-Ponty features prominently in François Jullien's chapter "The Great Image Has No Form" for offering a theory of perception that resonates with the thought that Jullien finds in Chinese landscape painting.[4] Some, like Stathis Gourgouris, would no doubt question whether what I present as core features of Western thought are indeed central to that tradition: Gourgouris' reading of ancient Greek philosophy seems to bring the roots of Western thought in close proximity to ancient Chinese thinking.[5]

Working within these rough outlines, then, and aware of the problems posed not only by generalization but by orientalist approaches that all too easily oppose "China" to "the West," I have nevertheless tried to think through the relations between thought, art, and politics between these divergent traditions, suggesting that specificities of thought may be reflected in specific artistic practices (and tendencies in art that can become clear over time, in art history) and even specific political formations (ways of conceiving power and practicing specific forms of government). While much of that project has operated within what I perceive to be a tension between China and the West, the sage as the most "Chinese" of my three figures immediately breaks down the understanding of such tension as simple opposition, because there is clearly an exceptionalism associated with the figure of the sage. If we stick only with the daoist sage, who entered upon the scene of this book in the previous chapter, Roger Ames and David Hall draw out in their translation and commentary of chapter 41 of Laozi's *Dao De Jing*—the very chapter that I focused on in this book's Part II—the sage's "cultural elitism" and tie it back to "classical Confucianism."[6] In other words: if the sage features here as a figure of post-exceptional thought, it does so not so much in opposition to exceptionalism but with a prominent trace of exceptionalism within it. Like the forger and the vandal, then, the sage operates in this book as a critical figure, one whose relations to exceptionalism and post-exceptionalism need to be critically negotiated—exactly as I have done previously with forgers like Zhang Daqian, Han van Meegeren, or Elmyr de Hory, or artist-vandals like Marcel Duchamp or Banksy.

Critique will in fact be prominently featured in the two chapters that comprise the book's third part, first in a chapter that considers the politics of post-exceptionalism—what I call, specifically, post-exceptionalism's political formalism—and then also in a chapter that through two established case-studies (one by Bianca Bosker, on architecture, and another by Winnie Wong, on painting) revisits several of the claims previously made in this book. In this chapter, I continue the discussion of the daoism-influenced artist Song Dong's work in Chapter 4, by considering one of his more political works, *Traceless Stele*. Situating this work, which in its very title reveals itself to be inspired by the wisdom of the sages, between the criticism of exceptionalism and its preservation, this chapter highlights post-exceptionalism's political dimension—in *Traceless Stele*, its realization as an art of the smooth that ultimately leaves sovereignty intact and can be said to operate in tandem with it, even as part of a single practice of aesthetico-political power. This reading invites something I have been hinting at in the preceding pages, namely a deeper inquiry into the particular politics that post-exceptionalism names. So far, much of this book's energies have been spent on demonstrating what kind of politics post-exceptionalism is against; this chapter, however, seeks to articulate positively the politics of post-exceptionalism, and specifically the risks that it entails. If I pursue such a project first and foremost to extend my thinking about post-exceptionalism, this chapter will also further my understanding of the political form of sovereignty that has been central to my work.

Ultimately, I am interested in this chapter in articulating post-exceptionalism as a political formalism; that is, as a political practice that advocates what I have previously discussed as "the ideal of form" in markedly material ways, thereby breaking down the distinction between form and the formless. After the discussion of Song's work *Traceless Stele*, I will lay out such an approach in part with reference to my own book *Plastic Sovereignties* (2016), but especially through a detailed discussion of political formalism in two works of literary scholarship, namely Caroline Levine's *Forms* (2015) and Anna Kornbluh's closely related *The Order of Forms* (2019). Both books diagnose the tension between form and formlessness in contemporary criticism, the tendency towards a politics of the formless in contemporary thought, and seek to defend the importance of form as life-enabling rather than as antithetical to life. They analyze a present torn between what Tobin Siebers understands to be the project of art vandalism—to "breach aesthetic form"[7]—and Hao Jingfang's imperative, in her science-fiction novel *Vagabonds*, to "*Care about the form of the world*."[8] While those approaches relate to a discussion about art more generally, beyond the strict confines of the Victorian literature that both those scholars consider, they also pertain to the debate about sovereignty as a political form that I opened up in *Plastic Sovereignties* and continue to pursue here as part of a question about the politics of unexceptional art. In the words of Emily Apter in *Unexceptional Politics*, this chapter seeks to demonstrate how through the vandal, the forger, and the sage I unexceptionalize what Apter calls "transcendent modes of the Political" and articulate instead "a 'small p' politics . . . that defines distinct modes of acting and articulating politically that evolve and mutate"[9]—in other words, that are plastic, plural, unexceptional, yet formal. It is along those exact same lines that I have sought to rethink here our thinking about artists and art.

Politics of Daoism

The work by Song Dong that was included in the show "The Allure of Matter: Material Art in China" at LACMA was titled *Traceless Stele*. It stands in some contrast to Song's private water diary, which I discussed in the previous chapter:

> In this work, Song invites the public to draw or write on the blank stele using brush and water from the trough at its base. A hidden heating device speeds up the evaporation of the water marks, returning the stele to its blank state.[10]

While the word "stele" is Greek, the work needs to be situated very much within Chinese history. Its inspiration, Lin notes, was the so-called "wordless stele" ("wu-zi bei" [無字碑], in Chinese—and I have already highlighted the importance of the character "wu" [無] in daoist thought), "a Tang dynasty monument for Empress Wu Zetian that was left without inscriptions."[11] Song's *Traceless Stele*, however, "functions as a counter-monument," as Nancy P. Lin points out: "Instead of reaffirming authority and single-authorship, the work invites all members of the public to participate."[12] Lin is clearly inscribing Song's work in a thought that is critical of exceptionalist sovereignty, pointing out how the work seeks to undermine such a form of power. "Rather than asserting permanence," she continues, this work "evokes the ephemerality of words and deeds; and in place of a single didactic message, it is open to new commentary and interpretations."[13]

Yet Lin is also aware that ultimately, something about this critique does not work: while the stele is a work that promotes "free expression and subversive critique,"[14] that critique is also expressed as quickly evaporating messages written in water, and so the stele ends up appearing as a figure of authority that "is shown to be immune to all critique."[15] It ends up, to return to the terms developed earlier in this book, looking quite smooth.

This is the precise point where the question of the politics of daoism, and by extension of post-exceptionalism, opens up—a complicated question that I can hardly pretend to be able to answer. Still, it is worth pointing out a couple of key things. When Ames and Hall comment on the already discussed chapter 41 of the *Dao De Jing*, they associate it with political "anarchism."[16] It is unclear what they mean by this exactly, perhaps especially because earlier in the book they also insist that "the *Daodejing* still assumes the need for a hierarchical political structure, with rulers above and the common people below."[17] There is, as I have already indicated, cultural elitism in daoism; chapter 41 begins by distinguishing between the very best students, mediocre students, and the very worst students—so it clearly maintains a sense of hierarchy.

Based on a reading of the *Dao De Jing* as well as Confucius' *Analects* and other texts of Confucianist and daoist thought, one can conclude that the idea here is that within the hierarchy of power, "the ruler above" acts virtuously—virtue is captured by the character "de" [德] in chapter 41—so that the ruler's subjects (the common people below) will *imitate* such virtuous behavior, and all will be well in the state. It is, in other words, a political order that rests on *both* the exceptionalist, sovereign status of the ruler acting virtuously, *and* the unexceptional commoners *copying* such virtuous behavior. Governing in this way is considered to be much more effective than the typically sovereign rule through law and punishment. It exercises sovereign control, but it is nevertheless subtly—yet crucially—different from sovereignty, a difference that I attribute to Chinese thought's post-exceptionalism and the crucial presence of the practice of copying in the political order just described.

Importantly, we are talking about a very specific kind of copying here: one that, in its motivation to act virtuously, must nevertheless be original and real—*it can not be mere performance.*[18] Daoism in particular harshly criticizes the hollowed-out performance of ritual. It was, in fact, one of the key issues for which it took Confucianism to task, arguing that much of Confucianism ultimately became meaningless ritual. (The criticism can be summed up by the story about Confucius refusing to sit down unless his mat was perfectly straight.)

One thing is certain: we are by no means in the anarchist understanding of democracy that Stathis Gourgouris, whose work I referenced in my Introduction, has articulated in his thought about unexceptional politics. Gourgouris is interested, rather, in a regime where the people alternate the role of ruling and being ruled—a regime that is autonomous in the sense that the rule that the people follow is one that they gave to themselves. The Chinese distinction between the ruler above and the people below does not exist here: instead, Gourgouris' unexceptional understanding of democracy—derived from Aristotle—has a flattening effect on such a hierarchy. Gourgouris can characterize such an understanding of democracy as anarchic because its rule is radically shared, and not experienced as a heteronomous command. When I follow the law, I am simply following the law that I have given to myself. Such a thought is, in Gourgouris' view, anti-monarchical. "*[A]narchy*," he writes, "*is the* arche *of democracy*."[19]

The fact that the stele, ultimately, appears to be immune to critique could be read as a marker of the remainder of sovereign power in daoist thought. Still, Song's work also participates in the post-exceptionalist dimension of such thought and the criticism of sovereignty that it exercises. If it contains a remainder of sovereignty, it is clearly a sovereignty that operates otherwise, not so much through law and punishment but through a kind of "trickle-down morality" (the copying of virtue) and the observance of ritual—through rites rather than laws.

Within Western thought, this recalls aspects of the kind of power that Michel Foucault in *The History of Sexuality: Vol. 1* called biopolitical: a power that operates not so much through laws but norms, disposing of things and spaces in such a way that people's freedom becomes a mere correlative of power.[20] Unlike sovereign power, governmental and biopolitical power is everywhere: it seeps through the most intimate aspects of one's life. Foucault allowed us to understand it as the micropolitics of sexuality, or also of race—two aspects of human life that the state, as Foucault shows, becomes progressively more interested in. If sovereign power thought of the body as a tomb for the soul, and sought to govern the soul by seizing the body (following the ancient Greek "soma sèma" adage), modern power understood that it is in fact the other way around: it is the soul that is a tomb for the body, and in order to truly control the body, one needs to control the soul. For that, rites—not laws—are crucial.

It's worth noting that this other type of power, the one Foucault calls governmental and associates with biopolitics, has also been understood as neoliberal, in the sense that it is a power that operates not so much by sidestepping sovereignty entirely—neoliberalism and sovereignty are not opposites, as scholars have shown—but by making strategic use of it, by allowing just as much as it needs of it to get its policies realized or enforced. Power, in this model, is exercised not so much by elected officials who have the people's support, but by non-elected petty sovereigns who are representatives of international capital. This is the *contemporary* dynamic of exceptionalist sovereignty and what Michael Hardt and Antonio Negri called "empire,"[21] two forms of power—sovereignty more formal than empire, to be sure—between which one doesn't have to choose but whose dynamic relationship contemporary politics requires us to chart. Between exceptionalist sovereignty and the risk of authoritarianism and a neoliberalism that is often conceptualized as flattening the relief of sovereignty, there has emerged something like "authoritarian neoliberalism" or "neoliberal authoritarianism"[22] that follows the imperatives of both. In the language I have developed in this book, it's exceptionalism and post-exceptionalism at the same time.

Rephrasing this theory of contemporary power in the language of exceptionalism and post-exceptionalism, however, draws out post-exceptionalism's potential association with neoliberalism—due to the challenge to sovereignty's relief that post-exceptionalism brings. (It's worth noting in this context that some work has been done on daoism's connections to neoliberalism—indeed the typical association of daoism to political anarchism has undergone an expansion towards the neoliberal in recent years.) This political approach to post-exceptionalism can be associated with my investigation of the smooth (and smooth art's close connections to economic value[23]) earlier on in this book as well: isn't the smooth the aesthetic realization of the global flow of capital that neoliberalism seeks to accomplish, beyond the limits of sovereignty—or by turning sovereignty into the handmaid of global capital?[24]

Some may argue that it makes no sense to tie a philosophy as ancient as daoism to a theory and practice of power as contemporary as neoliberalism, but such an argument can be countered in two ways. First, scholars have observed that "because elements of Chinese belief structures have remained consistent over time, many of the principles that underlie these systems of thought are applicable to modern thinking."[25] As Bianca Bosker remarks, Jonathan Hay for example suggests that "Chinese tradition has been consistently 'reprocessing' itself, giving an elastic quality to its historical evolution."[26] Compared to European history,

> China's history . . . seems far more homogeneous. Even though historical study is constantly revealing a far more complex edifice than that allowed by the conventional account, there indubitably was a more significant homogeneity over a far greater stretch of time and place than was ever the case in Europe.[27]

As such, it doesn't seem entirely unorthodox first, to find traces of daoism in contemporary China and second, to tie daoism to other, more contemporary thought-systems (and neoliberalism certainly is a thought-system, as Philip Mirowski among others has argued[28]) that are present in China. In addition (and this would be the second way of countering the argument against associating ancient Chinese thought with neoliberalism), neoliberalism's supposed contemporaneity should also be drawn into question. Dotan Leshem, for example, has traced back its philosophical origins to the times of Jesus,[29] so while we are familiar with it as a contemporary formation, its roots arguably reach far beyond the time-frame in which it is usually situated (1970s–present).

Needless to say, while there is truth to the association of the smooth to neoliberalism, or for example of neoliberalism to global capital, my very presentation of sovereignty and neoliberalism as profoundly imbricated rather than opposed draws those associations into question, and shows once more that, rather than dealing with oppositions, we are confronted with realities that are part and parcel of each other. In the next section of this chapter, I would like to rephrase this conversation about power as a conversation about political form. Working within the tension between form and the formless that has been present in this book, and engaging with ongoing contemporary debates about political formalism, I will take my cue from other scholars who have tried to overcome the conflict between form and the formless that has weakened contemporary political struggle, and propose—based on the work on post-exceptionalism that I have done in this book—a dynamic understanding of form that would lead out of this frustrating impasse.

After all, and in spite of the *Dao De Jing*'s emphasis on formlessness, one cannot help but note when reading chapter 41 that it is a carefully formed chapter: delivering its teaching through a carefully constructed text that uses repetition and musicality, rhythm and sound, Lao Zi's plea for the formless depends on its text's form and solicits, when it comes to the articulation of its politics, a theory of political formalism that would attune us to the formlessness that the *Dao De Jing* foregrounds.

What We Talk About (When We Talk About Form)

To consider the politics of the critique of exceptionalism in the arts—or the politics of the plea for post-exceptionalism in the arts—that I have laid out in the previous chapters, let me now focus on the term "form" which has already received some discussion in this book. Indeed, to the attentive reader my discussion of exceptionalism and post-exceptionalism may very well appear to be caught up in the tension between form and the formless that has arguably determined much of contemporary thought, with the notion of form currently trending upwards after several decades of being under attack (by Nietzscheans, Benjaminians, Foucaultians, Derrideans, feminists, and more).

That is the picture that literary critic and theorist Anna Kornbluh, a specialist of Victorian literature as well as Marxist and psychoanalytic thought, sketches in her book *The Order of Forms: Realism, Formalism, and Social Space*.[30] Calling out critical approaches that "exalt unmaking and unbuilding,"[31] a certain enamoredness with "formlessness" that she associates (a little crudely, in my view[32]—but the crudeness is useful as a provocation) with the anarcho-vitalism of Giorgio Agamben's influential thought and its insistence on "destituent potential," Kornbluh tends towards political formalism. She is careful to point out, however, that she doesn't agree with the latter's "descrying"[33] what political form enables—life—either. Instead, Kornbluh is interested in taking it up for forms and the life they enable: hers is a formalist approach that is able to accommodate life. *Order of Forms* reads like a manifesto that wants to be done with the hackneyed notion that forms "oppressively contain";[34] at the same time, it distances itself from formalism's equally tiresome allergy of life. Instead, it is time for critics to start building—because form enables life. A plea for form then, but not for form's sake; and a sharp criticism of formlessness, but not at life's expense. As such, this has something "utopian"[35] to it, as Kornbluh (with a reference to Ernst Bloch) acknowledges. "Freedom"[36] needs to be disassociated from formlessness and rethought in relation to form.

Kornbluh's book explicitly situates itself after Caroline Levine's *Forms: Whole, Rhythm, Hierarchy, Network*,[37] which provides a similar map of the contemporary critical situation (Levine in fact provides one of the back cover recommendations for Kornbluh's book). "I want to make the case here," Levine writes in a discussion that negotiates between form and formlessness in our critical approaches to institutions, "that these formless or antiformal experiences have actually drawn *too* much attention from literary and cultural critics in the past few decades."[38] Levine, while acknowledging the formless, seeks to take it up for form against that critical trend. All the same, it's worth noting that her defense, if it is one, very much continues the negotiation I just mentioned: "this book puts an emphasis on social *dis*organization," Levine writes later, even if it argues that "disorganization is not always better than order";[39] "too strong an emphasis on deep structures," she warns further down on the same page, "is disabling for radical politics"[40]—another gesture towards formlessness in this defense of form. Along similar lines, it's worth noting that form always has to be pluralized in Levine's perspective—her discourse is one of multiple forms, and disorganization haunts each individual form in addition to also coming about through the collision of forms. In Sophocles, for example, Levine thus finds "a conflict among contending forms."[41] Following Mary Poovey earlier on in the book, Levine reformulates her approach to form as a "dynamic" one that insists on "'*formation*' as an active concept—not on culture or formation as nouns of stasis or realization."[42] The issue that Levine ultimately foregrounds about Poovey, however (and she also considers here the work of other historicists like Meredith McGill and Don Pease), is that Poovey and co. continue "the tradition of unifying and containing form in the making of their own arguments"[43] even as they, rhetorically, advocate for formlessness. Thus, the argument for antiformalism rests on a formalism that makes it possible—and that's what Levine seeks to draw out. Levine's own approach, then, while taking a dynamic approach to form as formation nevertheless keeps the focus on form, on the dynamism of form that form enables. For such a dynamism, "use" becomes an important notion;[44] form is always necessarily under distress because multiple forms cannot be resolved "into a single containing unity."[45] For Levine, this becomes a key aspect of form, a distress that only is one because of how form has often been conceived—in opposition to the formless, as a static realization. The form of the network, the last form Levine discusses in her book, is particularly fruitful here to discuss the dynamic between form and formlessness since it is a form that is often thought of as formless.[46] As such, it does not allow for something like "the final word" on form or the formless: indeed, the network is always both.

Kornbluh distinguishes her own approach from Levine's early in her introduction precisely by drawing attention to the negotiation between form and formlessness in Levine's discourse. As Kornbluh notes, in *Forms* Levine

> defines "form" as "all shapes and configurations, all ordering principles, all patterns of repetition and difference" and reconstructs formalism as a crucial tool for social analysis, since it has

> "the potential to unsettle conventional, rigid social and conceptual forms"; she similarly concludes her book by according the savvy formalist the emancipatory political agency of "refusing to join hierarchies and escaping from enclosing shapes."[47]

Kornbluh continues: "Against this ubiquity of unsettling and unmaking, *The Order of Forms* embraces projects of building."[48] In other words, there is something about Levine's continued emphasis on formlessness even in her book on *Forms* that Kornbluh wants to move beyond. This is one of the reasons why her book, which covers some of the same territory as Levine, reads more like a manifesto; indeed, it intensifies Levine's claims. This doesn't mean that Kornbluh is a formalist who denies life—she also attacks formalists who do not recognize the life that forms enable (even if her main target is the anarcho-vitalists who see only form's constraints).

Provocatively, Kornbluh finds the life-enabling formalism that she defends in Victorian realist novels, in a form and an aesthetic that is often—wrongly, in Kornbluh's view—understood as formless and mimetic. (Mimesis is a key target in Levine's book as well.) Kornbluh points out that this begins with Ian Watt's *The Rise of the Novel* and continues in critics like Franco Moretti and Catherine Gallagher.[49] In Fredric Jameson, a Marxist theorist whose work she admires very much, it leads to the claim—in *The Political Unconscious*—that the novel should be understood "as process rather than as form,"[50] terms that resonate in the framework that I have construed in this book. But the realist novels that Kornbluh considers turn out to be nothing of the kind, at least in her refreshingly original readings: obsessed with form, or at the very least with the tension between form and formlessness (as in her reading of the limit-case of Charles Dickens' *Bleak House*, one of Levine's case-studies as well), these novels are precisely not mimetic—Kornbluh suggests "speculative" and "abstract" as good descriptors instead[51]—but realist in the sense that they are writing the (formless) gap that lies at the core of all our political forms and thereby enables them to generate life—the groundlessness of any political form and the life it enables. Writing for Kornbluh thus becomes "an act of formalizing that performs the contingent structuration of the rift."[52] How to combine the Marxist Jameson's claim about the novel-as-process with Kornbluh's own Marxist commitment to political formalism?[53] That is the question.

One of Kornbluh's central, original contributions is that mathematical formalism is crucial to such a project. This is so because it makes a kind of impossible, "nonmimetic"[54] writing possible: it allows us to write infinity, for example, even if we cannot count it—and it is this different sense of "writing," and ultimately of "accounting for" in the sense of "telling a tale," that Kornbluh explores (a storytelling that can write what cannot be counted). Remarkably, Kornbluh writes in this context of the realist novel as an "original copy,"[55] a term that resonates in the framework of this book and that will return as the title of Bianca Bosker's book in my next chapter. As such, the realist novel's non-mimetic storytelling has something to do with modeling. It turns out to have something to do with architecture as well—the non-mimetic art *par excellence*—as the practice of building social spaces for human beings.[56]

With all of that though comes a shift in focus: from a literary critical practice that "[does] not generally think of [its] work as building,"[57] to an approach that is interested in "the work of building—not just resisting but reconstituting; not just breaking forms but making new ones; not just performative disruption but scaled construction" that thus "founds affirmative orders."[58]

It's realism not as a mode of reflection but a mode of production,[59] as Kornbluh succinctly puts it.[60] While Kornbluh's focus is on literature, she also suggests it applies to the arts more generally: "The forms in art may themselves theorize the forms in life," she writes, "and questions of social configuration may be abstractly posed in art in ways that the concretude of experience blocks."[61] Towards a political formalism not just of the realist novel, then, but also of art at large. Art, too, ought to rethink its work as building—as form rather than formlessness. To rephrase what Kornbluh writes about novels as a programmatic statement about art:

> Artworks know that the worlds they build are artificial, artifacted, designed, and this is how they know that the same is true of any world; in their self-concept, they effectuate political formalism. We owe it to them to persuasively advocate for the making of new worlds as the very work of literature.[62]

On Sovereignty as Political Form

As I see it, *Order of Forms* helpfully makes clear some of the stakes of the conversation about art and sovereignty that I have engaged with in this book so far. From a certain point of view, I have tried in the previous chapters to break down the continued hegemony of the concept of sovereignty in the arts, an approach that has some affinity with a by now decades-long tradition of attacking form in criticism and theory, and one that has become tied in the previous chapter to the ancient Chinese philosophy of daoism through Laozi's line that "the greatest image has no form." Kornbluh (and, before her, Levine) invites me to pause, however, and ask about the political importance of form, and, put in a different way, about the political importance of art. That does not mean, of course, that Kornbluh is somehow with sovereignty and specifically the concept of sovereignty proposed by Carl Schmitt that my engagement with the formless here sought to attack. Kornbluh's insistence on form reminds us, rather, as political theorists and other critics of Schmitt have also done, that Schmitt does not have the monopoly on the concept of sovereignty, and that while specific aspects of sovereignty are clearly under close scrutiny in this book—exceptionalism, notably—that does not mean the concept of sovereignty in all of its articulations is done away with in these pages.

Indeed, Schmitt is a particularly interesting case to consider, through the lens of the debates on form and the formless: a political formalist who recognized—indeed, philosophically *defended*—the "life" that the exception brought to the legalo-political order. As such, the exception wrests the legal apart from the political and legitimates the absolute power of a sovereign that would safeguard the constitution by temporarily acting outside of the law, within the realm of the law's suspension. As I detailed in my Introduction, Schmitt was a conservative who brought the life of the exception *within* the legalo-political order, paradoxically by legitimating a concept of sovereignty that is able to politically act *outside* of the law. Form, then, as Schmitt sees it, ought to be particularly interested in the political formalism that enables form to be temporarily suspended—though not destroyed—in response to the formlessness of life. Such a political formalism is not anarchy, it is not chaos; for Schmitt, it is the form of the legalo-political order.

Schmitt's political formalism, however, is not Kornbluh's: whereas Schmitt's seeks to contain life (this is, indeed, the very tension between his conservative approach to sovereignty which he developed in response to the more radical politics of Walter Benjamin's "Critique of Violence" essay), Kornbluh insists on a political formalism that enables it.[63] If Schmitt has often been countered by those Kornbluh refers to as anarcho-vitalists, that is, scholars who choose life against political formalism, Kornbluh counters Schmitt with her own political formalism—one that *also* chooses life. This becomes an interesting way of dismantling Schmitt, of taking political formalism as well as life back from a dubious political theorist whose conservatism ultimately turned fascistic.

In *Plastic Sovereignties*, I too positioned myself critically in relation to Schmitt while nevertheless arguing at length for the continued importance of sovereignty as a political form. My use of the term "post-exceptional" in this present book, a word that in its very constitution retains the word "exceptional," indicates (as I have suggested previously) that not all exceptionalisms are bad, and that it is worth holding on to political relief in an era that often appears to be dominated by a politics of the flat. For me, it was crucial to rethink the concept of sovereignty as plastic, in other words as a political form that, while it obviously makes us, is also made by us—and my recommendation was for us to engage in "better building,"[64] to borrow the closing words of Kornbluh's book. In more technical terms, I was arguing, in an implicit tension with Benjamin's charge (in his "Work of Art" essay) that the aestheticization of politics leads to fascism, that our concept of sovereignty precisely ought to be aestheticized so as to draw out its plastic dimension, its shape-ability as a political form. By defending a plastic concept of sovereignty that was crucially plural, by thinking what I named in my title as "plastic sovereignties," I sought to offer both a deconstructed, aestheticized sovereignty that unworked some of sovereignty's most problematic theologico-political aspects (its logic of the one, its exceptionalism first and foremost, related to its transcendentality) while at the same time theorizing a plasticity that claimed sovereignty, and was thus more politically robust.

As was already becoming clear in that book, and has become explicit in my more recent work,[65] I now consider these tensions between the transcendental, absolute, exceptionalist notion of sovereignty and my own plastic and plural concept of sovereignty as a tension between what the Greeks called *eidos*, or ideal form, and *morphè*, or plastic form (in its relation with *ulè* or matter)—and the nude, in this present book, has thus come to operate as a figure of sovereignty and of how what I consider to be some of its most problematic aspects have been celebrated aesthetically in the West. It's between *eidos* and *morphè/ulè* that the two bodies of the king are to be played out: symbolic and material/biological. The nude reigns sovereignly in art history, and if sovereignty continues to be dominant in Western political life one can understand this as the continued political dominance of an aesthetic figure like the nude.

As I see it, Levine is closer to *morphè*, Kornbluh to *eidos*. Levine notes the multiple meanings of form on the second page of her introduction, distinguishing Plato's immaterial *eidos* from Aristotle's understanding of form as material shape (*ulè* and *morphè*; but what happens to *eidos* in this configuration? Levine doesn't clarify). However, she does not situate herself clearly in relation to both those terms or indeed other understandings of the notion of form—it's a conceptual history that she characterizes as "chaotic."[66] This, of course, adds to the complexity not only of her own book but also its reception, given that readers—and critics with whom Levine is in conversation—are part of this "chaotic" history and are, in the midst of it, trying to make sense of the term "form," which is at the center of their conversation.

As Barbara Cassin puts it in a reflection on *eidos* in *Dictionary of Untranslatables*: "To situate *eidos* in its place, one has to render it simultaneously operative on different levels of intelligibility"[67]—a place that is not exactly a single place, then. That is, in my view, one of the most difficult things to negotiate in a book: a concept's life across multiple semantic realities. Such a plural life can facilitate, of course, a great many conversations; but it also becomes increasingly difficult to say what those conversations are actually about, since they all use the same common term—"form"—but mean something very different by it. Levine ultimately settles for one commonality in all of the meanings: "'form' always indicates *an arrangement of elements, an ordering, patterning, or shaping*"[68]—and that will be the broad definition that runs through Levine's book. Still, if the implication is that such a meaning of form applies to the Platonic *eidos* as well, much of what Levine says about form in the book that follows doesn't: if Levine situates herself in a Platonic tradition,[69] it is only to insist on form as bringing conceptual unity, "imposing order on disparate materials," the chaos of experience (sense-experience without concepts, and concepts without sense-experience, as the old story goes . . .). Levine adds though that "few critics in our time would join Plato in imagining that our concepts [*eidos*; form; ADB] inhabit an ideal and timeless sphere."[70] But this changes something to Plato's notion of form, of course—it pushes it more towards Aristotle, and (I would argue) the history of form as *morphè* that becomes dominant downstream from Plato (neo-Platonist and Christian revivals of *eidos* notwithstanding). Levine's discourse about colliding forms, formation, the dynamics of form—nothing of that is particularly platonic, we'd have to admit. That is form as *morphè*, not *eidos*.

Kornbluh too explicitly notes the importance of Plato in her discussion of forms, acknowledging now—unsurprisingly, given how her work intensifies Levine's appreciation of form—her own proximity to Plato, and even recognizing that the "Platonic overtones"[71] of her discourse "will likely aggrieve some readers" (she has in mind specifically her preference for abstraction). "I find [those overtones] useful," Kornbluh continues, "in illuminating why form has both ontological quiddity and political contestability"—with the latter informing Aristotle's departure from Plato, his "insistence that form is something materially available."[72] Again, the exact relations between form, *eidos*, *morphè*, matter, *ulè*, are not spelled out—but based on the importance of mathematical forms in Kornbluh's study (the component of *Order of Forms* that most clearly sets it aside from Levine's book), one would have to acknowledge a closer proximity to Plato in Kornbluh than in Levine. Kornbluh's use of the term "original copy" to capture her understanding of the realist novel and the particular modeling that it does, takes on new meaning, as a notion that manages to combine the ideality of *eidos* with the materiality of the eidolon or image (form as contour [*morphè*] and matter [*ulè*]). Kornbluh's discourse too, however, evidences the pull of *morphè*, for example when she talks about "the plasticity of form,"[73] and perhaps silently evokes the work of the French philosopher Catherine Malabou when a few pages later she considers form's "explosion" as well.[74]

As I indicated in *Plastic Sovereignties*, Malabou has done very important work in the discussion about form, even if, curiously, she gets no mention in either Levine's or Kornbluh's books. In "Grammatology and Plasticity," for example, Malabou labors hard to distinguish her theory of plasticity, and the formation of form that it seeks, from Derridean deconstruction, pointing out that the formation of form entails "a power to shape meaning that exceeds [the] graphic displacement"[75] that is central to deconstruction and that is perhaps most memorably captured by Derrida's notion of "différance," a neologism that marks through a difference that is visible/written yet not audible/spoken (the famous "a" instead of the "e" of "difference"), a displacement or deferral of meaning. Even though Malabou obviously does not deny such graphic displacement, she evidently also wants more—and thus she arrives, I have argued, from Derrida's deconstruction (marked by his theory of graphic displacement) at a formalism that (as I showed in *Plastic Sovereignties*) has great political potential. It's important to note, and Kornbluh is very helpful on this,[76] that as such, a formalism like the one I find in Malabou does not leave Derrida behind—it places a different emphasis, rather, foregrounding construction after several decades of critical praises of formlessness (when Levine discusses Derrida he is associated with those praising formlessness; Kornbluh is more nuanced on that count).

Future Formations

What are we talking about, then, when we talk about form? Something plastic that is nevertheless "ideal" enough to provide a structure, model, or limit to shape life while it is also shaped by it. If both Levine and Kornbluh point us towards decades of criticism that has emphasized the formlessness in all of this, the ways in which life escapes form, they also allow us to highlight form, the life it enables, and call on us to build better forms (to echo Kornbluh's closing sentence once more). Humans make their own forms and those forms are necessary for living. But why, then, if my own thinking about this is largely in line with Kornbluh and Levine, have I emphasized formlessness more in this book? The emphasis was targeting, specifically, the exceptionalization of form—a thinking about form that follows the logic of the one, and has (as a consequence) become a rather easy target for criticism. Once that exceptionalism is removed, however, form remains—unexceptionally.

In her book *Unexceptional Politics*, Emily Apter has described and analyzed such a project with reference to my work, but in the first instance in a discussion of Bruno Latour's criticism of Carl Schmitt in his book *An Inquiry into Modes of Existence*. There, Apter perceptively writes about how Latour "unexceptionalizes transcendent modes of the Political," advocating what Apter calls a "'small p' politics that speaks its own language, that defines distinct modes of acting or articulating politically that evolve and mutate."[77] It's at this point that the reference to my *Plastic Sovereignties* comes in, a book that's aligned here with part of an approach that, in Apter's closing words in the chapter from which I have been quoting, "promotes thinking pragmatically and philosophically."[78] This works well to describe, I think, the political formalism of post-exceptionalism, the way it can do *eidos* materially and thereby overcome the age-old distinction between form and the formless that has hindered not just thought but also politics.

The challenge I propose in this book by thinking about post-exceptional art, is precisely to think about post-exceptional form—to pursue the unexceptionalization of form so as to facilitate future formations. This is also to point towards a risk (something that Levine's book is better at than Kornbluh's): in the contemporary emphasis on form, we want to avoid, surely, theorizing form in ways that would simply revitalize the age-old debates between form and formlessness. Rather, the goal would have to be to understand form otherwise, with a deep awareness of the criticisms that have already been leveled at it, so as to reformulate it beyond both those approaches that reject form in the name of life, and those that choose form at the expense of life. For such a project, both Kornbluh's and Levine's books are crucial.

For better or for worse, the sage as a figure that hovers between exceptionalism (hierarchy and elitism) and post-exceptionalism (the dao as way-making, always under construction, and unexceptional like water) helps us to negotiate the tension between form and the formless. As such, the sage becomes both a figure of a political formalism that I seek to promote, and a figure that in its combination of sovereign and neoliberal aspects, may also be connected to the authoritarian neoliberalism that has emerged in our time. There is a reason why, in *To Our Friends*, The Invisible Committee can refer to neoliberal government—and not their own anarchist practice—as "flexible, plastic, informal" and "Taoist."[79] Daoism may, for anarchists, not be anarchist enough—it may remain too close still to actually existing forms of government. Anarchists, however, are with life—against form, in Kornbluh's set-up. (At most, they would allow for what Agamben in his work calls a form-of-life.) Whatever the politics of daoism may be, it will be evident that on the count of formalism and form, it is not anarchist, but something else—and in that may precisely lie its value, as a post-exceptional political formalism. The choice is no longer between political formalism and anarchism, but for a political formalism that operates unexceptionally. One way to look at contemporary history would be to say that neoliberalism figured this out a long time ago. The political left, on the other hand, has hobbled behind, incapable of overcoming the form vs. formlessness distinction.

Following in Kornbluh's footsteps still, one could tie the distinction between form and formlessness to another one that comes up in the opening pages of Kornbluh's book, namely the distinction between critique and post-critique. The former is most frequently associated with ideal form, with the sovereign rupture of a decision, verticality; the latter is horizontal rather, immersed in the surface materiality of the text, formal but not at all in an idealist way—it is flat, as Kornbluh points out. While such distinctions are, like the distinction between form and the formless and exceptionalism and post-exceptionalism, ultimately difficult to maintain—if one follows one of post-critique's most celebrated proponents, Rita Felski, it is quite obvious, for example, that post-critique is anything but entirely flat—they still strike a chord. If critique is form and post-critique formlessness, then the project here has been to not advocate the former at the expense of life, or—when it comes to the latter—celebrate life at the expense of form. A critique, then, that would enable life, and a post-critique that would not be against form. Once again, as was the case with postmodernism, it appears that the prefix "post" in such a formation would name something that, as per Wendy Brown's useful gloss on the prefix in a book about waning sovereignty, may come temporally after critique, but not be over it.[80] Later, in both of Brown's books *Undoing the Demos* and *In the Ruins of Neoliberalism*, this gloss will develop into a measured defense of sovereignty—popular sovereignty, the sovereignty of the people—against neoliberalism and, in *Ruins of Neoliberalism*, a description of contemporary neoliberalism as a hollowed-out version of an older neoliberalism that had more relief built in. At some distance then from both contemporary neoliberalism and traditional sovereignty, post-critique would precisely name a continuation of critique *transformed*. It would draw out, precisely, the plasticity of critique, a critique "small c" that would, to paraphrase Apter, define distinct modes of acting and articulating critically that evolve and mutate.

Unfortunately, this is not the understanding that post-critique has received, nor the understanding of critique that post-critique has offered, and so we find ourselves in a moment where various factions "strike clumsily"[81] (as Kornbluh puts it) at the difference, a difference that is tied up in the distinction between form and formlessness. To talk about form, then, is also to recognize this clumsiness and articulate instead other ways of acting and articulating critically, which also means: politically.

To conclude, then, I think that Western political thought has much to learn from Laozi's wisdom that "the great image has no form." Since Plato, Western politics has been dominated by form (*eidos*, idea) and its tension with the formless. Form's reach far exceeds politics, however, and can—as I have shown—be found in philosophy and the arts as well, where form is frequently advocated at the expense of life or else relentlessly attacked in life's name. Both approaches are, I have suggested, ill-guided and Laozi's claim—which depends on the unifying form of rhythm and sound to deliver its praise of formlessness—can help one see instead how form and life enable each other. The future of democracy and the life of our institutions depend, I would propose, on being able to move outside of the opposition of form and formlessness to explore their dynamic interaction. It is not about sovereignly choosing between verticality or horizontality, state or non-state, rule or anarchy, but about openly exploring, after Laozi, how "the great democracy has no form." While that claim is political, I approach it through the arts and philosophy. Such a path reflects the provocative guiding premise of my work, namely that culture operates upstream from politics. To change the future of politics we must first change how we think and how we make art.

Laozi's wisdom has been tremendously influential in the arts. In the water works of Song Dong, which took up an important place in this chapter, one can see the tension between form and the formless negotiated. By using water as his medium, Song brilliantly foregrounds the formless as part of a series of artworks that inevitably depend on form to realize themselves as art. In Western art history, curators and art critics Rosalind Krauss and Yve-Alain Bois have uncovered the importance of the formless in a modernist tradition that is generally considered to emphasize form. Raphael Rubinstein has, with reference to the very same line from Laozi that I quoted, highlighted this in contemporary Western painting as an inclination towards "the provisional." But as François Jullien has noted in his study of Chinese "shanshui" landscape painting, such a negotiation between form and the formless also poses a demand on thought, specifically on a "Greek" thought that—again, since Plato—has tended towards form. The challenge becomes, rather, to think the dynamic interaction between form and the formless that leads from philosophies of the event (decision) that are common in the West to philosophies of process (deliberation) that are less common, and that resonate with ancient Chinese thought. In such a thought, forms like "whole," "rhythm," "hierarchy," and especially "network" become crucially important, as Caroline Levine's work demonstrates.

Political thought has something to learn from those philosophical and aesthetic approaches as they are played out between the West and China. Thinking the dynamic relation of form to formlessness is key to the life that political form enables. Too much form kills life; too much life is detrimental to form. Democracy is the regime that, in my view, strikes a balance between both—but as such it is perpetually at risk of becoming unbalanced. By developing a theory of unexceptional art, I have sought to act on the foundations of our political imagination, and the formal limits that have been set on political thought. Such an approach would bring creative and critical experimentation to a contemporary political project to design life-enabling institutions. Following Laozi, then, I have sought to expand contemporary political thought by thinking a political formalism between the West and China that highlights the importance of culture by taking its cues from the arts and philosophy.

Notes

1 I have commented on the distinction between the Western philosopher and the Chinese sage in the final chapter of my book: Arne De Boever, *François Jullien's Unexceptional Thought: A Critical Introduction* (New York: Rowman & Littlefield, 2020).

2 Gilbert Simondon, *L'individuation psychique et collective, à la lumière des notions de Forme, Information, Potentiel, et Metastabilité* (Paris: Aubier, 2007).

3 Byung-Chul Han, *Shanzhai: Deconstruction in* Chinese, trans. Philippa Hurd (Boston, MA: The MIT Press, 2017).

4 François Jullien, *The Great Image Has No Form, or On the Nonobject through Painting*, trans. Jane Marie Todd (Chicago, IL: University of Chicago Press, 2009), p. 43ff.

5 Stathis Gourgouris, "Arche," in: J. M. Bernstein, Adi Ophir, and Ann Laura Stoler, eds., *Political Concepts: A Critical Lexicon* (New York: Fordham University Press, 2018), pp. 5–24.

6 Laozi, *Dao De Jing: A Philosophical Translation*, trans. Roger T. Ames and David L. Hall (New York: Ballantine, 2003), p. 141.

7 Tobin Siebers, *Disability Aesthetics* (Ann Arbor: University of Michigan Press, 2010), p. 92.

8 Jingfang Hao, *Vagabonds*, trans. Ken Liu (New York: Saga Press, 2020).

9 Emily Apter, *Unexceptional Politics: On Obstruction, Impasse, and the Impolitic* (New York: Verso, 2018), p. 34.

10 Nancy P. Lin, "Song Dong: Water," in: Wu Hung, ed., *The Allure of Matter: Material Art from China* (Chicago, IL: Smart Museum, 2019), pp. 187–191, here p. 189.

11 Lin, "Song Dong," p. 189.

12 Ibid.

13 Ibid.

14 Ibid.

15 Ibid.

16 Roger Ames and David Hall, eds., *Dao De Jing: "Making This Life Significant" (A Philosophical Translation)*, trans. Roger Ames and David Hall (New York: Ballantine Books, 2003), p. 141.

17 Ames and Hall, *Dao De Jing*, p. 102.

18 Note that this is a distinction that is important in the Western tradition as well, in particular in the work of Saint Paul. See: Arne De Boever, "Bio-Paulitics," *Journal for Cultural and Religious Theory* 11.1 (2010), pp. 35–51.

19 Gourgouris, "Arche," p. 8.

20 Michel Foucault, *The History of Sexuality. Vol. 1: An Introduction*, trans. Robert Hurley (New York: Vintage, 1990).

21 Michael Hardt and Antonio Negri, *Empire* (Cambridge, MA: Harvard University Press, 2002).

22 On this, see: Grégoire Chamayou, *La société ingouvernable: Une généalogie du libéralisme autoritaire* (Paris: La Fabrique, 2018).

23 This is the other side of the consideration, which I raised in Chapter 1, that Han's description of injury can be associated with the rupturing logic of the exception. I am instead aiming here for a rewiring that would associate injury with post-exceptionalism.

24 In view of the figure that was central to the second part of this book, it's worth noting also that the fake has been associated with neoliberalism's close cousin, "finance." Whereas I have considered the fake as posing a challenge to sovereignty, I am now considering how that may push the fake into the realm of neoliberalism. Lily Cho has situated the fake in the realm of finance and understood it as a derivative. In my view, this cedes too much to the derivative, or does not give enough credit to the fake: unlike the derivative, the fake is still a commodity that, as a means to generate

value, fits in Marx's general formula of capital, M-C-M'. The derivative operates according to another logic altogether—it includes futurity into its structure, while the fake does not. In short, I'd take a shanzhai product over a derivative any time; the fake, as I see it, maintains a critical edge over neoliberalism. See: Lily Cho, "Fakes, Counterfeits, and Derivatives in Tash Aw's Five Star Billionaire," *Ariel* 49:4 (2018), pp. 53–75.

25 Bianca Bosker, *Original Copies: Architectural Mimicry in Contemporary China* (Honolulu: University of Hawai'i Press/Hong Kong University Press, 2013), p. 22.

26 Hay qtd. Bosker, *Original Copies*, p. 22.

27 Hay qtd. ibid., p. 135.

28 See: Philip Mirowski and Dieter Plehwe, eds., *The Road From Mont Pèlerin: The Making of the Neoliberal Thought Collective* (Cambridge, MA: Harvard University Press, 2015).

29 Dotan Leshem, *The Origins of Neoliberalism: Modeling the Economy from Jesus to Foucault* (New York: Columbia University Press, 2016).

30 Anna Kornbluh, *The Order of Forms: Realism, Formalism, and Social Space* (Chicago, IL: University of Chicago Press, 2019).

31 Kornbluh, *Order of Forms*, p. 1.

32 Kornbluh writes, for example, that "anarcho-vitalism refuses form" but this statement cannot hold in the context of Agamben's work, where the status of form is much more complicated. Consider, for example, the notion of form-of-life (*eidos tou biou*), which Agamben's work celebrates. Does Agamben, as Kornbluh charges, indeed "repudiate . . . form in life" (Kornbluh, *Order of Forms*, p. 29)? It would have been good to consider these terms and questions in relation to the claim Kornbluh makes in her introduction that for Marx, form is the matter of life. Overall, one feels that the relations between these various terms—form, matter, life—could have been spelled out more clearly in Kornbluh's book.

33 Ibid., p. 79.

34 Ibid., p. 3.

35 Ibid., p. 5.

36 Ibid., pp. 57, 81.

37 Caroline Levine, *Forms: Whole, Rhythm, Hierarchy, Network* (Princeton, NJ: Princeton University Press, 2015).

38 Levine, *Forms*, p. 9.

39 Ibid., p. 17.

40 Ibid.

41 Ibid., p. 92.

42 Poovey qtd. ibid., p. 33.
43 Ibid., p. 34.
44 It's evoked on p. 37 and p. 87, and named explicitly on p. 39.
45 Ibid., p. 42.
46 Ibid., p. 112–113.
47 Kornbluh, *Order of Forms*, pp. 3–4.
48 Ibid., p. 4.
49 Ibid., p. 44.
50 Jameson qtd. ibid., p. 49.
51 Ibid., p. 33.
52 Ibid., p. 148.
53 Ibid., p. 49.
54 Ibid., p. 33.
55 Ibid., p. 97.
56 Kornbluh discusses here some architects that I also engaged with in my book *States of Exception* and to which I will return in my final chapter, which partly engages with architecture.
57 Kornbluh, *Order of Forms*, p. 1.
58 Ibid., p. 6.
59 Ibid., p. 41.
60 This expresses succinctly the idea I sought to express in the closing paragraph of my book *Finance Fictions: Realism and Psychosis in a Time of Economic Crisis* (New York: Fordham University Press, 2018).
61 Kornbluh, *Order of Forms*, p. 6.
62 Ibid., 55; minor modifications, ADB.
63 Andreas Kalyvas has done a reading of Schmitt that finds this life in his democratic theory as well. This is closer to Kornbluh, but it is an idiosyncratic reading of Schmitt. See: Andreas Kalyvas, "Carl Schmitt and the Three Moments of Democracy," *Cardozo Law Review* 21:1525 (1999–2000), pp. 1525–1565.
64 Kornbluh, *Order of Forms*, p. 166.
65 See: *Against Aesthetic Exceptionalism* (Minneapolis: University of Minnesota Press, 2019) and *François Jullien's Unexceptional Thought* (New York: Rowman & Littlefield, 2020).
66 Levine, *Forms*, p. 2.
67 Barbara Cassin, ed., *Dictionary of Untranslatables*, trans. Steven Randall, Christian Hubert, Jeffrey Mehlman, et al., ed. Emily Apter, Jacques Lezra, and Michael Wood (Princeton: Princeton University Press, 2014), p. 1032.
68 Levine, *Forms*, p. 3.

69 Ibid., p. 28.
70 Ibid., p. 33.
71 Kornbluh, *Order of Forms*, p. 27.
72 Ibid., pp. 27–28.
73 Ibid., p. 82.
74 Ibid., p. 84.
75 Catherine Malabou, *Changing Difference: The Feminine and the Question of Philosophy*, trans. Carolyn Shread (Cambridge: Polity, 2011), p. 63.
76 Kornbluh, *Order of Forms*, p. 41.
77 Apter, *Unexceptional Politics*, p. 34.
78 Ibid., p. 36.
79 The Invisible Committee, *To Our Friends,* trans. Robert Hurley (Los Angeles, CA: Semiotext(e), 2015), p. 68.
80 Wendy Brown, *Walled States, Waning Sovereignty* (New York: Zone Books, 2010), p. 21.
81 Kornbluh, *Order of Forms*, p. 1.

6

From Duplitectures to Dafen

Transgressive Critique

In this final chapter, I consider two case-studies that can help further the thinking I have developed in this book by highlighting some of its most important critical aspects: first, the ways in which my thought has pushed against an orientalist framework that would create an all-too-easy opposition between the West and China when it comes to assessing the role that the original and the copy have played in these diverging cultures. Second—and more fundamentally—this chapter further questions the understandings of the original and the copy that have informed this book, that is to say in their specific relation to exceptionalism and its politics. Overall, this chapter aims to critique and transgress: to critique what has already been said so as to push my thought into new directions.

The first case-study is taken from the realm of architecture, which has appeared in this book but has received no in-depth consideration so far. Part of the reason why the consideration of architecture is important is because of the central role that the architect has played in the transformation of the artist from a technician into a quasi-theological (and exceptionalist) figure.

It is because of this centrality that the architect cannot be missing in any critique of exceptionalism in the arts. That case-study involves, specifically, what Bianca Bosker has dubbed the "duplitecture" phenomenon, the copying of a Western building, style of building, or in some cases an entire city neighborhood or town, in China. Bosker shows, importantly, that such copying should not be understood as a sign of architectural self-colonization (thus confirming the superiority of the original Western culture) but rather as a demonstration of cultural superiority (thus using the copy to confirm the exceptionalism of China).

The other case-study comes from the realm of painting, which has been prominently present throughout this book. It involves what is often presented (through a Western lens) to be the mass copying of Western paintings in Dafen Village in China, a phenomenon that has been studied by Winnie Wong. Wong's work offers convincing grounds for disputing such a Western presentation of Dafen. While Bosker provides us with a case of exceptionalist copying, in other words a case in which the practice of copying is motivated on exceptionalist grounds, Wong shows that when it comes to China, a Westerner may see copies where there are none—where there is truly only the cult of the original, which can be found in the West just as much as it exists China. The former—Bosker's case—shakes up my association of the original with exceptionalism and of the copy with unexceptionalism. The latter—Wong's case—goes against an orientalist framework that would oppose the West and China when it comes to the valuation of the original and the copy. Wong's work is, in that sense, anti-orientalist, and considering it here will introduce fundamental uncertainties into our very understanding of the original and the copy as well, thus further destabilizing—from a global point of view—art's politics after political theology.

I intend to push those uncertainties away from a concern with the original and the copy to ask instead another question that has been present throughout this book: not whether a work of art is an original or a copy, but whether it is art. The foundational premise of this book is that we have tended to think of art as exceptional. From that it follows that if a work of art is not exceptional, we would conclude that it is not art. In this chapter, however, we will be confronted with works that are exceptionalist but are not considered art, and this complicates the issue even further. Thus, both of the case-studies that I consider in this chapter ultimately open up a vision onto an understanding of art—as well as architecture—outside of exceptionalism, an art and architecture that would no longer be exceptional art and architecture—but be considered art and architecture nevertheless. This is the realm, I have argued, of post-exceptional art: of an art after exceptionalism, a post-exceptionalist art that remains unthinkable within an aesthetic regime in which the force that Caroline Jones calls "auratic authorship"[1]—which includes the auratic work of art—remains strong. Even today, in what will soon be a century after Walter Benjamin's "Work of Art" essay, and after artists and scholars like Hito Steyerl have updated Benjamin's work into a digital age and—anno 2024, when I am completing this book—an age that is marked by the reemergence of fascism and the clash between fascism and communism (specifically, "anti-fa"), what both Steyerl and Benjamin before her are fighting remains very much in force: aesthetically, but also politically, as I have suggested. Is it any wonder that fascism continues to reemerge politically if it has continued to thrive aesthetically, in the ways in which we think and talk about artists and art? On this count, we have never been postmodern, as I have already indicated: we have never realized the death of the author and the celebration of the copy that were the hallmarks of the postmodern era. Michel Foucault, in his study of power in the field of sexuality and race, was indeed correct when he indicated that "we have never cut off the head of the king": the concept of sovereignty has continued to reign victorious, in art as well as in politics. It's political theology all the way down.

My argument is not that this is entirely a bad thing. In the previous chapter, I made the case for the relief that the exceptionalist notion of sovereignty can bring to a contemporary political situation that is in the thralls of the flat. Indeed, if post-exceptionalism can be useful as a term, it would only be in the sense that for example Wendy Brown has developed of the prefix post, as qualifying something that may come temporally after, but is not entirely over, what it qualifies. My choice for the term "post-exceptional" was made in this light, as a choice not so much against the exceptional (as I have, polemically, put it elsewhere) but to unwork the exceptional—to put into motion strategies of thought and practice that would lead away from an aesthetic that is centrally organized around an idea that is deeply problematic from a political point of view. That does not mean doing away with exceptionalism altogether: it does not mean doing away with all the elements of verticality that can bring welcome relief in a neoliberal society that is in the process of becoming post-critical. But it does mean, as post-critique ought perhaps more precisely to be understood, to work against the problematically sovereign structures that dominate not only our thinking about art, but also about politics. Indeed, these are structures that, while they are political and aesthetic, are operative within our very ways of living and thus concern the realm of ethics as well.

Exceptionalist Copying

In a chapter titled "The Fascination with Faux" from her book *Original Copies: Architectural Mimicry in Contemporary China*,[2] Bianca Bosker observes something that by now should be obvious: that the West and China value the copy differently. Like other scholars whose work I have discussed in this book, she adds nuance to this claim, noting for example—outside of an all-too-easy opposition of the West and China—that the West itself has valued the copy differently in different phases of its development. Bosker recalls these commonplaces, however, because she wants to make them apply in a different domain: architecture. Her book is interested in particular in the Chinese phenomenon of copying a Western style of building, a Western building, or even an entire Western neighborhood or a significant part of a city. How are we to understand these "themed residential landscapes," these "counterfeited environments," or "theme cities"?[3] Going with what I have suggested in this book, namely that the copy can be understood as a form of vandalism that undermines the exceptionalist sovereignty of the original, one could suggest that architectural copies undermine the stability and even eternity with which architecture is often associated.

In a discussion of architectural modernism, for example, the philosopher Mark C. Taylor suggests that modernism's dematerialization—its strategies for making bodies disappear, and the concomitant emphasis on surface that this has produced—can be read as "the desire to escape time by securing stability in the midst of flux."[4] He proposes that we understand the ancient pyramid as a figure for such a longing for transcendence. Although the postmodernist aesthetic retains many aspects of the modernist one, it nevertheless also marks important differences, one of which has to do with architecture's longing for transcendence, eternity, stability, and security: with postmodernism, Taylor argues, "eternity is over" and "a labyrinth undermines every pyramid."[5] Taylor refers on this count to the work of the Swiss architect Bernard Tschumi. In a 1995 interview, Tschumi observes that:

> For six thousand years, architecture as always the symbol of stability, of permanence, of eternity [even modernism is, in Taylor's view, caught up in this] . . . Architecture is always about stability, either structural stability or the stability of the institution. It's frozen, it's there, it never changes . . . One thing that struck me early on was that architecture simultaneously was always challenged by the movement of bodies going through architecture, by various activities in it.[6]

Tschumi relates this movement of bodies through space to film:

> I was trying to learn about architecture through the cinema, through film, because I felt that the film space was telling me something about architecture, because you had always movement of bodies in space. Space was constantly activated by movement.[7]

"In the shifty structure of film," Taylor concludes, "Tschumi discerns a way of smuggling time into architecture."[8] One can call this postmodernism, but in this book it also carries the name of daoism, and—ultimately—post-exceptionalism: Taylor is thinking about the tension between the flow and fixed form.

Looking back at Walter Benjamin's "Work of Art" essay, one might say that for Taylor and others, postmodernism with its preference for the labyrinth ends architecture's potentially fascistic desire for eternity, stability, security, and challenges it with the flow of life, the movement of bodies through space, which for Tschumi is also the flow of film—of "the movies." That hardly means, though, that Tschumi—or Taylor for that matter—would label postmodernism as "communist," even if there arguably is something "communist" about buildings being shaped by the collective movement of the people's bodies in space. If the political charge of fascism or my use of the term "communism" may strike one as a little ungrounded here—a hangover of the discussion of Benjamin earlier in this book—one can consider one of Taylor's other architectural case-studies, the work of Daniel Libeskind, as a pertinent example in this context.

In Libeskind's work, architectural postmodernism—and specifically deconstruction—has explicitly been presented as a political project against fascism. Libeskind's design *Between the Lines* for the Jewish Museum in Berlin famously explores the complicities between the history of modernity and the extermination of the Jews. Internally, the design puts in tension "two lines of thinking": organization ("a straight line, but broken into many fragments") and relationship ("a tortuous line, but continuing infinitely").[9] This results in an empty, excessive space in the middle of the museum. Externally, "Libeskind locates three further elements that are 'integrated' into the building: the Holocaust Tower, the E.T.A. Hoffmann garden . . . and the Celan Hof."[10] In addition, by triangulating the addresses of among others Hoffmann, the composer Arnold Schönberg, and Walter Benjamin, "Libeskind defines a star, which establishes the coordinates that situate his addition to the Berlin Museum,"[11] a star that obviously recalls "the yellow star that was so frequently worn on [the] very site [where the museum was built]."[12] In this way, Libeskind aims to create a space in which the repressed history of the Holocaust can return, a space that would provide refuge for Berlin's "schizoid memory."[13] In his architectural work, then, Libeskind explicitly pays homage to Benjamin while critically positioning himself in relation to fascism. Postmodernist architecture and the "daoist" critique it develops of eternity, stability, and security explicitly become part of a critique of totalitarianism here. This critique arguably extends throughout Libeskind's work.

But how do we get from here to the copy? Consider, for example, Libeskind's early project *City Edge*, which can be understood as a critique of the Berlin Wall and the twentieth-century's other totalitarian disaster: communism. As Taylor points out, Libeskind "uses the structure of the wall to subvert the ideology of the Wall."[14] He addresses the wall's "violent slicing up of territory" by making drawings of a wall that is "lifting itself up and creating a new public street below," in other words by "turning the wall against itself" and by "deconstruct[ing] the binary logic of [the wall's] either/or."[15] This deconstruction is continued within the structure of the wall itself, which when one looks at it closely is revealed to be a "montage of edges," of pieces of other walls. Taylor notes that paradoxically, "this inward dehiscence does not destroy structure but is a condition of possibility."[16] This is a project that explicitly targets, then, the wall as a technology of sovereignty. And it does so, in Berlin in 1987, it is worth noting, *as a copy*: as a perverse copy of the Berlin Wall, suspended, not operating as a wall at all. Internal deconstruction and flow undermine the exceptionalism of architecture: its stability, permanence, eternity. Expanding the argument's reach, one may take this to suggest that the architectural copy could be read along similar lines, as a postmodernist phenomenon that through its strategy of duplication undermines architecture's exceptionalism.

This is not, however, what we find in Bosker, and Bosker's specific argument about duplitectures can help us develop a truly critical position with respect the copy, its relation to exceptionalism and post-exceptionalism, and their politics. At first sight, it appears that Bosker will follow the postmodernist path that I have opened up. Bosker starts by referencing Western postmodern theory and notes the anxiety that is expressed there about the copy and the breakdown between the authentic and the fake, or even the real and the fake (to put it in more ontological terms) that it brings. While there are connections between postmodern theory and Chinese thought, ultimately China does not share the Western anxiety about the copy, and Bosker is interested in that difference and how it applies in architecture. From Umberto Eco's work on the copy, Bosker moreover derives what she suggests "might be seen as a Promethean moment in the creation of a perfect copy": a perfect copy presents "an advance of culture above nature" and "in this respect, the generation of perfect copies of Western achievements . . . can serve as a potent symbol of the civilizational superiority of the 'counterfeiters.'"[17] Here the argument shifts away from the understanding of the copy that has been developed in this book so far. "To be able to make a perfect copy," Bosker concludes, "is to be able to take control of the world."[18] While this view differs from the politics of the copy as I have articulated it so far, it also helps us understand the importance of copying in the Chinese political hierarchy—a peculiar mix of sovereign and neoliberal elements—that I described in the previous chapter. While copying challenges exceptionalism, it can also represent its own power-practice,[19] and it might, in fact—and my discussion of Bosker's work is meant to expose this—represent *its own form of exceptionalism.*

Bosker summarizes the distinction that I have just laid out neatly—a little too neatly, no doubt—as follows: in the West, the copy represents inferiority; in China, it can be associated with superiority, "and the coexistence of an original and its virtually indistinguishable double does not trigger the ontological crisis that is characteristic of the West."[20] Bosker mentions *shanzhai* culture as reflecting "the skill and zeal with which the Chinese replicate, as well as the widespread tolerance for the practice."[21] Interestingly, she traces this back to traditional Chinese landscape painting and the idea that a copy seeks to be as close as possible to an original because it seeks "to capture the essence of the original," its "'life force' or *qi*."[22] This does not necessarily mean, I would add, providing a mimetic copy of the landscape (Bosker's book is not always clear on this);[23] but it does mean providing a copy of the dao flowing through the landscape. In such a thinking, already when it came to traditional Chinese landscape painting, the border between original and copy was less determinate than in the West.

Note that with the indeterminacy of the original and the copy comes an indeterminacy of the origin or the beginning (the words are used as synonyms by Bosker) as well: "Existence and reality are defined not according to their origin but consist of partaking in the universal, continuous process of 'coming into being.'"[24] Given the importance of Benjamin in this chapter so far, it's worth pointing out the similarities between this understanding and Benjamin's notion of origin, as he lays it out in *The Origin of German Tragic Drama*:

> Origin, although an entirely historical category, has, nevertheless, nothing to do with genesis. The term origin is not intended to describe the process by which the existent came into being, but rather to describe that which emerges from the process of becoming and disappearance. Origin is an eddy in the stream of becoming, and in its current it swallows the material involved in the process of genesis.[25]

Benjamin's description of origin is remarkable in that it moves us away from a (typically Western) understanding of origin as event towards a process-thought of origin, a thinking about any origin as always already caught up in a process. As I have shown in this book, such a process-thought, while present in the West, is central to ancient Chinese thought.

Bosker feels comfortable tracing a line from the Chinese attitude towards copying in ancient times to today because as she sees it, "long-standing attitudes about creating simulacrum landscapes have not disappeared but rather have evolved to better suit contemporary pressures and needs."[26] (As I have noted earlier in this book, it's worth pointing out that the Chinese government too has been interested in insisting on the continuity between ancient times and the contemporary both to legitimate its authority and unify China as a nation-state in its relation to the West.) As such, "the classical Chinese thinking on landscape re-creation" associated with the landscape painting that we have discussed previously "represents a valuable portal for analyzing contemporary events."[27] One thing is certain—and it might surprise a reader not familiar with these debates: the argument that the Chinese duplication of Western architecture is a symptom "of the West spreading its influence eastward"[28] should very much be drawn into question. Bosker's book contributes to such a project.

This becomes particularly clear in Bosker's Chapter 4, where she seeks to understand "the Chinese motivation for replicating the alien."[29] Embedding the phenomenon of what she dubs "duplitectures" in China's economico-political situation, specifically its development towards an open market, Bosker notes four factors that help explain the rise of copy-cat architecture in China:

> the rise of its newly minted middle and upper classes and their desire for branded luxury consumer goods and, more important, symbols of self-cultivation; the flexing of the national soft-power muscle; a "yes-we-can" boosterism bloated on a decade of unprecedented economic growth and increasing prestige and power in the global arena; and a deeply rooted tradition of celebrating cultural achievements by constructing gigantic monuments.[30]

Pushed by a mixture of private and public real estate companies as well as state-owned enterprises, duplitectures respond to "a confluence of pragmatic requirements and symbolic needs."[31] China, after a "decades-long moratorium on innovating residential construction,"[32] was eager to improve its building techniques, and for that it could learn from the West. Bosker points out that people were seeking out a higher standard of living as well. By copying Western buildings, China could provide that standard and demonstrate "that they had attained a certain level of sophistication."[33] Clearly, the duplitecture phenomenon partly came about due to a general disorientation in Chinese architecture after China opened up. Western technology was brought in "to bridge the gap between an outmoded construction technology and the burgeoning demand for housing."[34] In short: "Western architectural approaches can benefit China's architects"[35] at a time when they need it. Bosker frames this within a larger Chinese attitude "to embrace the skills of outsiders when they stand to benefit China."[36] Embrace the alien when you can learn and benefit from it.

However, Bosker also points out that functionality cannot possibly provide the whole story. Especially when the architecture copied is "antiquarian,"[37] the idea that Chinese architects are learning from the West seems tenuous at best, since some of the architectures that they copy are, "by Western standards . . . unsustainable and inefficient."[38] This leads Bosker to argue that copying a historical style is important not so much from a functionalist but from a commercial point of view: it helps to sell real estate that would otherwise be nondescript. But according to Bosker, there is more: "the fundamental motives driving the creation of simulacra colonies are less pragmatic than they are symbolic and have to do with reflecting and shaping attitudes toward what it means to be Chinese in a world in which China is competing with the West for economic dominance."[39] And this is, in fact, where things get interesting, because copying becomes part of an attempt to stand out—to obtain the exceptionalist position. It is part of a strategy not so much to unwork exceptionalism, but to obtain it.

Indeed, and going back to the perhaps surprising point that I already highlighted above, Bosker argues that duplitectures are precisely *not* "a form of 'self-colonization,'" as one might at first be inclined to think. "A more careful, nuanced look at these projects suggests otherwise," she writes.[40]

> Instead, the themed townscapes are able to serve as a symbol of the country's progress in the post-Reform era and of the successes of the Communist Party's leadership. In replicating Westerners' homes, city plans, and lifestyles in the context of these suburban micro-territories, the Chinese are exhibiting two of their most important accomplishments: their accumulated wealth and their technical prowess. In this way, the replication of alien landscapes may be a product of China's desire to assert, for domestic and international onlookers, its ascent and entry into the ranks of global, developed nations.[41]

Echoing the language of theology, duplitectures thus need to be read as "symbols of the country's recent economic miracle."[42] China builds them "Because it can."[43] Furthermore, and now explicitly pushing the reading in the direction of sovereignty, Bosker ties the phenomenon of duplitectures to the idea that "the age of monumental and ideology-inflicted architecture is *not* behind us" (emphasis mine).[44] By that, she counters the Dutch architect Rem Koolhaas' claim that the age of "ideological architecture" is over.[45] "The simulacrascape movement goes to show," Bosker concludes, "that in China . . . it is still possible to construct not just private but also public mythologies on a grand scale,"[46] and she explicitly contrasts such sovereign, imperial projects to the supposed dominance of the market mechanism of supply and demand. The latter does not govern the phenomenon of duplitectures; instead, a more sovereign force is at work. And it expresses itself through the copy, which I had pitched in this book so far as critical of Western exceptionalism. Clearly, the copy and its economic, political, and philosophical force needs to be carefully negotiated to see exactly how it is at work in a particular context.[47]

Bosker arguably draws out in architecture what I have previously called (after Ames and Hall) the "cultural elitism" in ancient Chinese philosophy, an exceptionalist aspect of ancient Chinese thought that cannot be denied. On the other side of such a hierarchical reading of daoism and, by extension, of the copy, would stand the association (also made by Ames and Hall among others) of daoism and the copy with political anarchism—their association with post-exceptionalism, which I have pushed in this book. To look at deconstructivist architects like Tschumi and Libeskind to understand this anarchic dimension in architecture may ultimately not go far enough; one might want consider instead the "anarchitecture" of Gordon Matta-Clark. Trained as an architect, Matta-Clark's work consisted in so-called building cuts through which architectures (specifically, buildings marked for demolition) were transformed into art—into what he understood to be anarchical architectures that no longer depended quite so much on the logic of the *archè*. To make art by cutting into a building scheduled for demolition challenged both the idea of a beginning, as captured by the notion of *archè*, but also undermined any suggestion of rule (another meaning of *archè*), given that the work of art that Matta-Clark created was already destined for demolition. There is thus a deliberate attempt to avoid what Benjamin called outdated and potentially fascistic notions like creativity or eternity in favor of something, still architectural but anarchic—anarchitectural.

Dafen Village

A second example that brings home the need to carefully negotiate the copy and its economic, political, and philosophical force, and that also helps us to further reassess the all-too-easy opposition of the West and China when it comes to the copy, is Winnie Wong's study of the reproduction of Western paintings in China.

To begin, it's worth noting that Wong has written about architectural copying as well. Importantly, and in contrast to Bosker, Wong does not think "the notion of counterfeiting" applies in architecture. This is

> because imposter structures are rarely if ever exact replicas of an original . . . and the history of the discipline can be understood as one long story of stylistic influence and imitation. Architecture thus resists assimilation into the legal and conceptual frameworks through which we understand the phenomenon of copying.[48]

"Even in the notoriously litigious US, where there is a long tradition of intellectual-property law," Wong adds, "it wasn't until 1990 that architecture was accorded copyright protection."[49] With respect to duplitectures, Wong argues that "despite superficial visual similarities, the buildings in these themed developments are not actually copies of European architecture at all: They are uniquely Chinese constructions serving a wide range of local needs across social strata."[50] In other words: they might look like copies, but they aren't.

To develop such a reading resolves the contradiction between Bosker's approach and mine: for if these duplitectures aren't copies, Bosker's argument that they are marking a cultural superiority does not undermine the unexceptionalist approach to the copy that I have developed so far. Indeed, Wong argues that these duplitectures are originals; and in that sense, they simply confirm the exceptionalist thinking about the original that I have diagnosed. Importantly, however,

Wong's argument thus breaks down the orientalist framework that would oppose the West to China when it comes to the copy. Rather than finding in duplitectures a confirmation of such a framework, Wong in fact argues that the exceptionalism of the original can be found *across the board*—in the West *and* China.

The implications of Wong's thinking exceed the mere focus on architecture, and by considering some of Wong's other work such an *anti-orientalist* reflection on the original and the copy between the West and China can be further developed. Wong's line of argument—that what we perceive to be a copy in fact isn't one—is familiar to those who have read Wong's book about the copying of Western paintings in the city of Dafen, often referred to as "Dafen village" and often understood as a kind of factory where paintings are mass-produced on an industrial scale (assembly-line painting is the dominant image). In the introduction to her book, Wong seeks to counter those as well as other assumptions about Dafen and its model of production. She points out, first of all, that while Dafen occupies the historical site of a "rural village," "[forms] a migrant workers' urban village" (as Wong explains, "urban villages" are a common model of development in South China that involves villagers leaving their homes for nearby high-rises built for them, and then allowing their land to be redeveloped into "multistory walk up and residential buildings," thus producing an "urban village"), and is "promoted [by the government] as an artists' village," it is "no more 'rural' than is the East Village in Manhattan."[51] Second, Wong emphasizes that Dafen is not "a single [painting] factory" as is sometimes suggested in the media but "made up of hundreds of small studios, workshops, and self-described 'factories,'" employing maximum—and this only in very few cases—"a few dozen employees."[52] Third, while there are a lot of painters and paintings in Dafen, "it would be wrong to assume [Wong argues] that this high quantity *alone* signifies mass production on a monolithic scale, resembling an assembly line factory or requiring specific kinds of factory discipline."[53] Finally, and from my point of view most importantly, Wong argues that the paintings that are made in Dafen are not "forgeries" that would "fool only the most uneducated consumers."[54] As Wong's book shows, this is simply the wrong lens through which to view Dafen's painting production. When sellers advertise their paintings in Dafen as "'Hand-painted Originals,' 'Original Oil on Canvas,' 'Many Unique Exclusives,' 'All Originals . . . No Prints of Any Kind,'"[55] they are not wrong. Evoking Walter Benjamin's analysis of the copy as having a "withering" effect on the aura of the original work of art, Wong points out that the works for sale in Dafen actually participate in the artwork's "auratic traditions,"[56] even if they are often associated with their elimination.

What might be the reasons, Wong asks in this chapter, *not* to call the work that is made in Dafen "art"?[57] She points out the resemblances of the conditions under which paintings are made in Dafen to the painting workshops that we are familiar with in the West, for example "the souvenir painting production of Canaletto, the custom-service portrait studios of John Singer Sargent and Gilbert Stuart, the speculative series of paintings of the impressionists, the 'factories' of Andy Warhol and Damien Hirst, and the custom production studios of Zhang Huan and Takashi Murakami."[58] In other words: if we call all of the latter art, why not the paintings made in Dafen? It's worth pointing out Wong's observation—for which she provides plenty of evidence later in her book—that "[t]he practices of both ink and oil painters in Dafen . . . in fact closely echo those described in James Cahill's groundbreaking study of the unspoken professional lives of Chinese literati painters from the Sung to the modern period."[59] If literati paintings are art, *why not Dafen paintings*? They share very similar conditions of production. Rather than coming down on the side of the copy, in Wong's analysis the paintings made in Dafen interestingly appear to be caught up in between what Benjamin calls "mechanical reproduction" (which you won't find in Dafen) and the auratic artwork with its associated notions of creativity, originality, et cetera. It's almost as if Dafen, in Wong's analysis, *dramatizes* the tension between the original and the copy that structures Benjamin's text; in Dafen, and the discourse that it has produced, this tension feels alive—contested, rather than set.

Wong shows this not only through a critical analysis of what has been said about Dafen, but also through a discussion of artworks that have been made about Dafen. One of the most interesting ones that she discusses is "The Benjamin Project" by an "artist duo named Empfangshalle and a German video artist, Thomas Adebahr."[60] Based in Munich, Germany, these artists asked Dafen painters to reproduce on thirty-eight large canvases and with oil paint all of the pages of Walter Benjamin's original essay on "The Work of Art in the Era of Mechanical Reproduction." This outsourcing of artistic labor is—as I have noted earlier in this book—a move that is typical of much contemporary art, and especially of conceptual art. Elsewhere, Wong sharply comments that "In some respects, conceptual artists are simply new clients with new sales tactics."[61] She is highly critical of Christian Jankowski's and especially Michael Wolf's work on this count. But what was the specific rationale for "The Benjamin Project"?

As Wong explains, these artists (like many others) "conceived of Dafen painters as alienated Chinese copyists of original Western masterpieces, and sought to engage with Dafen painters in a newly conceptual fashion":

> These German artists thus made a special effort to ask the painters to put their signatures on the back of each painting [that they had asked them to make], insisting that these paintings were "their own work." They also invited the Dafen painters—as well as approximately twenty pairs of identical twins—to personally attend the exhibition opening when the paintings were exhibited at an art museum in Shenzhen in 2010.[62]

The project is interesting for a couple of reasons, not in the least because through it, the artists claimed to "[invert] Benjamin's thesis,"[63] thereby explicitly taking the side of aura (never mind aura's association with what Benjamin perceives to be very outdated notions like authenticity or genius—and ultimately fascism). Instead, and somehow in ignorance of the role of politics in Benjamin's essay, Adebahr and Empfangshalle (like many other contemporary artists) can be said to *promote* aesthetic exceptionalism—leaving intact and even confirming what Caroline Jones, pushing us closer to the notion of sovereignty, calls "the regime of auratic authorship."[64]

In the context of Wong's reading of Dafen, "The Benjamin Project" seems interesting in particular because it *misreads* the artwork and the situation of artists at Dafen. The choice for the Benjamin text of course makes explicit the artists' Western theoretical lens. But Wong's book shows, precisely, that such a lens does not apply to Dafen—not to its painters, and not to its paintings. Thus, "The Benjamin Project" becomes a symptom for the West's misperception of what goes on in Dafen, which is precisely *not* the mechanical reproduction that Benjamin writes about.[65] Dafen precisely does *not* offer us a model of the lonely, alienated painter who is mindlessly churning out copies of Western masterpieces. Particularly interesting on this count is an observation that can be found later in Wong's book, namely that "[c]ontrary to the narrative of mass production requiring 'mindless imitation,' then, at the highest volume of production painters [in Dafen] actually abandoned the practices of copying and instead painted 'from the mind.' In other words, and counterintuitively, we might say that the greater the number of paintings the painter makes, the more 'spontaneous,' the more 'freehand,' and the less 'mechanical' his techniques are."[66] Wong characterizes this as a "reversal" of "the Romantic anxieties" around copying, particularly present in the work of "trade painters."[67] But this raises another issue: that even in Dafen, the auratic traditions of the work of art remain very much alive. And furthermore: that it will not do to call the paintings that are made in Dafen "fakes." Another kind of thinking, and another terminology, seems required.

Wong points out that we are dealing here with a "bewildering situation,"[68] in which we are faced with paintings that undisputably have aura—that are unique, hand-painted, exclusive originals—yet whose status as artworks is uncertain. If Benjamin had us think about *the mechanical copy's withering effect on the aura of the original work of art*, here we are dealing with *an auratic work whose status as a work of art is nevertheless in doubt.* Wong's book ought to be understood as a far-reaching shake-up of the very framework of Benjamin's thinking. Dafen paintings "are not just reproductions," she writes, "but are fixed markers of the distance between imitation and appropriation, between classes, modes, and markets of production and consumption":

> The central question that China's painting factories raise, then, is not whether China's export art products are mere copies of objects of another origin, whether Western, traditional, ethnic, or native, but, rather, why and when the layering of origins is important to the consumption and production of the work of art in the globalizing frame.[69]

Wong in fact discusses some of the terminology that's in use in Dafen and that might help us think through the particular situation of the work of art there. This starts with her thinking about the term "gao," which she translates as "the copy." "The copy" is "the source image from which paintings are painted, while the circulation of the *gao* forms the basis of professional transactions between clients and painters."[70] The term "copy," then, weirdly refers to "the image source" (as Wong points out) and any painting that happens in Dafen strictly speaking takes place after the gao, or "*after the copy*," as Wong writes. The gao could be a photograph of a work of art, or also a painting of that work of art. Even more strangely, gao can also refer to an original work of art that is realized as part of a series, with the entire series being referred to as hua, but each work in the series as gao. In this case, then, the hierarchy between original and copy is very much in question—the terms come to refer to nearly the same thing. Wong notes the use of the term "yuangao" in this context, which she renders as "original copy" (which, recall, is also the title of Bianca Bosker's book). Once an artist has completed their version of a gao, they can take a picture of their own painting and thus acquire a gao of their own. But this of course starts a game of telephone where, progressively, we end up farther and farther removed from whatever the original was (and Wong in fact points out that in almost all cases, the original was already a copy).

The transformation that this implies, however, is a key aspect of what goes on in Dafen: gao in fact also means "'a draft,' as in a provisional text or a preparatory sketch."[71] "In this sense," Wong writes in a wonderful passage,

> a *gao* offers only the compositional basis of an artistic work across time, media, and authors. Almost always, Dafen painters freely alter any given gao's dimensions, proportions, palette, style, brushwork, medium, and even content and subject matter. *Mona Lisas* painted in Dafen are almost always larger, *Starry Night* always thicker, David's *Napoleon* smiles more, and Yue Minjun's pink faces smile less cynically. Lichtenstein's comic strip bubbles can be updated with new jokes, and Warhol's contrast color stylization is applied to family portraits. The removal of undesirable details, the replacement of figures, reproportioning for different compositional formats, alterations to the entire tone or style of an image: these are all artistic practices in which Dafen painters are habitually and extensively engaged.[72]

A little later, Wong points out—wait for it—that Warhol's *Marilyn* is in fact painted by Dafen painters *by hand*.[73] Against the background of my discussion of both internal and external criteria used for the authentication of a work of art in both the West and China, it's worth noting that in the above passage, Wong runs through some of the internal criteria that Cahill considers to determine whether "Riverbank" is a forgery by Zhang Daqian or an original by Dong Yuan. The question this triggers should be obvious: *If all of the above are up for transformation, can we still speak of Dafen paintings as copies?*

Wong's conclusion is clear. "Thus," she writes

> Dafen paintings are in fact the very opposite of forgeries, because very often neither painter, seller, nor buyer is even aware what

> the paintings are a "copy" of. Such an unencumbered and transformative practice closely resembles postmodernist ideas of the endless variability and iterability of the image, freed from historical chronology and the anxiety of influence. In Dafen, the detachment of painting from history and precedent . . . enables and fuels free (uninfluenced) adaptation. Here we are in terrain far from the conventional figuration of Chinese "copying" as rote and mimetic reproduction of "the" Western original.[74]

But what is "the very opposite of forgeries"? In this context, it's not quite the original work of art, although the notion of the original very much remains intact in Dafen. Another way of summarizing Wong's argument could be that Dafen does not so much challenge our understanding of the original but our understanding of the copy.

Taken together, these two examples—Bosker and Wong—add new dimensions to the thinking that I have laid out in the previous chapters. Bosker's work on duplitectures has us consider how the copy, considered inferior in the West, can actually become a mark of superiority in the East, and part of an exceptionalist project. In other words, the copy is not essentially unexceptionalist, even if—in the West—that is how it can generally be read. One of the most valuable aspects of Winnie Wong's intervention is that it deconstructs the oppostion between West and East that has been operative in this book and that can be found in Bosker's work as well, by deconstructing not only the opposition of original to copy but the very notion of the copy itself, in particular how it is often all too easily assumed to apply in China. Wong's work on the copy in both architecture and art makes the case that neither duplitectures in China nor the paintings in Dafen are copies—that something more complicated is going on in both these cases than what can be captured by the

Western term "copy." Certainly Walter Benjamin's essay "The Work of Art in the Era of Mechanical Reproduction" cannot be a suitable lens through which to study Dafen village. While it has been the go-to reference for many contemporary Western artists making work about Dafen, Wong's book shows that these artists fundamentally misread what is going on in Dafen; specifically that Dafen is not the regime of alienating, mechanical reproduction that those artists want to make it out to be. Drawing out parallels with the conditions of production under which paintings were and are made both in the West (the artist's studio from the Renaissance to today) and in China (the lifestyle of literati painters), Wong is interested rather in drawing out the continuity of Dafen in the painterly tradition and what she also calls (after Benjamin and others inspired by Benjamin) *the auratic traditions of art and authorship*. But this, then, leaves us with further questions: Does this mean that the Chinese tradition of art and authorship *is* auratic, like the Western one? Does it mean it is *not* post-exceptionalist, as I have been arguing on the basis of works by Han, Jullien, Bosker, and others? Does it mean that Chinese art is, like Western art, exceptionalist?

No Longer Art, No Longer Architecture (#NoLA)

As I see it, Wong's argument does not necessarily lead to that conclusion—in other words, *both* the post-exceptionalist argument *and* Wong's reading of the copy in art and architecture may be true. When Wong is establishing a continuity between Dafen and literati painters, she is not so much talking about the auratic tradition of art and the artist, but asking the question—which Thierry de Duve has argued becomes prominent after

Duchamp—of whether the paintings made in Dafen *are art*. That question asks about a different kind of aura than the question about a work of art's originality, even if the latter is obviously imbricated in the former (in other words: someone may deem a work not to be art if it is a forgery—it should be clear from this book that I am obviously not that someone). Dafen confirms, Wong's research allows her to conclude, the auratic tradition of the original in its insistence on the fact that its painters make original, hand-painted, unique, exclusive works. When it comes to the aura of the work of art, however, Wong herself notes that this is very much uncertain at Dafen; that is, in fact, the true question that Dafen poses: not so much that of the original (Dafen challenges our understanding of the copy, rather—it confronts us with works that look like copies but aren't), but of whether the works one finds in Dafen are *art*. In the terms of this book: while Dafen does not challenge the exceptionalism of the original, or even of the artist—it very much participates in it and confirms it, it makes it its selling point—it does have an unexceptionalizing influence on the privileged status of the work of art.

One can reflect this question back onto duplitectures as well. Wong argues that in fact, these are not copies but uniquely Chinese buildings. We can then discuss whether they are original buildings or not. But we could also ask, as I believe a reading of those buildings after Wong forces us to, whether they are *architecture*—and that is a different question.

Wong's book offers us a variety of reasons—historical, material, related to both the artwork and the artist—that would allow us to conclude that, yes, the paintings made in Dafen are art; and that, yes, duplitectures are architecture. To be clear, we are not arguing about whether they are good or bad art or architecture:

we know that our aesthetic judgments might very well differ, even if we make those judgments as if they are universally shared. But it seems that by the accepted criteria of what, in the West but not only in the West—Wong in fact shows that these criteria apply in China as well—we have deemed to be art, the paintings in Dafen would need to be considered art as well. The same is arguably true for duplitectures, and their inclusion in the realm of architecture.

Still, there remains just the vaguest hint—Wong calls it an uncertainty—that this conclusion is in fact false, that *in spite of* fitting all the criteria, Dafen paintings *aren't art*. The same goes for duplitectures: somewhere, we think they don't quite qualify as *architecture*. My suggestion has been that this very uncertainty, the remainder of this vague hint, points us not just towards the unexceptional but towards what I have called unexceptional art (and now also architecture)—an art that is somehow not quite art, and specifically not art in an exceptionalist way (idem ditto for architecture). Elka Krajewska calls this kind of art "No Longer Art"; Ben Lerner—writing about a fictionalized version of Krajewska's *Salvage Art Institute* in his novel *10:04*—narrows this down to "zero-value art." We could consider "No Longer Architecture" in this context as well, and it would be worth pursuing the thought experiment that imagines the equivalent of Lerner's "zero-value art" in architecture: a building that has become damaged to such an extent that is deemed beyond repair, and worthless—even if it may still be perfectly usable as an architecture, and even if nothing may appear to be visibly wrong with the building. This is perhaps more difficult to do with architecture than with art because architecture has to be functional (its purpose is not, as with art, that it has no purpose). In other words, the unexceptionalizing aspect of use is stronger in architecture than in art. This leads to the reverse situation that if architecture is damaged, and thereby removed from use, it may actually begin to approximate art, and become more exceptionalist. Such architecture may no longer be architecture, but as such it may become art, and the issue of exceptionalism gets deferred in such a process from architecture onto art. This justifies our focus on art throughout this book, even if (as I have shown) architecture has played a major role in art's exceptionalization.

One is reminded in this context of a project like Robert Smithson's *Island of the Dismantled Building*, from 1970, a ruin that Smithson was going to create deliberately on a deserted island in Vancouver Bay—but the project ultimately wasn't realized "because of opposition by local residents and ecologists" for whom the creation of an architecture "without the slightest economic justification, as pure loss, was too much!"[75] If Smithson's project sounds like an affront to architecture, it's worth noting that from another angle, it's art. And it's the pure loss of *architecture-as-art* that becomes excessive here. From post-exceptional architecture to exceptional art—that is very much how I would characterize Smithson's project. On this critical count, Smithson's work couldn't be more different from that of the already mentioned Gordon Matta-Clark, who only works in buildings that are marked for demolition and whose work has a transiency to it that is quite different from Smithson's. Even with *Island of the Dismantled Building*, Smithson seems to be seeking the trace rather than its disappearance; while Matta-Clark operates in ruins as well, ultimately what he seeks is disappearance—and not the trace. As I already discussed in the previous chapter, this also marks the difference between Smithson's work and work by Song Dong, which at first sight may show some similarities to Smithson's earlier projects.

By now, I think it's Krajewska's phrase—"No Longer Art"—that has become the more interesting one—more interesting, I think, than "zero-value art," or the idea of art before or after capital that is the focus of Lerner's investigations. Indeed, in the case of Dafen, we appear to be dealing with a kind of art that is no longer art, an art that is not only "after the copy," as Wong has it, but also—and more radically—"after art." If the phrase sounds like a contradiction in terms, reminiscent of theoretical cop-outs like "messianism without messianism," that is—I would argue—because the word that is elided in that phrase is "exceptional": Dafen offers us "art after *exceptionalist* art"—post-exceptional art. Such exceptionalism may be economic—and Lerner is very much interested in that, hence his focus on value, aesthetic, or political (in the sense that an exceptionalist understanding of art implicitly promotes a political exceptionalism). If the target of the phrase "art after art" is exceptionalism, however, then we would do better to shorten "art after exceptionalist art" not to "art after art" but to "art after exceptionalism." And given that we are talking about "art," a discursive realm in which such terms have proliferated, why not propose "post-exceptionalism" as the next new thing—a term that has been used in policy studies but that has—so far—not made the transition into art (and one understands why—because the force of exceptionalism is much too strong there!)?

Ultimately, the prefix post- is related to the prefix un- which is, in turn, associated with the prefix de-: each of these evokes an unworking or what the philosophers have called "désoeuvrement" of the exceptional. They each evoke a work, or perhaps better a kind of practice or doing: something that is not an established fact, but remains to be accomplished, is ongoing, in-the-works, and solicits your participation. This is also to say that post-exceptional art is explictly not an essentialist notion—it captures an ongoing process. Indeed, post-exceptional art is ultimately not an indexical notion. By this I mean that one cannot in each case point to some art and say it is post-exceptional, and then point to some other art and say that it is not. As opposed to an ontology of post-exceptional art, as opposed to a metaphysical approach that would capture its idea, one should think of the post-exceptional as naming a procedure or operation that unexceptionalizes the exceptionalism constituting the art world. The post-exceptional is in that sense a negative, indeterminate and unfinished concept that cannot be positively defined.

However, there are certain people and realms in which the force of the post-exceptional is potentially strong. Whereas aesthetic exceptionalism exists first and foremost on the side of the spectator, who takes in and fetishizes the work of art, the procedure or operation of the post-exceptional takes place first and foremost with artists themselves, with those who make the work and know how the work was made. It also takes place with the art handlers, those who pack up and ship the work and install it in galleries, museums, or private homes. It takes place with those who work in art environments (not only galleries or museums but also art schools for example) and encounter art while it is being made, before it goes on show, and after the show is taken down—those who are close to it. It can take place with those who sell artwork—although it's against their economic interest, of course, to fully acknowledge art's post-exceptionalism. It can even take place with those who own artwork—although as with those who sell it, the realization of art's post-exceptionalism will bring a fundamental crisis not only to art as property but to the notion of property itself and the capitalist economy that is built upon it.

It appears, however, that the aesthetic exceptionalism associated first and foremost with the spectator has pervaded all of the above, in a kind of spectator-ization (to follow a famous analysis) of the art world.[76] Such a becoming hegemonic of the spectator's experience of art as exceptional has undone the post-exceptionalism of art on all fronts. If this was already part of Friedrich Nietzsche's argument against Immanuel Kant in the third essay in *On The Genealogy of Morals*, it is worth rehearsing it here again in praise of a post-exceptionalism that would challenge the exceptionalization of the artist that Nietzsche supported.[77]

Let us suggest a polemical reversal of the logic governing the world of art: *to be close to art is to be in proximity to the post-exceptional.* This does not require *connoisseur*-ship, at least not of the kind associated with aesthetic exceptionalism. It requires a kind of knowing, to be sure, a kind of *connaître* or *savoir*, but a knowing whose verticality has been thoroughly unworked, even if traces of it remain. It is to be hoped that the post-exceptionalism of such a knowledge will one day take over the experience of the spectator, unworking their exceptionalism into the post-exceptional, so that they will be able to see art for what it is: *just art.* There is something "secular" about this, in Edward Said's sense of the term, in that it asks us to acknowledge first and foremost art's worldliness.[78] In the end, the artist at work is just that: at work in the world, doing what they do every day. Their art is just that: the post-exceptional, worldly—secular—product of their labor. The rest is aesthetic exceptionalism.

I will leave the last word to the art forger Ivan Friedland, from Daniel Kehlmann's novel *F*:

> All museums are full of fakes. So what? The provenance of each and everything in this world is uncertain; there is no particular magic involved in art, and the works that are ranked as

great have not been brushed by an angel's wings. Art objects are objects just like everything else: some are extraordinarily accomplished, but none of them springs from a higher universe. That some are linked with the name of this or that person, that some of them fetch high prices and others don't, that some are world-famous and most are not, is due to a number of different forces, but none of these is otherworldly.[79]

Notes

1 Jones qtd. Winnie Wong, *Van Gogh on Demand: China and the Readymade* (Chicago, IL: University of Chicago Press, 2013), p. 12.
2 Bianca Bosker, *Original Copies: Architectural Mimicry in Contemporary China* (Honolulu: University of Hawai'i Press/Hong Kong University Press, 2013).
3 Bosker, *Original Copies*, p. 20.
4 Mark C. Taylor, *Hiding* (Chicago, IL: University of Chicago Press, 1995), p. 239.
5 Taylor, *Hiding*, p. 239.
6 Tschumi qtd. ibid., p. 241.
7 Tschumi qtd. ibid., p. 242.
8 Ibid., p. 243.
9 Libeskind qtd. Mark C. Taylor, *Nots* (Chicago: IL: University of Chicago Press, 1995), p. 140, p. 141.
10 Taylor, *Nots*, p. 147.
11 Ibid.
12 Libeskind qtd. ibid.
13 Ibid.
14 Ibid., p. 134.
15 Ibid.
16 Ibid.
17 Bosker, *Original Copies*, p. 24.
18 Ibid.
19 Ariella Aïsha Azoulay has developed such a reading of reproduction specifically with respect to Benjamin's "Work of Art" essay. See: Arielle Aïsha Azoulay, *Potential History: Unlearning Imperialism* (New York: Verso, 2019).

20 Bosker, *Original Copies*, p. 25.
21 Ibid., p. 25.
22 Ibid., p. 27.
23 In an excellent article, Chang Tan points out that the "nature" that is rendered in Chinese landscape painting is not so much mimetically rendered as invented. Among other works, Tan looks in the article at landscape paintings that look traditional but are in fact "collages of scenes of urban congestion and pollution" (p. 223), noting the great skill it takes "to create such deceptively 'real' *shanshui* [landscapes; literally: mountain(s)-water(s)]" (p. 227). While Tan's point is about the breakdown of nature and culture in such landscapes—Tan's title is obviously inspired by the work of Timothy Morton, whose book *Ecology Without Nature* is referenced in the article—it participates in a criticism of a mimetic reading of Chinese landscape painting as well. Chang Tan, "Landscape Without Nature: Ecological Reflections in Contemporary Chinese Art," *Journal of Contemporary Chinese Art* 3:3 (2016), pp. 223–241.
24 Bosker, *Original Copies*, p. 28.
25 Walter Benjamin, *The Origin of German Tragic Drama*, trans. John Osborne (New York: Verso, 1998), p. 34.
26 Bosker, *Original Copies*, p. 22. Interestingly, landscapes themselves are also being copied today. Ethan Tucker reports about how "[i]n the high-end residential districts of Seoul, South Korea," you can find "replicas of some of Korea's most famous natural sites, rendered in miniature for the enjoyment of the city's rising upper class." Tucker points out that "this trend of reproducing famous landscapes" is called "jingyeong sansu" and that the roots of this style "are in 18th-century Korean landscape painting, when artists who had previously depicted idealized landscapes began to turn their attention to the Korean landscape as it actually was, and strove to recapture the exact qualities of real mountains and landscapes in the country," a style that was called "jingyeong sansuhwa" or "true-view landscape painting." See: Ethan Tucker, "Famous Landscapes Are Being Recreated Around Korea," *Architectural Digest* December 10 (2019), accessible: https://www.architecturaldigest.com/story/famous-landscapes-recreated-luxe-homes-south-korea
27 Bosker, *Original Copies*, p. 22.
28 Ibid., p. 36.
29 Ibid., p. 67.
30 Ibid., p. 68.
31 Ibid., pp. 69–70.

32 Ibid., p. 70.
33 Ibid.
34 Ibid., p. 73.
35 Ibid.
36 Ibid., p. 75.
37 Ibid., p. 74.
38 Ibid., p. 76.
39 Ibid., p. 80.
40 Ibid., p. 86.
41 Ibid., p. 87.
42 Ibid.
43 Ibid.
44 Ibid., p. 88.
45 Koolhaas qtd. ibid, p. 92.
46 Ibid., p. 92.
47 I have found useful here, as a comparative case where one can see similar dynamics at work, Andrew Morris' article "'I Believe You Can Fly': Basketball Culture in Postsocialist China" (in: Perry Link, Richard P. Madsen, and Paul G. Pickowicz, eds., *Popular China: Unofficial Culture in a Globalizing Society* [New York: Rowman & Littlefield, 2002], pp. 9–38). I owe this reference to Robeson Taj Frazier, who assigned this text as required reading when he visited my graduate seminar in Spring 2020.
48 Winnie Wong, "Creative Commons," *Artforum* 03 (2014), pp. 117–120, here p. 118.
49 Wong, "Creative Commons," p. 118.
50 Ibid., p. 120.
51 Wong, *Van Gogh on Demand*, p. 26.
52 Ibid.
53 Ibid., p. 27.
54 Ibid., p. 28.
55 Ibid.
56 Ibid.
57 The Chinese government is in fact quite interested in calling it art. This can be understood as the government's broader interest in its citizens becoming "members of a new creative class" (Silvia Lindtner, "Making Subjectivities: How China's DIY Makers Remake Industrial Production, Innovation & the Self" [June 15, 2013]. Presented at the Eleventh Chinese Internet Research Conference (CIRC11), Oxford Internet Institute, University of Oxford, June 15, 2013, accessible: SSRN: https://ssrn.

com/abstract=2282420 or http://dx.doi.org/10.2139/ssrn.2282420). The government's tolerance towards, and even support of, shanzhai can also be understood in this way.

58 Wong, *Van Gogh on Demand*, p. 8.

59 Ibid.

60 Ibid., p. 11.

61 Winnie Won Yin Wong, "Framed Authors: Photography and Conceptual Art from Dafen Village," *Yishu: Journal of Contemporary Chinese Art* 7:4 (2008), pp. 32–43, p. 37.

62 Wong, *Van Gogh on Demand*, p. 11.

63 Ibid.

64 Jones qtd. ibid., p. 12.

65 See: Wong, *Van Gogh on Demand*, p. 13.

66 Ibid., p. 53.

67 Ibid.

68 Ibid., p. 16.

69 Wong, "Framed Authors," p. 38.

70 Wong, *Van Gogh on Demand*, p. 17.

71 Ibid., p. 20.

72 Ibid., pp. 20–21.

73 Ibid., p. 21.

74 Ibid.

75 Yve-Alain Bois and Rosalind Krauss, *Formless: A User's Guide* (New York: Zone Books, 1999), p. 187–188.

76 This was, as others have pointed out, precisely the issue that Nietzsche had with Kant. Kant's theory of aesthetics, he argued, operated from the point of view of the spectator. It is of course in Kant's time that many of the issues I have discussed here are born. Nietzsche responds to all of this—the institution of the exceptional realm of art in the eyes of the spectator—with an exceptionalism of the artist. But this did not solve the core of the problem he had identified. Nietzsche too is within the realm of aesthetic exceptionalism—but from the artist's side.

77 Friedrich Nietzsche, *On the Genealogy of Morals*, trans. Walter Kaufmann (New York: Vintage, 1989), pp. 103–106.

78 See: Edward Said, *The World, the Text, and The Critic* (Cambridge, MA: Harvard University Press, 1983).

79 Daniel Kehlmann, *F*, trans. Carol Brown Janeway (New York: Vintage, 2015), pp. 188–189.

Conclusion: Variations on Post-Exceptional Art

Ghostwritten

Methodologically, much of this book has sought to break down the all too easy, orientalist opposition between the West and China when it comes to the aesthetic, philosophical, and ultimately political distinctions that I have sought to draw between exceptionalism and post-exceptionalism. While it would be wrong to oppose the West to China on that count, I have nevertheless highlighted divergences between the two that have enabled me to lay bare the prominence of exceptionalist thinking in the West and the importance of ancient Chinese thought as a resource for thinking the post-exceptional. That said, daoism, or the ancient Chinese thought that I have focused on, clearly contains exceptionalist traits, in the same way that post-exceptionalist thinking can be uncovered in the West.

In this Conclusion, I want to pursue three closely related variations on those themes, mobilizing the distinction between exceptionalism and post-exceptionalism between those areas—the West and China—to put some of the thinking that I have developed in this book to work in relation to three new topics of inquiry that have not been a focus in the book so far, but are germane to it (as will become clear): the art of calligraphy; artificial intelligence art; and debates about art restoration. Considered between the West and China, all three enable us to deepen and further complicate the main concepts and structuring divergences of this book, both confirming the theoretical framework that I have laid out as a fruitful lens for further inquiry and shaking it up in ways that invite us to consider its validity anew. That describes, in my view, the practice of critique, as subversively operating within and at times at the limit of a theoretical framework that it considers legitimate, and thus both confirming a world of thought and potentially leaving it behind.

In the previous chapters, I have built upon the work of other scholars to suggest that the nude in Western art history is a realization, aesthetically, of a model of thought that I have called exceptionalist. I have, furthermore, associated a politics with such thought by approaching it through the lens of disability studies, for example, or connections between aesthetics and politics in the twentieth century (whether it is fascism's rejection of a modern art which, aesthetically, shows connections to disability, or fascism's celebration of an aesthetic of shock as captured in this book by Carl Schmitt's concept of sovereignty). Such an aesthetico-political thought has been countered through an engagement with landscape, specifically so-called monumental Chinese landscape ("shanshui," "mountain[s]-water[s]") painting as a productive site to unwork Western exceptionalism. That does not mean, as I have also indicated, that Chinese landscape painting is free from exceptionalism; indeed, it is still called monumental, and it too seeks to project sovereign—and specifically imperial—power. Whether such power is captured by the mountains in those landscapes or by the water and clouds is another question, as I have indicated; even what to understand by the mountain—a symbol of oneness and eternity in the West—is under discussion here (for since the mountain changes every time one looks at it, perhaps it is more appropriate to think of it as plural rather than as unique and one). Such questions may also evoke, as I have suggested, a different practice of power—sovereign, as in the West, but exercising that sovereignty differently. Rather than qualifying as "post-exceptional," then, Chinese landscape painting reconfigures the relation between the exceptional and the post-exceptional and invites one to think sovereign power anew, in a different aesthetic and even cosmic context.

In such a context, it is worth considering Chinese landscape painting's close relation to calligraphy, or the art of beautiful writing. After all, calligraphy is housed in art departments in China and its practice is considered a branch of aesthetics.[1] Landscape painting developed out of it, with many of calligraphy's techniques migrating into landscape painting.[2] As such, calligraphy too navigates the tension between the exceptional and the post-exceptional. If exceptionalism was captured in this book by the nude in Western art history, then it's worth pointing out that calligraphy does not seem to follow the same logic as the nude. The exceptionalism of the nude, as I have discussed, is the result of mathematics and perfect geometrical proportion—plus some other, "natural" element, as Kenneth Clark argues, that is difficult to capture. Overall, however, math predominates, either as a (flawed) architectural model for the nude, or as a geometric understanding of the human body as a model for architecture.[3] Hence, the nude's association with Plato earlier in this book. In his discussion of beauty in his novel *Essays in Love*, for example, Alain de Botton discusses the Platonic notion of beauty, specifically its "mathematical basis,"[4] and the effect it has had on idealizations of women's bodies.[5] The nude is the "Greek," mathematical standard of beauty. This standard presents itself as universal—the universal of math and geometry—but I mark it here as "Greek" to draw out its geographical specificity: not all standards of beauty are mathematical.[6]

There is no equivalent science of calligraphy. This also divorces calligraphy from the universalism of the Western ideal. Indeed, calligraphy generally does not stand apart from the individual calligrapher's emotional state. Calligraphy is, rather, an extension of the writer's inner state, and thus a form in process rather than a mathematical, geometrical ideal.[7] Recall that in the *Dao De Jing*, "the great square has no corners." It's François Jullien who suggests that this may be "the non-Greek formula par excellence."[8] One might thus develop different calligraphies for different moods—but the same can't be done with the nude: mathematics and geometrical proportion allow for only one.

But why this comparison of calligraphy to the nude, other than the fact that landscape painting developed out of calligraphy and was put in a certain amount of tension in this book with the nude? Indeed, calligraphy is likely more closely related to Western handwriting, which—although it hardly marks the same unicity as the nude—is still uniquely yours (one could call this "plural" exceptionalism—"plural" in the sense that everyone has it; this is a "weak" exceptionalism compared to the "strong" exceptionalism of the nude). Calligraphy's closer proximity to exceptionalism becomes clear precisely in what sets it apart from Western handwriting: it obviously exists at a much higher level of art than the latter. As such, it is closely associated with the idea of the sage—one only becomes a calligrapher after a life dedicated to meditation—which (as I've already pointed out) certainly has traces of exceptionalism (cultural elitism) to it, even if much sagely thought seeks precisely to undo the exceptional.

It may be useful to recall in this context the example of a historical figure like Emperor Huizong (who made a brief appearance in the second chapter of this book). Emperor Huizong employed several "lady ghostwriters"[9] who would do his handwriting for him. Hui-Shu Lee discusses a story that indicates that Huizong instructed these ghostwriters himself:

> After the year 1116, Huizong's officials apparently began to notice that the imperial handwriting was somewhat different from what they were accustomed to seeing. And after 1119, the emperor's hand seems to have undergone another subtle stylistic shift. The officials began to hear that eunuchs, such as the favored Liang Shicheng (d. 1126) might be involved, since these writings did not appear to be "feminine" and consequently unlikely to be from the hands of the palace ladies. When their concerns were brought to Huizong's attention, the emperor explained, "In the past, the palace ladies' manner of writing was not particularly good, so I instructed them personally. Now their writing is just like that of men, and they truly deserve praise. You gentlemen have really blundered!"[10]

Lee draws out the gendered dimension of this account, but the overall tenor is nervousness about the uncertainty of calligraphy's authorship. Already the palace ladies represent that uncertainty: it's their "ghosting" that opens up the possibility of *yet another someone* ghosting in *their* stead. Since the calligraphy in question relates to issues of state, Lee points out that such uncertainties "would have been a matter of great concern."[11] The copy, more specifically the practice of what Lee refers to as "imperial ghostwriting,"[12] thus poses a great political threat, one that is caught up here in the exceptionalism of handwriting and the post-exceptionalism that is brought to it through the copy. *Sovereignty can't be ghosted.*

Today, it is interesting to learn in this context about experiments in "Automatic Artistic Calligraphy Generation"—AI-generated calligraphy.[13] As was to be expected, such experiments proved offensive to some: because the writing that calligraphy realizes is so intensely personal, and tied to lived, human experience and wisdom, its generation by AI seems to hollow it out to such an extent that one can no longer really speak of calligraphy. If from a Western point of view AI-generated handwriting already seems a bit of a travesty given handwriting's unique association with an individual, AI-generated calligraphy definitely appears to be a contradiction in terms. Of course, my use of the word "definitely" in this context depends on the exceptional status of calligraphy, and the unexceptionalizing effect that the introduction of AI into its generation would have. This is moderately disturbing with respect to Western handwriting; but it comes as a shock with respect to calligraphy. It is worth noting by the way that Chinese landscape paintings, too, are being reproduced by AI and can only be distinguished from human-made Chinese landscape paintings less than 55 percent of the time.[14]

Laura Vermeeren's fieldwork in Beijing has foregrounded a number of important aspects of this problematic. In an article titled "Chinese Calligraphy in the Digital Realm,"[15] she starts by considering the widespread concern and even "moral panic" that is triggered by the digitization of Chinese handwriting, specifically the "character amnesia"[16] that it risks to produce. This is partly tied to the idea that an important aspect of high culture is going to be lost when the artistic skill that is needed for calligraphy is lost (in this case, through digitization). Many also see the practice of calligraphy as a mark of culturedness and appreciate its associations with upward mobility: the ordinary Chinese, too, can enjoy this art of the elites![17] This clearly draws out the exceptionalist dimensions of calligraphy. In the context of her discussion of calligraphy in relation to digitization, however, Vermeeren is interested specifically in practices of calligraphy appearing in what she calls "the everyday."[18] It is these post-exceptional uses of calligraphy that stand out to her—"[e]merging quotidian calligraphic practices"—as being able to continue the practice of exceptionalist calligraphy in the digital era.[19] While Vermeeren considers these as "interruptions"—in other words, as exceptions to the norm—it would be more productive to read them as unexceptionalizations that continue calligraphy by challenging, precisely, calligraphy's possible association with exceptionalism. In such a context, the digital realm too can emerge as a space where calligraphy is unexceptionalized. Far from unilaterally leading away from calligraphy, and thus proving right the fear of character amnesia that Vermeeren mentions, Vermeeren shows how the digital can in fact become a component in what her article's title terms calligraphy's "remediation":[20] she points out, for instance, how the digital is used to promote the study and practice of calligraphy today. In these ways, the digital can also come to enhance the techniques that are necessary for calligraphy.

As was perhaps to be expected, Vermeeren eventually arrives at a discussion of Walter Benjamin's "Work of Art" essay in this context. She uses the essay to make a historical and deconstructive point: rather than oppose calligraphy to the copy, she writes, we would do well to consider how calligraphy was always considered "reproducible,"[21] and how calligraphy students in fact learn by reproducing the calligraphy of their masters. "The copy," as Rosalind Krauss already put it in *The Originality of the*

Avant-Garde, is "*the underlying condition of the original*."[22] This is an unexceptionalizing move that is worth noting. Chinese calligraphy, Vermeeren writes, "has remained strikingly homogenous in both form and shape."[23] But this is not what determine's calligraphy's exceptionalism. "Authenticity . . . should be sought," rather, "in the execution of the calligraphy: the choice and interpretation of the models, the speed of the brush, and the display or deliberate disguise of personal expression or spirit."[24] It is in a painter's choice of model and way of painting that originality resides. Calligraphy then needs to be understood as a navigation "between the copying of a model and the use of 'personality' and 'own style' . . . a balance dictated by the ruling regime and tastes of the scholarly elite of the time"[25]—a navigation between aura and its loss. Vermeeren notes that while this is more easily done in the realm of the analog, the digital too is characterized by this dialectic.

At the origin of landscape painting, calligraphy proves to be a remarkable site, then, to think through the tension between exceptionalism and post-exceptionalism in Chinese aesthetics. A practice associated with exceptionalism and elitism, it relies for its continued existence on the copying of a model, a copying that in the case of the Emperor Huizong for example can become politically threatening as undermining or even vying with the sovereign authority of the one. Still, such authority depends for its continuation on the practice of copying, and as such post-exceptionalism turns out to be vital for the remembering of calligraphy, especially in the era of the digital where it risks to become forgotten—because artificial agents can practice the art of beautiful writing just as well (landscapes, as I have indicated, are also caught up in these developments). Digital technologies ought to be put to use, then, in the post-exceptionalizing study of calligraphy—to both continue the cultural relief of its tradition and leave its exceptionalist aspects behind.

Automatic Painting

In the West, it's worth considering in this context the work of Jackson Pollock. I turn to Pollock—whose painting has been referenced not just by Ben Lerner in the context of his discussion of art vandalism[26] but also as a possible inspiration for the diasporic Chinese master-painter and possibly forger Zhang Daqian[27]—because his aesthetic seems to share something with calligraphy: it strikes one as the anti-nude because it does not seem to paint a mathematical or geometrical ideal form ("seem"—soon I'll have to reconsider this claim); and, like calligraphy for the calligrapher, it captures Pollock's inner state. The latter is in fact why people have characterized Pollock's painting as "automatic": it's work of abstract expressionism that renders Pollock's mental state and even his unconscious directly onto the canvas.[28] As such, it would seem that no two Pollocks could ever be the same, and *also* that it would surely be madness to try to copy a Pollock—because one would be copying not merely an aesthetic, but also a mental state or even an unconscious.[29]

And yet, people *have* copied Pollocks (and perhaps one would need a psychoanalyst to tell us which is the original, which one the copy). Moreover, the idea of *mechanically* reproducing a Pollock has also exercised some influence over the popular imagination, perhaps precisely because Pollock's painting was called "automatic." In the script of Alex Garland's film *Ex Machina* (A24/Universal Pictures, 2014), for example, in which several conversations about artificial intelligence take place in a room referred to as "the Pollock room" and in front of what in the film appears to be a Pollock painting, there is a scene—not present in the final cut of the film—in which the AI-creator Nathan Bateman explains that he had an AI repaint one of Pollock's famous paintings. This led to an identical painting, and Bateman then supposedly destroyed one of the two paintings, leaving it forever uncertain which one survived: the real one, or the fake. Bateman's story brings together discussions about the fake, copying, mechanical versus manual reproduction, and art's economic value. But that's the movies, right? Surely no AI could copy a Pollock? Surely that would be the wrong interpretation of "automatic painting"? A painting *without* an unconscious behind it?

Pollock's work may in fact surprise us here. In a chapter from his book *The Creativity Code* titled "Learning from the Masters," Oxford-based mathematician Marcus du Sautoy writes about the mathematician Richard Taylor, who "revealed that the arcs of paint Pollock let fall are not unlike the looping lines traced by a chaotic pendulum, which has a pivot that moves around instead of remaining fixed."[30] "Taylor had designed," he continues, "a contraption called the Pollockizer to confirm his theory about Pollock's painting style."[31] In this way, Taylor is able to reproduce the fractals that Pollock, through his idiosyncratic painting style, also produced: "Pollock's unique fractal quality [turned out to be] something you could measure."[32] In other words: Pollock is math, but it's a different kind of math than the nude. The nude, as I have shown, presents us with exceptionalist math—the perfect geometric proportions of the Vitruvian Man. But in Pollock we find what one might call the post-exceptionalist math of the fractal, which is structured by the copy. (The structuring principle of the fractal is nothing but the copy.) Du Sautoy interestingly describes the effect of this in terms that recall but also subtly shift my discussion of Chinese landscape painting: "Approaching the painting," he writes, "you lose your sense of place in relation to the canvas and begin to mentally fall into the image."[33] The spectator (rather than the painter) disappears into the painting.

Interestingly, it's "[w]ith this insight [into the fractal nature of Pollock's paintings] [that] mathematicians have been able to pick out the fake canvases [in other words, fake Pollocks *made by humans*] 93 percent of the time"—because they did *not* produce the fractals that Pollock (and the Pollockizer) both produce.

In spite of the Pollockizer being the better copier, however, a new problem emerged:

> Locally the paint on the canvas looks like a Pollock but the problem is, it has no structure. The chaotic pendulum produced drip fractals but it was incapable of creating that overall impression of something more that Pollock was able to convey.[34]

So, in the end, even if the machine-element appeared to win at first, it is the human element that has the last word: the Pollockizer cannot bring Pollock's sense of composition to the larger canvas, even if locally, it reproduces Pollock's painting *exactly*. What that sense of composition is remains frustratingly vague in du Sautoy's chapter. Here too, then, an element of human exceptionalism remains. There evidently persists a difference between a canvas made by Pollock, and one made by the Pollockizer. The Pollockizer unexceptionalizes (locally, Pollock is math—the math of fractals, that is, structured as a copy) but its shortcomings also confirm Pollock's exceptional status (when it comes to overall composition).

A particularly interesting project in this context is the post-conceptual artist Warren Neidich's work *Accidental Paintings* (1993–1994), which presents itself as a "catalogue raisonné" of paintings not included in Pollock's oeuvre. It consists of photographs Neidich took of paint splatter at Pollock's studio, next to his East Hampton home (which currently houses the Pollock-Krasner Foundation): the splatter that landed next to the canvas on the wall, or on the floor. Before taking his photographs, Neidich removed all the works that are on the studio's walls, leaving only the splatter and the labels that accompanied the works on the wall. In this way, the labels—for example, "Jackson and Lee [Krasner] by the studio door"—come to operate as titles for these accidental, and abstract, works.

What to make of Neidich's work? *Accidental Paintings* developed out of several of Neidich's previous projects in photography. The work can be traced back, Neidich suggests, to the doctored images titled *The Unknown Artist Warren Neidich*, in which he inserted himself in famous photographs of American (U.S.) history. A more direct antecedent for *Accidental Paintings* came about later, when Neidich removed images from the walls of the German artist Martin Kippenberger's Paris Bar in Berlin to replace them with his own. Neidich was struck by the discoloration that the removed frames left on the walls—and he photographed those. For his project *Metamaterial*, finally, Neidich photographed the objects that were left after the parties that accompany exhibition openings or closings. The photographs were meant to draw out the aesthetic dimension of those objects: a stack of beer crates left in the middle of a gallery appears like a work by Donald Judd. Like Neidich's *Accidental Paintings*, all of those projects were based on accident, chance, contingency, and in that sense they resonate with the aesthetic of unexceptional art.

Neidich's *Accidental Paintings* makes several interesting interventions: on the one hand, the project unexceptionalizes Pollock's work by including in it what fell just outside of its frame—a remainder that was still made by Pollock, and reproduces the effect of his technique, but is nevertheless not a Pollock, even if he made it. The goal here is not to unexceptionalize by reproducing the mastery of the painter in some other way, but by showing the by-products of the painter's mastery and allowing those to undermine the work's exceptional status. This goes further than François Jullien's interest in the sketch, which I discussed earlier in this book. It is about recuperating something that has no value at all, as art. Its nearest counterpart in the pages of this book would be the works collected in Elka Krajewska's *Salvage Art Institute*. *Accidental Paintings*, however, is not so much art that is no longer art, art before or after capital, but art's material remainder—*what remains of art*.

From another point of view, of course, one might also say that the recuperation of such a remainder as art is possible only because of the exceptionalism attached to Pollock: even his unintended splatter becomes art, in spite of it having no aesthetic value. Moreover, it is of course Neidich who, through his gesture of photographing the splatter, turns it into art, and adds an exceptionalism to it. (This returns us to the Banksy dilemma that I discussed in Chapter 1.) *Accidental Paintings* can thus be said to negotiate the difference between exceptionalism and post-exceptionalism in art.

When it comes to assessing the politics of Pollock's art, as I have tried to do with various examples of exceptional and unexceptional art in this book, things get complicated. It might surprise those who know Pollock as one of the most expensive contemporary painters, but Pollock's work is historically associated with the Depression Era. From 1935 until 1943, Pollock was employed by the United States government (as part of the Works Project Association of Roosevelt's New Deal Federal Arts Project). As Frances Stonor Saunders notes in her seminal "Yanqui Doodles" essay, Pollock (like other ab ex'ers) was "producing subsidized art for the government and getting involved in left-wing politics."[35] This was particularly true for Pollock, "who in the 1930s had been involved in the Communist workshop of the Mexican muralist David Alfalo Siquieros"—and Saunders adds that "several other Abstract Expressionists had all been Communist activists."[36] Overall, people considered his work to be about the freedom of human expression, a reading that's doubly interesting given Pollock's own insistence that his work was "No chaos, damn it!"

To see Pollock's work in a film like *Ex Machina* be brought in conversation with AI, which tends to be associated first and foremost with a surveillance society in which freedom becomes a mere correlative of government, as Michel Foucault lecturing in the mid-1970s put it,[37] seems a bit odd, then, to say the least. One can think also of Gilles Deleuze's "society of control"[38] or the Belgian researcher Antoinette Rouvroy's notion of "algorithmic governance":[39] these appear to be theories that cannot be brought in conversation with Pollock. Nevertheless, it should be noted that whereas to some, "Abstract Expressionism [was] evidence of a Communist conspiracy," to others it represented something entirely different: "a specifically anti-Communist ideology, the ideology of freedom, of free enterprise,"[40] which of course would ultimately deliver precisely the very cynical notion of freedom—neoliberal freedom—that can be paired with the digital age. This dramatically unexceptionalizes our notion of freedom.

If Foucault at the end of the famous fifth section of *History of Sexuality: Volume 1*, in which he proposes the notion of biopolitics, imagines people in the future being amused by the obsession with sex as a site where our liberation could be found—if only we could get at the bottom of sex, then we would be free!—one could perhaps imagine a similar amusement with or even laughter at what is left of freedom in the digital age. If we can agree that the disciplinary power that Foucault associates with an anatomo-politics of the body may have waned, while the biopolitics of the population ("focused on the species body . . . and effected through an entire series of interventions and regulatory controls"[41]) has intensified into the psycho- and even neuro-politics of the mind and the brain, we can see that our notion of freedom has morphed along the way. It has transformed into something that is not so much disciplined or even the target of intervention or regulation (both of which Foucault associated with biopolitics[42]) but has rather become premediated. Deleuze concisely anticipated all of this, *after* Foucault, in his "Postscript on the Societies of Control." The data that we provide just by carrying our digital devices or through our activity online are gathered and used to establish a pattern that predicts what we might do tomorrow; today, our individual and collective free actions are used to bring tomorrow's freedom within the limits of control. Patterns—established through the most advanced computer science—are used for example to predict market behavior and guarantee trading profit.[43]

Pollock, one may be surprised to hear, is part of the history of such patterning. Art historian Pamela Lee has drawn out, not in a direct way but by carefully mapping out Pollock's historical moment, Pollock's place in the history of contemporary algorithmic culture—the "digital legacy," as she calls it, of the historical moment of which Pollock was very much a part.[44] In her work on "Think Tank Aesthetics," Lee puts Pollock's painting, which Pollock himself situated entirely within the representational and not the abstract (Pollock rejected the term abstract expressionism, as Lee points out), in dialogue with a Cold War intellectual and military culture. Thus, she lays bare Pollock's role in what in another chapter of the same book project she calls "the military-aesthetic complex."[45] Here, Pollock's non-chaotic painting becomes part of a Cold War obsession with patterning, with the deciphering of abstract form into representation so that, for example, enemy behavior could be predicted (and it is, of course, Saunders who has most convincingly laid out ab ex's tie to the Cold War and the CIA in particular; Eva Cockcroft had already done as much in 1974[46]). Lee finds this discourse in anthropology, and notes the government's interest in it around 1947: Pollock's painting and the discourse around it, she suggests, need to be read within the same context, with a methodological overlap between all three—anthropology, the military, and art. At stake in a Pollock are the very same issues that fascinate those other fields at the time. And those issues continue, Lee argues, all the way into today's digital age.

In other words, while Pollock may be placed on the other side of fascism, a closer albeit brief historical look—with I provided via Lee's work—forces one to see the other side of that position, and consider its relations to neoliberal government in the digital age. Such a digital, neoliberal, "dematerialized" reading of Pollock goes against the mythology that is usually construed around him. As Saunders points out in "Yanqui Doodles," the myth of Pollock is very much a "material" one: "Everything about Pollock was right. Born on a sheep ranch in Cody, Wyoming, he entered the New York scene like a cowboy—hard-talking, heavy-drinking, shooting his way from the Wild West."[47] Saunders adds, however: "This was, of course, a mythical past. Pollock had never ridden a horse, and had left Wyoming as a young child. But the image was so apt, so *American*, and no one disbelieved it."[48] Although echoes of this kind of masculinity continue today in the neoliberal era, the materiality of the image (which can be tied to Pollock's insistence on representation versus abstraction when it came to the characterization of his work) also stands in tension with the abstraction of the age.

The time seems to have finally come, then, to start "disbelieving": it seems clear that Pollock's work participated in the abstract, dematerialized culture of neoliberalism and the digital that the myth (as well as Pollock himself through how he talked about his work) sought to keep at bay. Indeed, this may be a key component of its very post-exceptionalism—and this certainly has to be reckoned with in terms of the criticism of sovereignty that post-exceptionalism brings.

The Rembrandt Shudder

As a way to push this point even further, and to show specifically that such "neoliberal" post-exceptionalism does not necessarily stand in opposition to exceptionalist sovereignty, let us consider the smooth video in which the Dutch multinational banking and financial services corporation ING revealed how it had used AI (created on the basis of a three-dimensional computer analysis of all of Rembrandt's paintings) to generate a new Rembrandt. The video was to promote the work—and, of course, ING itself.[49]

It shows how a team of scientists "used technology and data," which are generally used "to improve business life," "as paint and brushes"—to make a work that reaches into the most intimate regions of human existence. A deep algorithm studied all of Rembrandt's paintings to derive from it a "profile" that would become the basis of what the video calls "the next Rembrandt." The profile's features are listed in the video as: Caucasian; male; facial hair; 30–40 years old; dark clothing; collar; wearing a hat; facing to the right. With those features "extracted" from Rembrandt's work, the team continued to pursue, among other things, a "height" analysis of Rembrandt's paintings, creating a 3D map that showed how Rembrandt applied and layered the paint in his work. It's out of such analyses that, eventually, a new Rembrandt came about.

For the critical viewer, however, such a project immediately raises numerous questions: What technologies were used—and, presumably, optimized—to measure the faces in Rembrandt's paintings? Who owns those technologies after the completion of the project? Could they be used by governments for facial recognition? Might the Rembrandt project in fact have operated as a kind of playing ground precisely for those interested in developing better technologies to recognize faces? The issue seems particularly present when computer analysis arrives at what the film calls the typical "profile" of the subjects in Rembrandt's portraits. While the technologies on show in the film are used to generate a Rembrandt, they are clearly also technologies of government, and it's difficult not to consider them as such. In other words, the unexceptionalizing technologies that enable us to copy a Rembrandt also operate in the service of the exceptionalist power called sovereignty that continues, in our day and age, to exercise its grip on the bodies of the people.

I ask these questions partly in view of other, similar connections that scholars have made—especially in the context of the overall problematic of the original and the copy that is central to this book: for example, the fact that, as John Brewer has noted, forensic techniques familiar from policing work seep into art history to determine the originality of a painting.[50] Brewer notes in particular how "the distinctive portrayal of hands, knees and ears" was used to "detect signs of authors," observing that "Alphonse Bertillon of the Paris prefecture of police used these same human features to perfect his system of anthropometric measurement designed to identify thieves."[51] Marcus du Sautoy in fact explicitly turns to policing in his discussion of the AI-generated Rembrandt discussed above: to successfully create a new Rembrandt, an AI cannot simply fuse the faces of all existing Rembrandts into one. "As Francis Galton discovered in 1877 when he tried to construct a prototypical image of a convict by averaging photographs of real convicts," du Sautoy writes, "the result produces something far removed from the original"[52]—or, in this case, the *originals*. Specifically, the composite turned out to be much more handsome than any of the originals: the average tended to "smooth out the asymmetries,"[53] he writes (and note, in view of my Chapter 1, the use of the verb "smooth out"). Indeed, we are returning here to the kind of measurement that Leonardo da Vinci already practiced when he came up with his *Vitruvian Man*: not so much the math of fractals, but the math of the nude. To generate a new Rembrandt, however, one would have to avoid such smoothness: one would have to have the AI paint "as if it could see the world through Rembrandt's eyes."[54] The overall point is clear: in order for AI-generated art to read as art, it cannot be too smooth. Good AI art will have to take this maxim—which leads us back to the Byung-Chul Han quote with which I began this book—into account.

Du Sautoy quotes one critic, Jonathan Jones, who thought the AI-generated Rembrandt failed miserably on this count:

> It's not style and surface effects that make [Rembrandt's] paintings so great but the artist's capacity to reveal his inner life and make us aware in turn of our own interiority—to experience an uncanny contact, soul to soul. Let's call it the Rembrandt Shudder, that feeling I long for—and get—in front of every true Rembrandt masterpiece.[55]

This recalls my discussion of Pollock's automatic painting, how it splatters Pollock's unconscious directly onto the canvas. An AI-generated Rembrandt could only succeed if the AI would also have experienced "plague, poverty, old age, and all the other human experiences that make Rembrandt who he was, and his art what it is."[56] This is how, in Jorge Luis Borges' story *Pierre Menard, Author of the* Quixote,[57] Pierre Menard at first considers recreating an exact copy of *Don Quixote*—but it is doubtful, for a critic like Jones, whether an AI could accomplish this (Menard ultimately decides against that method).

Making similar connections, Thierry de Duve has explicitly tied "the establishment of authorship" in art history to both "crime investigation" (the need to establish who committed a crime) and "criminology,"[58] a field that—he notes—"came into being when the identification of moral responsibility with the rational subject of the Enlightenment became shaky."[59] Whereas the former cannot allow for "epistemological doubts," the latter deals in those. Here is de Duve writing about crime investigation but making it sound like art history:

> Crime investigators cannot afford epistemological doubts. Their task is to find the culprit; they leave it to the psychiatric experts to try to convince the judge that psychological causality may be an attenuating circumstance for a lack of moral responsibility. For them, the author of a crime remains the individual who chose to commit it. The definition of his crime remains a deed to which a suitable name can be pinned: it is either murder or rape or arson or theft. And the proof of his crime is a signature: his fingerprints were found on the premises. And so for art historians: for them, a work of art is a thing an artist chose to make, and if he chose to choose it instead, it is still he who appropriated it. A work of art is something to which a suitable name can be pinned: it's either painting or sculpture, or music or literature; and if it's neither, perhaps a new category will do, supplied by the author himself, the category of readymades for example. For them, a work of art has to bear a signature, whether a name at the bottom of the painting or a recognizable brush stroke; and if the signature is forged, either the author worked under a pseudonym, or he is not the author. Van Meegeren is not Vermeer, but Rrose Sélavy is Duchamp.[60]

Strictly speaking, of course, we are not in the realm of the copy with ING's Rembrandt, since the Rembrandt generated is a new Rembrandt. At the same time, it's a Rembrandt that is based on features of previously painted Rembrandts, so whatever novelty it brings is very limited, exists within certain parameters only. The Rembrandt is not new in the sense that it can only exist based on previous Rembrandts—it copies the features of those. But doesn't every new work by an artist contain within it the previous work that this artist has made? Aren't artists themselves a kind of AI that continuously acts within, and creatively pushes the boundaries of, the parameters within which their previous work exists? Perhaps it is the "creative push" that makes the difference—but even on that count, as Marcus du Sautoy has shown, AI has been catching up. By tying such conversations to considerations about crime investigation or policing work, however, de Duve and Brewer make clear the relations between debates about originality and the copy, and specifically the methods and technologies that are used to separate the one from the other, and power. Indeed, an AI-generated Rembrandt, presented as an ad for a multinational banking and financial services corporation, and with ties to contemporary practices of government and control, may present the perfect mix of elements to understand contemporary power and the sovereign as well as neoliberal elements that (as I have discussed in Chapter 5) inform it. Importantly, such a Rembrandt would be doing so precisely as a post-exceptional work of art.

Some may be reminded here of Mike Kelley's *Craft Morphology Flow Chart* in which, as per Yve-Alain Bois and Rosalind Krauss' description "sixty found, handmade stuffed animals are laid out on thirty-two tables . . . some according to size, others according to on perceptible similarity at all, still others—becoming a category of the 'unique'—into a grouping of one."[61]

Bois and Krauss indeed explicitly tie Kelley's organization of the stuffed animals to Foucault's work—Foucault's work on knowledge, *The Order of Things*. When they also connect the project to "the operations of statistics," however, ranging "from intelligence tests, to police activities such as fingerprinting, to medical record keeping, to political census taking," this quickly leads them to Foucault's work on power and even Deleuze's already mentioned notion of the "societies of control."[62] Like du Sautoy, Krauss and Bois discuss Galton, and for the same reason: to point out that his superimposition of images averaged out the typical criminal's face too much. In the history of Western modernism, then, this shows that form is too ideal—what is needed is a bit of formlessness, and Kelley's work is brought in here in that spirit. But too ideal for what? For an effective exercise of power, which needs to be attuned to the formless. The interesting question that emerges, then, is to what extent today this element of formlessness has in fact been incorporated by the power-practices that are evoked here, and has even become the very basis upon which post-exceptional power operates: through formlessness.

Restorations

To end this series of vignettes, consider the following: in April 2018, it was reported that a self-portrait by the Flemish master Peter Paul Rubens had returned to the painter's old atelier in the Rubenshuis in Antwerp (Flanders, Belgium) after a year of restoration by Marie-Annelle Mouffe from the Royal Institute for Cultural Heritage. As part of that process, Mouffe had removed several layers of varnish, and multiple additional layers of paint, of a painting that was for 75 percent painted over. Many accents had been added to the original painting over time. The restoration also revealed that the painting had existed in different formats: it had been enlarged, for example, and even been turned from a rectangular into an oval shape, the trace of which is faintly visible in the restored original. Such material changes are related to changes in ownership. Those who owned the painting also left a material mark on it.

It is worth noting the different kinds of changes that are listed here, from changing the shape of the painting to adding accents to the painting, or even painting over parts of the painting. The value of the Rubens painting was, of course, never in doubt.

Nevertheless, the painting had—until now—only been showing about 25 percent of its original paint. Still, it was considered an original Rubens all this time, even if many others had also had a hand in it. Because it was a Rubens, the painting received the expensive restoration that revealed this. But all of this raises questions about many of the other paintings we see in museums as well: To what extent are they, too, painted over, and many layers removed from their original state? To what extent have they, too, had accents added, a layer of varnish added, or their format changed? To what extent do they, too, show, in their material history, the traces of their private owners, before they ended up as public property in the museum? To what extent do these material histories, these unexceptionalizing accounts of masterpieces, undermine the exceptionalist attachment to the original that structures Western museums today? To what extent, finally, do such material histories place Western art in close proximity to the ancient Chinese perspective that I have described in this book, a proximity that the art market would rather wish to deny?

And given that such a denial rests on a denial of painting, of the very worldly practice through which even a masterpiece such as Rubens' portrait came about, isn't it interesting that Rubens presents himself in the painting as a nobleman rather than a painter—that he did not want to be known as a painter—as if he was dissimulating the very worldly craft that was so obviously on display in this portrait of the master by his own hand? By wanting to be recognized as a nobleman, Rubens contributed to the institution of exceptionalist art, a development that the painting's material history unworks, all the way into the painting's original layer (which the museum's director in an interesting turn of phrase described as being close to Rubens' "skin"—showing a kind of bare or naked Rubens, in other words). Far from confirming the exceptionalist status of art, and Rubens' status as a nobleman, the painting's restoration draws out something utterly unexceptional about the painting, uncovering the painter underneath the nobleman, and reminding all of us through the painting's material history (which is also the history of its ownership) of how unexceptional, in the end, art really is.

If I'm suggesting that restoration, or the practice of conserving works of art, can unexceptionalize art, this can be considered a third path added to the two that Ben Lerner distinguishes in an article he wrote for *The New Yorker* on conservation.[63] There, Lerner shows—using terms that are familiar to us by now—that conservation does not just help "protect" the "aura of the original," but can also "help produce" it. Lerner arrives at this conclusion starting from a reflection he develops about Josh Kline's sculpture *Cost of Living (Aleyda)*, which he goes to see at the Whitney. This piece, which includes 3D prints of scans that have a resolution that is too high for 3D-printing technology at the time of Lerner's writing ("there is . . . a 'resolution gap' between the digital files and current 3D-printing technology"), is read by Lerner—in terms that are familiar to us from Byung-Chul Han's *Shanzhai*—as a work that "is reversing the traditional temporality of the 'original' artwork: what comes first are copies," Lerner writes. "[T]he real work will arrive in the future." Lerner is interested in the questions this work raises for conservation that, in the case of Kline's work, must consider for example whether it wants to conserve the imperfect 3D prints of Kline's work until the future time arrives when the resolution gap between the digital file and the 3D-printing technology will have been overcome. Before that consideration even, a museum would have to ask whether it will want to replace Kline's imperfect 3D prints with more perfect ones, or whether such a replacement would in fact produce a new work (a dimension of Kline's work would surely be lost with the loss of the "resolution gap" that, at least in Lerner's reading, structures the work). Such questions are within the purview of the Whitney's "Replication Committee," a unique institution that "convenes to determine when a work of art, or a part of a work of art, cannot be fixed or restored in the traditional ways—when and how it must, instead, be replicated."

Apart from the reversal of original and copy, Kline's work triggers other such reversals in Lerner's text. Discussing Andrew Petryn's peculiar approach to conservation, Lerner introduces the term "de-restoration" into the conversation: "advocating a purism then popular among some conservators [in the 1950s and 1960s]," Petryn "decided to remove previous restoration, leaving, or aspiring to leave, only the hand of the artist." Lerner adds: "And the hand of time: what conservators call 'losses'—lacunae, expanses of bare wood—overwhelmed the original images." Characterized by critics as "aggressive over-cleaning," and "part of a long history of 'cleaning controversies'" in conservational theory and practice, Petryn raises the issue, which is prominently present in architectural theory and practice as well, of whether works of art and buildings should be restored, and kept in a kind of ideal state, outside of time; or whether they "must be left to decline, even die" (as John Ruskin, whom Lerner quotes, argued) following the view that the "greatest glory of a building . . . is in its Age." Lerner recalls that "Picasso and Braque told friends that they would rather let their canvases deteriorate than have them varnished, which they felt would ruin the subtle texturing of the surfaces." Duchamp, who like Picasso plays a prominent role in this book, thought similarly:

"Art history only begins after the death of the work"; "to conserve was to embalm."

Lerner is struck in all of this by "how the work of a conservator can re-sacralize the original art object." Overall, however, Lerner's article drifts towards the unexceptional: towards the resolution gap in Kline's work, and the unexceptionalizing of the work of art that it produces. We are dealing here with a copy before the original, a peculiar entity that has some affinity with Krajewska's "No Longer Art" or Lerner's understanding of it in his article "Damage Control" as "art before or after capital." Lerner embraces artworks in their state of destruction: his text ends with a plea for abandoning the need to control the damage. If that means that "several of the defining aesthetic experiences of [his] life took place in front of canvases that were merely 'a false description of the thing destroyed'"—a Van Gogh ruined by wax lining, a Braque destroyed by varnish—so be it; Lerner finds it "enlivening rather than depressing" to realize "that a piece of art is mortal; that it is the work of many hands, only some of which are coeval with the artist; that time is the medium of media; that one person's damage is another's patina; that the present's notion of its past and future are changeable fictions."

As for the politics of such post-exceptionalism, that remains to be negotiated, from work to work, context to context, history to history. In Lerner's "The Custodians," it seems to go against the attempt to control the future—to determine, through the pursuit of what the Whitney Museum refers to as an artist's "living will," what a work should look like through time, irrespective of the unexpected transformations it may undergo within it. This is all about pursuing the artist's intention, the hand of the artist that finished the original work—and undoing everything that comes after: the hand of time, of restoration (even if it is restoration done by the artist himself—Lerner discusses a conservator's suspicion that Rothko may have done "a poor job" restoring his own paintings, producing a situation where the conservator may have to protect "the artist's hand from the artist's other hand," as the text puts it). As such, this may sound like an obsession with the present (a living artist's intention), or the past (in the case of dead artists, like Rothko). But part of what interests Lerner is that this is also about the future, about locking in *now* the future appearance of the work of art. This adds a science-fictional element to Lerner's text, which is made explicit when at one point in the writing Lerner compares the sixth floor of the Whitney, which is dedicated to restoration, to the observation deck of the U.S.S. Enterprise in *Star Trek.* The architectural comparison is not gratuitous, however: *Star Trek*'s "Prime Directive," that the officers of its fleet "may not interfere with the development of alien civilizations," is then compared to the "absolutism" of Petryn's conservationism and its "aggressive over-cleaning." In both cases, the goal is to not interfere—and of course in both cases, huge quandaries emerge from that.

Lerner's use of the term "absolutism" is worth noting in this context, because it evokes the politics of sovereignty that has been central to the discussion of exceptionalism in this book. Indeed, Lerner's suggestion that conservation, while being about the past and the present, is also about the future—about gaining a certain hold on the future—recalls my discussion of Carl Schmitt's concept of sovereignty in my Introduction. In Schmitt's *Political Theology*, sovereignty is conceptualized precisely as a power that would be able to conserve a situation that emerges from the future and is not codified by the law. Sovereignty, for Schmitt, is the power that the law can institute in such situations at the threshold of the law to decide on such an exceptional situation and contain it in order to safeguard the law. As such, sovereignty is a power that exercises a hold over the future. Schmitt's conservatism, then, which is keenly aware of the radicality of "the future" and "life," shows connections to the conservationism discussed in Lerner's text, and Lerner's preference for the unexceptional towards the end of his essay can, in the context of the provocative comparisons that I have set up in this book, be read in tension with the exceptionalism of Schmitt's concept of sovereignty, which would be closer to the absolutism of purist conservationist approaches. The fact that this is tied, in Lerner's text, to the image of a museum at sea (to recall the text's closing words), should not come as a surprise at this point: it is in line not only with the association I have established between water and unexceptionalism, but also with Schmitt's well-known anxiety about water as an anarchic element and his conservative preference for dry land. The Whitney building, as Lerner points out early on in his text, was designed by architect Renzo Piano as a "great ship," and the text suggests that this very design injects an element of unexceptional movement into exceptionalist understandings of art.

While some overall conclusions about the politics of post-exceptionalism can certainly be drawn—and I have on several occasions done that in this book—I have also tried to show that, as is perhaps the case with every politics, the politics of post-exceptionalism can only really be negotiated locally, with respect to a specific work of art in a specific situation. This is, in fact, what constitutes post-exceptionalism's critical core, the political equivalent of the fact that, in the realm of art, unexceptional art is not an indexical notion. Post-exceptionalism needs to be negotiated across aesthetics and politics—critically. Far from being post-critical, then, post-exceptionalism reveals to us the continued need for critique, within the West, within the East, from the West to the East, and vice versa. Contrary to what we are sometimes led to believe, it is not critique that tends towards exceptionalism but post-critique. To come after critique: that is precisely what the exceptional strives for. One can readily grant critique's possible appropriation by exceptionalism also—it is not as if critique is immune to it—but this is an appropriation that should be resisted. It is precisely this that has produced the current vogue of post-critique. Rather than making critique great again, then, or going post-critical, the point would be to *keep critique post-exceptional*. It would make a great slogan for an intellectual campaign.

Notes

1 It's worth noting that, in my experience, such departments are very hierarchically organized. In other words, the key orientations of Chinese thought and aesthetics do not translate, institutionally and politically, into a democratic or anarchic politics. Although on the Western side, democracy has become the dominant political regime, this orientation is in my view not generally reflected in Western thought and aesthetics. In other words, in both the West and China there is no direct transfer between thought and practice. Instead, we find a chiasmic relation that justifies an approach that situates itself between the two rather than comfortably on either side.

2 See, for example: François Cheng, *Empty and Full: The Language of Chinese Painting*, trans. Michael H. Kohn (Boston, MA: Shambhala, 1994), here p. 67.

3 For a discussion of this reversal, which Clark situates in Vitruvian man, see: Kenneth Clark, *The Nude: A Study in Ideal Form* (Princeton, NJ: Princeton University Press, 1972), p. 348.

4 Alain de Botton, *Essays In Love* (London: Picador, 1994), p. 94.

5 Men's bodies shouldn't be excluded from the argument—they too have been subjected to the idealized understanding of beauty.

6 As Clark shows, the history of the Western nude certainly includes that realization.

7 As such, it is in line with Chinese thought overall, which is a process thought.

8 François Jullien, *The Great Image Has No Form, or On the Nonobject through Painting*, trans. Jane Marie Todd (Chicago, IL: University of Chicago Press, 2009), p. 49.

9 Hui-Shu Lee, "The Emperor's Lady Ghostwriters in Song-Dynasty China," *Artibus Asiae* 64:1 (2004), pp. 61–101.

10 Lee, "The Emperor's Lady Ghostwriters," p. 61.

11 Ibid., p. 62.

12 Ibid.

13 It's worth noting that Chinese landscape painting has entered into the realm of the digital as well: Christin Bolewski, "Eastern Cultural Heritage, Digital Remediation and Global Perspectives" (conference paper), accessible: https://dspace.lboro.ac.uk/2134/25074

14 See: https://www.scmp.com/tech/innovation/article/3112358/ai-paintings-chinese-landscapes-pass-human-made-55-cent-time

15 Laura Vermeeren, "Chinese Calligraphy in the Digital Realm: Aesthetic Perfection and Remediation of the Authentic," *Concentric: Literary and Cultural Studies* 43:2 (2017), pp. 163–191.

16 Vermeeren, "Chinese Calligraphy in the Digital Realm," p. 165.

17 Ibid., pp. 165–166. Lee also comments on this: Lee, "The Emperor's Lady Ghostwriters," p. 67.

18 Vermeeren, "Chinese Calligraphy in the Digital Realm," p. 166.

19 Ibid.

20 Ibid., p. 163.

21 Ibid., p. 170

22 Rosalind Krauss, *The Originality of the Avant-Garde and Other Modernist Myths* (Cambridge, MA: The MIT Press, 1985), p. 162.

23 Ibid.

24 Ibid.

25 Ibid.

26 "As a kid, when I first saw images of Jackson Pollock at work, I thought I was watching somebody vandalize a painting, not create one: the canvas was on the floor, paint was splattered and poured, and he was indifferent to the ash falling from his cigarette. Trash—nails, tacks, button—can

be found encrusted in his paintings' surfaces": Ben Lerner, "Damage Control: The Modern Art World's Tyranny of Price," *Harper's Magazine* 12 (2013), pp. 42–49, here p. 43.

27 Shi Jia, "Zhang Daqian, Painter who Journeyed between East and West," *Shine: Beyond a Single Story*, July 5 (2018), accessible: https://www.shine.cn/feature/art-culture/1807058045/

28 Pollock's automatic painting was in that sense a little like the automatic writing of the Surrealists.

29 Certainly, one wouldn't go to the museum to sit down and copy one of his paintings; to copy a Pollock one would need to enter into the mental state that Pollock was in when he made the painting, or even to somehow paint from Pollock's unconscious.

30 Marcus du Sautoy, *The Creativity Code: Art and Innovation in the Age of AI* (Cambridge, MA: Harvard University Press, 2019), p. 116.

31 Du Sautoy, *The Creativity Code*, p. 116.

32 Ibid.

33 Ibid.

34 Ibid., p. 117.

35 Frances Stonor Saunders, *The Cultural Cold War: The CIA and the World of Arts and Letters* (New York: New Press, 1999), p. 253.

36 Saunders, *The Cultural Cold War*, p. 253.

37 Michel Foucault, *The Birth of Biopolitics: Lectures at the Collège de France 1978–1979*, ed. Michel Senellart, trans. Graham Burchell (New York: Palgrave Macmillan, 2008).

38 Gilles Deleuze, "Postscript on the Societies of Control," *October* 59 (1992), pp. 3–7.

39 Antoinette Rouvroy, "The Digital Regime of Truth: From the Algorithmic Governmentality to a New Rule of Law," trans. Anaïs Nin and Benoît Dillet, *La Deleuziana: Online Journal of Philosophy* 3 (2016), accessible: http://www.ladeleuziana.org/wp-content/uploads/2016/12/Rouvroy-Stiegler_eng.pdf

40 Saunders, *The Cultural Cold War*, p. 254.

41 Michel Foucault, *The History of Sexuality: An Introduction*, trans. Robert Hurley (New York: Vintage, 1990), p. 139.

42 Ibid.

43 Ulf Otto is one of the scholars who have considered the extent to which Byung-Chul Han in his work on neoliberalism relies on it (Ulf Otto, "Theatres of Control: The Performance of Algorithms and the Question of Governance," *TDR: The Drama Review* 63:4 (2019), pp. 121–138, here

in particular p. 131). As I've noted previously, however, Han does not connect his work on neoliberalism to his thinking about the fake.

44 Pamela Lee, "Pattern Recognition ca. 1947" (public lecture). Lecture delivered at the West Hollywood Public Library, at the invitation of the MA Aesthetics and Politics program at the California Institute of the Arts, on Friday, November 26, 2017.

45 Pamela Lee, "Aesthetic Strategist: Albert Wohlstetter, the Cold War, and a Theory of Mid-Century Modernism," *October* 138 (2011), pp. 15–36, here p. 29.

46 Eva Cockcroft, "Abstract Expressionism, Weapon of the Cold War," in: Francis Frascina, ed., *Pollock and After: The Critical Debate* (New York: Harper & Row, 1985), pp. 125–133.

47 Saunders, *The Cultural Cold War*, p. 254.

48 Ibid.

49 See: https://www.nextrembrandt.com

50 John Brewer, *The American Leonardo: A Tale of Obsession, Art and Money* (New York: Oxford University Press, 2009) (Ebook), chapter 6.

51 Brewer, *The American Leonardo*, p. 44.

52 Du Sautoy, *The Creativity Code*, p. 119.

53 Ibid.

54 Ibid., p. 120.

55 Jones qtd. ibid., p. 121.

56 Ibid.

57 J. L. Borges, "Pierre Menard, Author of the *Quixote*," in: J. L. Borges, *Collected Fictions*, trans. Andrew Hurley (New York: Penguin, 1999), pp. 88–95.

58 Thierry de Duve, "Authorship Stripped Bare, Even," *RES: Anthropology and Aesthetics* 19/20 (1990–1991), pp. 234–241, here p. 235.

59 De Duve, "Authorship Stripped Bare," p. 240.

60 Ibid., p. 241.

61 Yve-Alain Bois and Rosalind E. Krauss, *Formless: A User's Guide* (New York: Zone Books, 1999), p. 251.

62 Bois and Krauss, *Formless*, p. 251.

63 Ben Lerner, "The Custodians: How the Whitney is Transforming the Art of Museum Conservation," *The New Yorker* January 11 (2016), accessible: https://www.newyorker.com/magazine/2016/01/11/the-custodians-onward-and-upward-with-the-arts-ben-lerner

Coda: The End of Art (Once Again)

You Morons

In early March 2021, a group of "tech and art enthusiasts" who make up the company Injective Protocol[1] burnt Banksy's work *Morons (White)* (2006), which they had previously acquired from Tagliatella Galleries for $95,000.[2] At first sight, the burning could be read as performance art in the spirit of Banksy's *Morons (White)*, which shows an art auction where a canvas featuring the text "I CAN'T BELIEVE YOU MORONS ACTUALLY BUY THIS SHIT" is up for sale (and going for $750,450). As such, the performance would take further Banksy's own criticism of the art market, a market whose dialectic has easily reappropriated Banksy's criticism as part of its norm and turned it into economic value (as I discussed in my first chapter). The burning of the Banksy would then seek to more radically negate the value of the work of art that Banksy's *Morons (White)* challenges, but cannot quite escape as long as it remains a valuable work of art.

However, such negation was not the goal of the burning. As the tech and art enthusiast who set the Banksy aflame explained, the burning was in fact accomplished as part of a financial investment, and to inspire other artists. In other words, the burning in fact confirmed the art market's norm rather than challenging it, and it encouraged other artists to make work that does the same. You see, before Banksy's *Morons (White)* was burnt, Injective Protocol had recorded the work as what is called a non-fungible token or NFT in the blockchain. This means that for the work's digital image, a unique, original code was created; that code—which is what you buy if you buy an NFT—is the new, original, NFT artwork, henceforth owned by Injective Protocol even if digital copies of Banksy's *Morons (White)* of course still circulate as mere symbols of that code.[3] Such ownership, and the financial investment as which it was intended, required the burning of the material Banksy because Injective Protocol sought to relocate the primary value of the work into the NFT artwork—something that could only be accomplished if the original Banksy was destroyed. The goal of the burning was thus to relocate the value of the original in the derivative, which had a bigger financial potential than the original Banksy.

The Banksy burning was perhaps an unsurprising development for those who have an interest in art and cryptocurrencies and have been following the rise of cryptoart. Cryptoart is digital art that is recorded in the blockchain as an NFT. That makes cryptoart "like" bitcoin, which is similarly recorded in the blockchain: each bitcoin is tied to a unique, original code that is recorded in a digital ledger where all the transactions of bitcoin are tracked. As an NFT, a digital artwork is similarly tied to a unique, original code that marks its provenance. The main difference between bitcoin and an NFT is that the former, as currency, is fungible, whereas the latter, as art, is not.[4] Now, NFTs were initially created "next to" already existing non-digital art, as a way to establish provenance for digital images and artworks. But as such images and artworks began to accrue value, and began to comparatively accrue more value than already existing non-digital art, the balance in the art market shifted, and NFTs came to be considered more valuable investments than already existing works of non-digital art.

The burning of Banksy's *Morons (White)* was the obvious next step in that development: let us replace the already existing work of non-digital art by an NFT, destroy the already existing work of non-digital art, and relocate the value of the work into the NFT as part of a financial investment. It realizes the dialectic of an art market that will not hesitate to destroy an already existing non-digital work of art (and replace it with an NFT) if it will drive up financial value. The auction houses who have sold NFTs are complicit with this process.

Crypto Value = Exhibition Value + Cult Value

The digital may at some point have held the promise of a moving away from exceptionalism—the belief that the artist and the work of art are exceptional, which is tied to theories of the artist as genius and the unresolved role of the fake and the forgery in art history—as the structuring logic of our understanding of the artist and the work of art. The staged burning of the Banksy does not so much realize that promise as relocate the continued dominance of exceptionalism—and its ties to capitalism, even if the work of art is of course an exceptional commodity that does not truly fit the capitalist framework—in the digital realm. The promise of what artist and philosopher Hito Steyerl theorized as "the poor image"[5] is countered in the NFT as a decidedly "rich image," or rather, as the rich NFT artwork (because we need to distinguish between the NFT artwork/the code and the digital image, a mere symbol that is tied to the code). Art, which in the part of its history that started with conceptual art in the early 1970s had started realizing itself—parallel to the rise of finance and neoliberalism—as a financial instrument, with material artworks functioning as means to hedge against market crashes (as James Franco's character in Isaac Julien's *Playtime* [2014] discusses[6]), has finally left the burden of its materiality behind to become a straight-up financial instrument, a derivative that has some similarities to a cryptocurrency like bitcoin. Art has finally realized itself as what it is: non-fungible value, one of finance's fictions.[7]

Although the video of the Banksy burning might shock, and make one imagine (because of its solicitation to other tech enthusiasts and artists) an imminent future in which all artworks will be burnt so as to relocate their primary value in an NFT tied to the artwork's digital image, such a future actually does not introduce all that much difference with respect to today. Indeed, we are merely talking about a *relocation* of value, about a relocation of the art market. The market's structure, value's structure, remain the same. In fact, the NFT craze demonstrates how the artwork's structuring logic, what I have called aesthetic exceptionalism,[8] realizes itself in the realm of the digital where, for a brief moment, one may have thought it could have died. Indeed, media art and digital art more specifically seemed to hold the promise of an art that would be more widely circulated, where the categories of authorship, value, and ownership were less intimately connected, and could perhaps even—see Steyerl; but the argument goes back to Walter Benjamin's still influential essay on the copy[9]—enable a communist politics.

Such a communist politics would celebrate the copy against the potentially fascist values of authenticity, creativity, originality, and eternal value that Benjamin brings up at the beginning of his essay. But no: with NFTs, those potentially fascist values are in fact realizing themselves once again in the digital realm, and in a development that Benjamin could not have foreseen "the aura" becomes associated with the NFT artwork—not even the digital image of an artwork but a code as which the image lies recorded in the blockchain. Because the NFT artwork is a *non-fungible* token, one could argue that it is even more of an original than the digital currencies with which it is associated. After all, bitcoin is still a medium of exchange, whereas an NFT is not. In the same way that art is *not* money, NFT is *not* bitcoin, even if the NFT needs to be understood (as I suggested previously) as one of finance's fictions.

What's remarkable here is not so much that a Banksy is burnt, or that other artworks may in the future be burnt. What's remarkable is the power of aesthetic exceptionalism: an exceptionalism so strong *that it can even sacrifice the material artwork* to assert itself.

Of course, some might point out—taking Banksy's *Morons (White)* as a point of departure—that Banksy himself invited this destruction. Indeed, at a Sotheby's auction not so long ago, Banksy had himself already realized the partial destruction of one of his works in an attempt to criticize the art market[10]—a criticism that is evident also in the work of art that Injective Protocol burnt. But the art market takes such avant-garde acts of vandalism in its stride, and Banksy's stunt came to function as evidence for what has been called "the Banksy effect":[11] your attempt to criticize the art market becomes the next big thing on the art market, and your act of art vandalism in fact pushes the dollar value of the work of art. If that happens, the writer Ben Lerner argues in an essay about art vandalism titled "Damage Control,"[12] your vandalism isn't really vandalism: art vandalism that pushes up dollar value isn't vandalism. Banksy's stunt was an attempt to make art outside of the art market, but the attempt failed. The sale of the work went through, and a few months later one can find the partially destroyed artwork on the walls of a museum, reportedly worth three times more since the date when it was sold. For Lerner, examples like this open up the question of a work of art outside of capitalism, a work of art from which "the market's soul has fled,"[13] as he puts it. But as the Banksy example shows, that soul is perhaps less quick to get out than we might think. Over and over again, we see it reassert itself *through those very attempts that seek to push it out*. One might refer to that as a dialectic—the dialectic of avant-garde attempts to be done with exceptionalist art. Ultimately they realize only one thing: the further institutionalization of exceptionalist art.

That dialectic has today reached a most peculiar point: the end of art that some, a long time ago, already announced. But none of those arguments reached quite as far as the video of the Authentic Banksy Art Burning Ceremony that was released in March: in it, we are quite literally witnessing the end of the work of art as we know it. It shows us the "slow burn," as the officiating member of Injective Protocol puts it, through which Banksy's material work of art—and by extension the material work of art at large—disappears (and has been disappearing). At the same time, this destruction is presented as an act of creation—not so much of a digital image of the Banksy work but of the NFT artwork or the code that authenticates that digital image, authors it, brands it with the code of its owners. So with the destruction of Banksy's work of art, another work of art is created—the NFT artwork, a work that you cannot feature on your wall (even if its symbolic appendage, the digital image of the Banksy, can be featured on your phone, tablet, or computer and even if some owners of the NFT artwork might decide to materially realize the NFT artwork as a work that can be shown on their walls). But what is the NFT artwork? It strikes one as the artwork narrowed down to its exceptionalist, economic core, the authorship and originality that determine its place on the art market. It is the artwork limited to its economic value, the scarcity and non-fungibility that remain at the core of what we think of as art. This is not so much purposiveness without purpose, as Immanuel Kant famously had it, but non-fungible value as a rewriting of that phrase. Might that have been the occluded truth of Kant's phrase all along?

In *Kant After Duchamp*,[14] which remains one of the most remarkable books of twentieth-century art criticism, Thierry de Duve shifted the aesthetic question from "is it beautiful?" (Kant's question) to "is it art?" (Duchamp's question, which triggers de Duve's rereading of Kant's *Critique of Judgment*). It seems that today, one might have to shift the question once again, to situate Kant after Mike Winkelmann, the graphic designer/NFT artist known as Beeple whose NFT collage "Everydays: The First 5000 Days" was sold at a Christie's auction for $69,346,250. The question with this work is not so much whether it is beautiful, or even whether it is art; what matters here is *solely* its non-fungible value (how valuable is it, or how valuable might it become?), which would trigger yet another rereading of Kant's third critique. Shortly after the historic sale of Beeple's work was concluded, it was widely reported that the cryptocurrency trader who bought the work may have profited financially from the sale, in that the trader had previously been buying many of the individual NFTs that made up Beeple's collage—individual NFTs which, after the historic sale of the collage, went up significantly in value, thus balancing out the expense of buying the collage and even yielding the trader a profit. What's interesting here is not the art—Beeple's work is not good art[15]—but solely the non-fungible value.

It seems clear that what has thus opened up is another regime of art. In his essay on the copy, Benjamin wrote of the shift from *cult value*, associated with the fascism of the original, to *exhibition value*, associated with the communism of the copy. Today, we are witnessing the anachronistic, zombie-like return of cult value within exhibition value, a regime that can be understood as the *crypto value* of the work of art. That seems evident in the physical token that buyers of Beeple's NFTs get sent: in its gross materialism—it comes with a cloth to clean the token but that can also be used "to clean yourself up after blasting a hot load in yer pants from how dope this is!!!!!!111"; a certificate of authenticity stating "THIS MOTHERFUCKING REAL ASS SHIT (this is real life mf)"; and a hair sample, "I promise it's not pubes"—it functions as a faux cultic object that is meant to mask the emptiness of the NFT. Assuaging the anxieties, perhaps, of the investors placing their moneys into nothing, it also provides interesting insights into the materialisms (masculinist/sexist, and racist—might we call them *alt-right materialisms*?) that reassert themselves in the realm of the digital, as part of an attempt to realize exceptionalism in a commons that could have freed itself from it.[16] As the text printed on the physical token has it: "strap on an adult diaper because yer about to be in friggn' boner world usa motherfucker."

NFT-Elitism

It's worth asking about the politics of this. I have been clear about the politics of aesthetic exceptionalism: it is associated with the politics of sovereignty, which is a rule of the one, a mon-archy, that potentially tends abusive, tyrannical, totalitarian. That is the case for example with exceptionalism in Carl Schmitt, even if it does not have to be the case (see for example discussions of democratic exceptionalism).[17] With the NFT artwork, the politics of aesthetic exceptionalism is realizing itself in the digital realm, which until now seemed to present a potential threat to it. It has nothing to do with anti-elitism, or populism; it is not about leaving behind art-world snobbery, as some have suggested. It is in fact the very logic of snobbery and elitism that is realizing itself in the NFT artwork, in the code that marks originality, authenticity, authorship, and ownership. Cunningly, snobbery and elitism work their way back in via a path that seems to lead elsewhere. It is the Banksy effect, in politics. The burning of the Banksy is an iconoclastic gesture that preserves the political theology of art that it seems to attack.[18] This is very clear in even the most basic discourse on NFTs, which will praise both the NFT's "democratic" potential—look at how it goes against the elitism of the art world!—while asserting that the entire point of the NFT is that it enables the authentication that once again excludes fakes and forgeries from the art world. Many, if not all of the problems with art-world elitism continue here.

With the description of NFT artworks as derivatives, and their understanding as thoroughly part of the contemporary financial economy, the temptation is of course to understand them as "neoliberal"—and certainly the Banksy burning by a group of "tech and art enthusiasts" (a neoliberal combo if there ever was one) seems to support such a reading. But the peculiar talk about authenticity and originality in the video of the Banksy burning, the surprising mention of "primary value" and its association to the original work of art (which now becomes the NFT artwork, as the video explains), in fact strikes one as strangely antiquated. Indeed, almost everything in the video strikes one as from a different, bygone time: the work, on its easel; the masked speaker, a robber known to me from the tales of my father's childhood; the flame, slowly working its way around the canvas, which appears to be set up in front of a snowy landscape that one may have seen in a Brueghel. Everything is there to remind us that, through the neoliberal smokescreen, we are in fact seeing an older power at work—that of the "sovereign," authentic original, the exceptional reality of "primary value" realizing itself through this burning ritual that marks not so much its destruction but its phoenix-like reappearance in the digital realm. In that sense, the burning has something chilling to it, as if it is an ancient ritual marking the migration of sovereign power from the material work of art to the NFT artwork. A transference of the sovereign spirit, if you will, and the economic soul of the work of art. For anyone who has closely observed neoliberalism, this continued presence of sovereignty in the neoliberal era will not come as a surprise—historians, political theorists, anthropologists, philosophers, and literary critics have shown that it would be a mistake to oppose neoliberalism and sovereignty historically, and in the analysis of our contemporary moment. The aesthetic regime of crypto value would rather be a contemporary manifestation of neoliberal sovereignty or of authoritarian neoliberalism (the presence of Trump in Beeple's work is worth noting).

Art historians and artists, however, may be taken aback by how starkly the political truth of art is laid bare here. Reduced to non-fungible value, brought back to its exceptionalist economic core, the political core of the artwork as sovereign stands out in its tension with art's frequent association with democratic values like openness, equality, and pluralism. As the NFT indicates, democratic values have little to do with it: what matters, at the expense of the material work of art, is the originality and authenticity that enable the artwork to operate as non-fungible value. Part of finance's fictions, the artwork thus also reveals itself as politically troubling because it is profoundly rooted in a logic of the one that, while we are skeptical of it in politics, we continue to celebrate aesthetically. How to block this dialectic, and be done with it? How to think art outside of economic value, and the politics of exceptionalism? How to end not so much art but exceptionalism as art's structuring logic? How to free art from fascism? The NFT craze, while it doesn't answer those questions, has the dubious benefit of identifying all of those problems.

Notes

1 See: https://injectiveprotocol.com/
2 See: https://news.artnet.com/art-world/financial-traders-burned-banksy-nft-1948855. A video of the burning can be accessed here: https://www.youtube.com/watch?v=C4wm-p_VFh0
3 See: https://hyperallergic.com/624053/nft-art-goes-viral-and-heads-to-auction-but-what-is-it/
4 A simple explanation of cryptoart's relation to cryptocurrency can be found here: https://www.youtube.com/watch?v=QlgE_mmbRDk
5 Hito Steyerl, "In Defense of the Poor Image," *e-flux* 10 (2009), accessible: https://www.e-flux.com/journal/10/61362/in-defense-of-the-poor-image/

6 See: https://www.isaacjulien.com/projects/playtime/

7 I am echoing here the title of my book *Finance Fictions*, where I began to theorize some of what is realized by the NFT artwork: Arne De Boever, *Finance Fictions: Realism and Psychosis in a Time of Economic Crisis* (New York: Fordham University Press, 2017).

8 See: Arne De Boever, *Against Aesthetic Exceptionalism* (Minneapolis: University of Minnesota Press, 2019).

9 See: Walter Benjamin, "The Work of Art in the Era of Mechanical Reproduction," in: Walter Benjamin, *Illuminations: Essays and Reflections*, ed. Hannah Arendt, trans. Harry Zohn (New York: Schocken, 1969), pp. 217–251.

10 See: https://www.youtube.com/watch?v=vxkwRNIZgdY&feature=emb_title

11 Lexa Brenner, "The Banksy Effect: Revolutionizing Humanitarian Protest Art," *Harvard International Review* XL:2 (2019), pp. 35–37.

12 Ben Lerner, "Damage Control: The Modern Art World's Tyranny of Price," *Harper's Magazine* 12 (2013), pp. 42–49.

13 Lerner, "Damage Control," p. 49.

14 Thierry de Duve, *Kant After Duchamp* (Cambridge, MA: The MIT Press, 1998).

15 While such judgments are of course always subjective, this article considers a number of good reasons for judging the work as bad art: https://news.artnet.com/opinion/beeple-everydays-review-1951656#.YFKo4eIE7p4.twitter

16 The emphasis on materialism here is not meant to obscure the materialism of the digital NFT, namely its ecological footprint which is, like that of bitcoin, devastating.

17 See Boever, *Against Aesthetic Exceptionalism*.

18 On this, see my: "Iconic Intelligence (Or: In Praise of the Sublamental)," rev. Stathis Gourgouris, *The Perils of the One* (New York: Columbia University Press, 2019), *boundary 2* 49:2 (2022), pp. 129–151.

Index

EU Authorised Representative:
Easy Access System Europe Mustamäe tee 50, 10621 Tallinn, Estonia
gpsr.requests@easproject.com

Printed and bound by CPI Group (UK) Ltd, Croydon, CR0 4YY
06/08/2026
02188476-0001